The Concept of Body in Judaism, Christianity and Islam

Key Concepts in Interreligious Discourses

Edited by
Georges Tamer

Volume 12

The Concept of Body in Judaism, Christianity and Islam

Edited by
Christoph Böttigheimer and Konstantin Kamp

DE GRUYTER

ISBN 978-3-11-074817-8
e-ISBN (PDF) 978-3-11-074824-6
e-ISBN (EPUB) 978-3-11-074828-4
ISSN 2513-1117

Library of Congress Control Number: 2023946121

Bibliographic information published by the Deutsche Nationalbibliothek
The Deutsche Nationalbibliothek lists this publication in the Deutsche Nationalbibliografie; detailed bibliographic data are available on the internet at http://dnb.dnb.de.

Typesetting: Integra Software Services Pvt. Ltd.
Printing and binding: CPI books GmbH, Leck

www.degruyter.com

Preface

This volume at hand of the book series "Key Concepts in Interreligious Discourses" (KCID) documents the results of a conference which dealt with the concept of "Body" in Judaism, Christianity and Islam and was held at the Catholic University of Eichstätt-Ingolstadt. The conference was organized by the research unit "Key Concepts in Interreligious Discourses" and took place from June 26th to June 28th 2019.

The research unit "Key Concepts in Interreligious Discourses" was jointly run by the Friedrich-Alexander-University Erlangen-Nuremberg and the Catholic University of Eichstätt-Ingolstadt between June 2018 and June 2021. As the title already implies, the mutual project focused on interreligious discourse. However, it was not about conducting an interreligious dialogue, but rather reflection upon this dialogue, thereby facilitating a theologically well-founded interreligious dialogue. For only if every dialogue partner has a clear picture of what is discussed about, a dialogue can be conducted reasonably. It was the project's ambition to provide such clarification by examining concepts that are central for Judaism, Christianity and Islam, both historically and in terms of their interdependencies and by setting them in a relation to one another. By reflecting on central ideas and beliefs historically and comparatively, common values and origins, but also differences and contradictions between the three monotheistic religions are to be clearly elaborated. By disclosing key concepts of the three closely interconnected religions: Judaism, Christianity and Islam, a deeper mutual understanding is fostered, prejudices and misunderstandings are counteracted and thus a contribution is made to peaceful interaction based on respect and recognition.

Only through precise knowledge of the central ideas of the foreign as well as of one's own religion a well-founded, objective and constructive interreligious understanding can prevail. Conferences at which international experts from the fields of theology, religious studies and philosophy of religion intensively discussed and clarified core religious ideas from the perspective of the three religions served this purpose. Developments within religious history never proceed in isolation; rather, they interpenetrate each other and are mutually dependent. Thus, the research unit "Key Concepts in Interreligious Discourses" pursued fundamental research and aimed at an "archaeology of knowledge" with its comparative conceptual-historical investigations.

Inasmuch as world peace cannot be obtained without religious peace, the project contributed importantly to a peaceful social coexistence and thus corresponds to the obligation that has been newly assigned to the universities in recent decades, namely to engage in social concerns in addition to teaching and research. This is expressed by the term "third mission."

https://doi.org/10.1515/9783110748246-202

I wish to thank Dr. Wenzel Maximilian Widenka, who organized the conference, and Konstantin Kamp, who helped editing this volume. In addition to the cooperation partners of the Friedrich-Alexander-University Erlangen-Nuremberg and the de Gruyter publishing house for including this volume in the book series "Key Concepts in Interreligious Discourses," we would like to express our sincere thanks to the third party funders, Reinhard Cardinal Marx and the Archdiocese of Munich and Freising, the Karpos Foundation of the Diocese of Eichstätt, the Maximilian Bickhoff Foundation and the ProFor Program of the Catholic University of Eichstätt-Ingolstadt. Without their support, neither the conference nor the volumes would have been possible.

Christoph Böttigheimer,
July 2023

Contents

Preface —— V

Yakir Englander
The Concept of Body in Judaism —— 1

Gregor Etzelmüller
The Concept of Body in Christianity —— 29

Abbas Poya
The Concept of Body in Islam —— 99

Christoph Böttigheimer / Konstantin Kamp
Epilogue —— 155

List of Contributors and Editors —— 173

Index of Persons —— 175

Index of Subjects —— 177

Yakir Englander

The Concept of Body in Judaism: The Shaping of the Halakhic (Jewish Legal) Body from a Phenomenological Perspective

The perception of the body in Judaism is an extremely broad and fascinating topic. One of the compelling attributes of Jewish culture and religion is the choice to develop it around the halakha (Jewish law) – the physical act or praxis of a Jew. Observing the role of the body in halakhic literature thus contributes significantly to our understanding of Jewish body image in general.

In this article, I juxtapose certain choices about the shaping of the body among halakhic (Jewish legal) authorities and in the social-religious praxis with the phenomenological thinking of Maurice Merleau-Ponty (1908–1961). I do so out of an assumption that the perception of the body in Jewish halakha constitutes one of the central spheres within which the actual Jewish body takes shape. In so doing, I will point to the centrality of the body in halakhic literature as a source of the religious praxis, and to the contribution of reading halakhic literature about the body when applying phenomenological research. In the article, I will use several distinctions from Merleau-Ponty's research and will note insights that can be gained from his work about the halakhic body image.

A significant part of halakhic (Jewish legal) literature addresses the body (washing hands, ritual purity and impurity, circumcision, marital relations, head coverings) or acts performed with the body (tallit and tefillin, kiddush and Havdalah, Sukkah and Shofar).[1] The prayers and the various blessings that accompany halakhic practice are also performed with the body: they are recited out loud, i.e.,

1 The tallit is a kind of scarf worn by Jews on the entire upper part of the body during the morning prayer. Tefillin (two phylacteries) are also used during the morning prayer. Made from leather, one is placed on the head and the other on the arm opposite the heart. Inside the boxes of the tefillin are verses from the Torah written on parchment describing the relationship between a Jew and God. On the 7-day festival of Sukkot (celebrated in October), Jews build a booth

Note: The Hebrew version of this article was published in the book: Rosenak, Avinoam (ed.), *Halakha as an Event*, Jerusalem: Magnes Press, 2016. All translations of Hebrew sources are ours. I would like to thank Jeremy Kuttner for translating the article from Hebrew, and Dr. Henry R. Carse for translating some of the rabbinic sources. Special thanks to Prof. Avinoam Rosenak and to Dr. Dror Yinon for their support and dialogue during the writing of this article. I am grateful to Prof. Yael Zerubavel and to Prof. Azzan Yadin-Israel from the department of Jewish Studies at Rutgers University who hosted me. This article was written while benefitting from their generous hospitality.

https://doi.org/10.1515/9783110748246-001

via a physical action, and indeed, halakhic literature contains a consensus about the inability to fulfill a halakhic obligation merely through mental contemplation and emotional experience.[2] The choice of central halakhic authorities to focus on the physical act and to downplay the importance of thought and experience has many ramifications that I will examine below. Among other things, it enhances the standing of the body, enables the creation of a more equitable community in which a Torah scholar and an unlearned person are fundamentally equal, and where both perform their halakhic obligation as long as they perform the same halakhic act, even if the unlearned person is unaware of the act's intent.

The focus on the body indicates a positive approach towards the body in many sections of halakhic literature. This focus should not, however, lead to the conclusion that the halakha necessarily views the body in a positive light. One example is Rabbi Yechiel Michel Epstein (1829–1908), author of the *Arukh HaShulchan*. In the first section of the book, he described the relation between this world and the World to Come.[3] According to Rabbi Epstein, the relation between the two worlds is similar to the relation between walking along a passageway and arriving at the center of the house; in similar fashion, the significant essence of a person's life is in the World to Come, and not in this world. In his opinion, the primary difference between the two worlds is that in this world, a person is accompanied by a body, a kind of hindrance that does not exist in the World to Come: "He possesses an animalistic nature due to his physical body, which drives him to animal behaviors, such as eating, drinking, and sleeping. This reality gives rise to a constant struggle within man all the days of his life, with his animal nature pining for physical desires."[4] Nonetheless, the body also constitutes a relative advantage for life in this world – a person being bound to halakha that is performed with the body, for which he subsequently merits reward in the World to Come, unlike the angels.[5] Among other things, the words of the *Arukh HaShulchan* raise two assumptions: the first – it defines man as a bodiless entity. The body is an appendage that accompanies a person in this world whereas, in the World to Come, a person is simply himself/herself, without the body. The second assump-

---

in which they eat and sleep. The Shofar is a ram's horn that is blown during the prayers on the special days of forgiveness and introspection – Rosh Hashana and Yom Kippur.

2 Cf. *b. Ber. 20a-b*; Judah Loew ben Bezalel, *Netivot Olam*, Chapter 1 (Goldman edition, Warsaw 1872, 30–31).

3 Cf. *Arukh HaShulchan*, Orach Chaim 1.

4 *Arukh HaShulchan*, Orach Chaim, §1–2.

5 "Angels are intelligent, serve their Creator, and do not have a self-serving evil inclination. Animals, on the other hand, have such inclinations, but lack intelligence. The result is that angels cannot receive reward for their service" (*Arukh HaShulchan*, Orach Chaim, §2).

tion is that halakha is meaningless without the body, and it will, therefore, be impossible to observe the halakha in the World to Come. Rather, it can only be observed in this world where a person has a physical body.

I emphasize these assumptions specifically because of the tension between them. Rabbi Epstein's comprehensive halakhic composition thus primarily addresses the body of a Jew observing halakha. At the same time, the first section of his book stresses that the definition of a person does not include his body.[6] Perhaps it is possible to deduce then that the occupation of halakhists who devote most of their endeavor to body-related issues does not necessarily testify to them having a positive attitude towards the body to halakhic life in this world. This tension raises the need for a study that examines halakhists' attitude towards the body and the way in which they seek to form it, a process I will demonstrate in my article.

As I will illustrate, the physical halakhic act is not merely an accompanying feature of the halakhist's life, but rather constitutes the infrastructure within which life takes place. My claim is that the focus of Jewish life on the halakhic act is a cultural choice in the sense that a Jew will focus relatively more on their body and less on thought and experience. The halakha could have focused on each with equal emphasis to precisely describe how to create an experiential realm where God is experienced intensely in the lives of halakhists "between the pots and pans," in the words of Teresa of Ávila.[7] Instead, the halakha primarily focuses on just the physical act. For example, while there are countless halakhot relating to the ways in which a Jew should act on Shabbat, there is no exact instruction as to the way Shabbat should be experienced. Moreover, the fact that the halakha designates specific actions and times for observing the halakha also simultaneously creates neutral domains in which the halakha does not actively exist. This choice is so central and significant in halakhic literature that it caused Rabbeinu Bahya ibn Paquda (1050–1120), the author of *The Duties of the Heart* (in Hebrew: *Chovat HaLevavot*), to offer a critical response. In his opinion, the centrality of halakhic literature's focus on the physical act is such that it almost overlooks internal intent and experience.[8] A similar approach to that of ibn Paquda can be identified in kabbalistic (Jewish mystic) literature from the 12th century

6 This approach is not unique to Epstein. It also appears in contemporary Musar (Jewish ethics) literature. See Englander, Yakir, *The Male Body in Ultra-Orthodox Jewish Theology*, Eugene, OR: Pickwick Publications, 2021.

7 Teresa of Ávila, *The Collected Works of St. Teresa of Ávila*, vol. 3, Washington, D.C.: ICS Publications, 2011, 5.

8 Cf. ibn Paquda, Bahya, *Chovat HaLevavot*, Introduction.

until the modern era,[9] which mentions methods and ways to focus on different experiences and feelings in religious and halakhic life. Nevertheless, as mentioned above, the central focus of halakhic literature is on physical action and on the design of the private and public domains in which the body is active, and less on the details of halakhic intent.[10]

Among the wealth of halakhic literature focusing primarily on halakhic practice itself are books that also contain explicit reference to practical intent. One example, to which I will refer below, is the book written by Rabbi Yosef Chaim of Baghdad (1834–1909), known as the "Ben Ish Chai." The book is unique in that, unlike many other classic halakhic works, each chapter opens with a theological-kabbalistic reading of the reasons for the development of the halakhic act discussed in that chapter. In other words, the "Ben Ish Chai" restored the element of experience to Jewish life and sought to connect it to the physical act. The fact that his book is exceptional in halakhic literature only serves to emphasize the cultural-Jewish choice to focus exclusively on the physical act itself.

The need for a phenomenological theory about the body would seem to be nothing less than called for, in light of halakhic literature's focus on physical action. This is a research method that seeks to describe things themselves by observing data, while internalizing Kantian critique.[11] Merleau-Ponty devoted a significant portion of his work to examination of the human body and the way it operates in the world. According to him, phenomenological observation can serve as a vehicle for learning something about the nature of the body and delving beyond the cultural-social influence on it. Below, I will present several conclusions from Merleau-Ponty's research on the body itself and will use them to examine

9 Cf. Afterman, Adam, "Letter Permutation Techniques, Kavannah and Prayer in Jewish Mysticism," *Journal for the Study of Religions and Ideologies* 6 (2007), 52–78. See also the numerous references that appear in the article's footnotes. It is important to note that a similar approach to that of the Kabbalah already appears in the Talmud. See, for example, Naeh, Shlomo, "Creates the Fruit of the Lips: A Phenomenological Study of Prayer According to Berakhot 4:3, 5:5," *Tarbits* 63 (1994), 185–218 (Heb.). In his article, Naeh showed that the Talmud features opinions according to which the physical act is deeply and inseparably connected to experience. Moreover, a halakhic act is a tool for conveying a divine message; in other words, according to this approach, the centrality of physical acts stems precisely from their deep connection with experience.

10 It is not my intention to claim that intent is not important in halakhic literature, which features numerous references to intent and "the intention of the heart." Nevertheless, halakhic literature does not focus on this intent or on its meaning. Moreover, discussions pertaining to the role and significance of intent can be found throughout the history of halakhic literature. Frequently, the significance of intent in halakha is, simply, that a person knows they are performing a mitzva (a good deed) (see, for example, in the *Rashba Responsa*, Part 1, §344, Bnei Brak 1984).

11 Cf. Merleau-Ponty, Maurice, *The Phenomenology of Perception*, trans. Colin Smith, London: Routledge, 1962, 10.

the choices of different halakhic authors pertaining to body-related topics and to their choices regarding the way in which the religious domain should be shaped. I will claim that Merleau-Ponty's phenomenological description enables to trace the way in which different halakhic authorities are interested in casting the body (in accordance with or contrary to its nature) and the way in which those shaping religious society shape their own living space, a space in which the religious-physical praxis occurs.

1 Merleau-Ponty and the Phenomenology of the Body

The question of the body has occupied western thought since its inception.[12] Philosophy, theology, and science all addressed questions such as "what is a person?" and "what is the relationship between the body and the mind?". One of the central voices at the beginning of the modern era was that of Descartes. Descartes adopted the dualistic form of thought and created an absolute separation between the body, which he placed together with the other objects limited by time and space, and the mind, which has an independent existence.[13] This division created an unequivocal alignment of power, and the focus of human identity was diverted exclusively to the intellect. Cartesian philosophy did not accord any significance to the physical experience and claimed that human thought can, via philosophical contemplation, detach itself from the physical illusion and create pure thought.

Merleau-Ponty devoted most of his phenomenological research to the question of the body and the attempt to ascertain what can indeed be said about it. He criticized the prevalent philosophical and psychological approaches of his time.[14]

---

12 Cf. Goetz, Stewart / Taliaferro, Charles, *A Brief History of the Soul*, London: Blackwell, 2011; Corcoran, Kevin (ed.), *Soul, Body, and Survival: Essays on the Metaphysics of Human Persons*, New York: Cornell University Press, 2000; Baumgarten, Albert I. / Assmann, Jan / Stroumsa, Guy G. (eds.), *Self, Soul and Body in Religious Experience*, Leiden: Brill, 1998.

13 Cf. Baker, Gordon / Morris, Katherine, *Descartes' Dualism*, London / New York: Routledge, 1996. It is important to note that Descartes continued a longstanding tradition of a dualistic approach. Nonetheless, Descartes exerted a paramount influence on modern thinking. Traditionally, phenomenological theory from Husserl's school corresponded with Descartes, hence the reference to him in Merleau-Ponty's phenomenology.

14 The book *Phenomenology of Perception* was first published in French in 1945. The criticism voiced by Merleau-Ponty against the perception of the body in his time is the product of the research in his previous book, *The Structure of Behavior*, that was published in 1942, but which was

Merleau-Ponty claimed that, since Descartes' work, research has tended to examine the body in a manner similar to the way it observes the other objects in the world and in the laboratory – the view of the body is of a third person, as an external researcher.[15] Research consequently encounters difficulty, among others, in seeing the connection between physiological facts and psychological facts that occur in our consciousness.[16] In contrast, Merleau-Ponty claimed that it is impossible to compare events that take place in the lab and events which, while identical from a physical perspective to what takes place in the lab, actually occur in our body.[17]

According to Merleau-Ponty, there is therefore a difference between the way in which a person experiences their body and the way they experience all the other objects. With the other objects, a person observes, unlike the body where a person does not assume the position of an external observer, because the body itself is the point of view via which a person views and experiences the world.[18] According to him, it must be acknowledged that study of the body should begin from the phenomenon a person experiences. The Cartesian claim (known in research jargon as "the central theory" due to its focus on the brain as the center of a person), which believes that human existence is not dependent on the body, is therefore incorrect, because our experience and knowledge are created as the result of a person's physical encounter with the world. Nevertheless, Merleau-Ponty also criticized the peripheral theory that views a person as a biological object, similar to the other objects in the world. His criticism claimed that, because this theory describes the act taking place but does not provide an explanation as to why a person chose to do this particular physical act and why it is experienced in

---

known already in 1938. A summary of the study appears in the introduction to the 1945 book. Cf. Merleau-Ponty, *The Phenomenology of Perception*, 3–74. See also Carman, Taylor, *Merleau-Ponty*, London / New York: Routledge, 2008, 4–29.

15 Cf. Merleau-Ponty, *The Phenomenology of Perception*, 87; see also Carman, *Merleau-Ponty*, 88–89. Despite Merleau-Ponty's criticism of science, he collaborated throughout his life with scientific biological and psychological theories and placed great importance on meticulous study of the body and its function. His criticism is, instead, against the interpretation that scientists give to research results.

16 Cf. Merleau-Ponty, *The Phenomenology of Perception*, 89.

17 Cf. Kearney, Richard, "Maurice Merleau-Ponty," in: id. (ed.), *Modern Movements in European Philosophy*, New York: Manchester University Press, 1994, 73–74.

18 Cf. Merleau-Ponty, *The Phenomenology of Perception*, 104. Merleau-Ponty's work on the connection between a person and the world is based on Martin Heidegger who wrote, for example, that "Being alongside the world never means anything like the Being-present-at-hand-together of Things that occurs. There is no such thing as the 'side-by-side-ness' of an entity called 'Dasein' with another entity called 'world.'" (Heidegger, Martin, *Being and Time*, trans. John MacQuarrie / Edward Robinson, New York: Harper and Row, 1962, 81).

a specific way, it does not constitute a complete description of a person. According to Merleau-Ponty, it would be wrong to reduce the body to a point at which its physical and mechanical aspects are viewed separately: "the union of soul and body [. . .] is not an amalgamation between two mutually external terms, subject and object, brought about by arbitrary decree. It is enacted at every instant in the movement of existence."[19]

In my opinion, Merleau-Ponty's theory about the body can be used to understand a halakhic choice in relation to prayer. Prayer contains components that differ from those of every-day speech. The words of the prayer, i.e., their meaning, are not created by the person praying but rather appear in front of him. The worshiper must observe the words in front of him, be attentive to them and attempt to connect with and experience their meaning. According to the central theory, it would be better for prayer to occur without involving the body, without reciting it aloud, i.e., via a physical act, so as not to "sully" the intent. Indeed, Bahya ibn Paquda, the author of *The Duties of the Heart*, who distinguished between mind and body, expressed this puzzlement in writing that "the language of prayer depends on the intention of prayer, while the intention does not depend in the same way on language. This is because prayerful intention takes place not on the lips, but in the heart, and it is this intention that comprises the meaning of the words we pray."[20] For him, the halakha's choice that a person should recite the words of the prayer is a *post factum* ruling attributed to the inferior emotional state of many of the worshipers. However, unlike the spirit of Rabbeinu Bahya, it can be said that, based on Merleau-Ponty, the choice of halakhic literature to express the prayer aloud testifies to the need for the body's physicality so that certain experiences can take place in a person.[21] Emotions and thoughts are not enough for a person to pray with his entire being. Thoughts and feelings differ from what is said aloud. Words recited aloud are not an expression of the feeling of the heart but rather an articulated feeling. If so, prayer does not express the workings of the heart or the written text appearing in the pages of the siddur but rather constitutes a verbalized feeling.

A further claim arising from Merleau-Ponty's words is that our body's experience is dependent not only on its biology and the encounter with the objects in the world but also on the roles assigned to it. One such example is a person hold-

---

19 Merleau-Ponty, *The Phenomenology of Perception*, 102.

20 Ibn Paquda, *Chovat HaLevavot*, Sha'ar Cheshbon Nefesh, Chap. 3.

21 The creators of physical gestures in prayer were faced with several possibilities: prayer of the heart, verbalized but silent prayer, and prayer recited aloud. On the various choices and their cultural significance at the time, see Ehrlich, Uri, *"All My Bones Shall Say": The Non-Verbal Language of Jewish Prayer*, Jerusalem: Magnes Press, 1999, 163–179, esp. 165–167 (Heb.).

ing a pipe in his hand. When he does so, the hand is experienced differently than the other organs of the body. This is because while holding the pipe, the hand is not only a hand, one of the body's organs, but rather serves the role of "pipe holder." Consequently, when the body is "on duty," it is experienced differently than when it is free from duty.[22] In other words, a person's relation towards the world alters his physical experience. The same holds true when performing religious acts.[23]

This claim becomes important, even decisive, in the case of a religious society. As I will illustrate, a section of halakhic literature is interested in shaping the human body as a tool for implementing the halakhic act and for realizing the experience of God in a person's life (and thereby for limiting the realms in which God is absent from his life). The body that sways to and fro at varying rhythms during the prayer is not thus proof of emotional devotion. The body's movement is, itself, devotion, and the tool that enables a person to feel God's presence within him during prayer.[24] A Jew is not merely a praying "cogito." A person is prayer – "But I am all prayer" (Ps 109:4). It is unsurprising to find several rabbis encouraging people who pray but fail to have intention or feel a part of the prayer to perform physical acts while praying, such as body movements that imitate someone in a trance. They believed that such movements are meaningful, even though they are "external," i.e., performed without internal motivation. Imitating devotion in prayer can lead a person to feel a sense of devotion.[25] This principle appears in the *Sefer HaChinukh*:

> And even he who in his heart is a complete sinner and all the desires of his heart are only for evil; if his spirit shall be enlightened and he will put his efforts and actions to persist in Torah and commandments – even if not for the sake of Heaven – he shall immediately incline towards the good. And from that which is not for its own sake comes that which is for its own sake; for the hearts are drawn after the actions.[26]

22 Cf. Merleau-Ponty, *The Phenomenology of Perception*, 114–115.
23 Cf. Merleau-Ponty, *The Phenomenology of Perception*, 246. Further development of Merleau-Ponty's claim in theological thought appears in Kearney's work. See Kearney, Richard, *Anatheism*, New York: Columbia University Press, 2010, 85–100.
24 This claim is influenced by Michel Henry's interpretation of the relations between body and soul. See Henry, Michel, *I am the Truth: Toward a Philosophy of Christianity*, trans. Susan Emanuel, Stanford: Stanford University Press, 2003, 30.
25 Cf. Schwartz, Yoel, *Avodat HaLev: Ma'alat HaTefilla V'Inyana*, Jerusalem: Mishnat Rabbi Akiva Institute, 1981, 84.
26 Aaron Halevi of Barcelona, *Sefer HaChinukh*, Mitzva 17.

Another significant point in Merleau-Ponty's phenomenology is that the body operates in the world independent of a person's intention.[27] In other words, not only is a person not found outside his body (similar to Descartes' claim) but, rather, he is also not in control of his body which operates of its own accord. This is correct not only in the context of the body's autonomous workings – the blood flow, the contraction of the heart and other muscles – but also in the context of its controlled movements. A person does not routinely instruct his hand to pick up a certain object such as a book, rather, he simply picks up the book. In other words, the physical act of picking up the book is generally performed together with the desire to pick it up and the two cannot be separated.[28] According to Merleau-Ponty, if a person seeks to control each and every movement of his hand (similar to the central theory that focuses on the brain's instruction), his body's movements will bear no resemblance to the natural body movement which moves autonomously and without the need for assistance from the brain. In other words, the hand of a person who moves his hand knows how to move in the world because it is part of the world. It should be noted that Merleau-Ponty did not oppose the Cartesian theory, and that his claims whereby the body has independent knowledge distinct from the "cogito" were not directed against it. Merleau-Ponty rejected the division between the body and the "cogito," in the sense that the "cogito" with which a person is identified is the intellect as opposed to the body. In his opinion, a person is a "bodily being," in the sense that his physicality engages in a dialogue that influences and is influenced by the consciousness. A person's conscious readiness towards the world therefore influences the way in which the body experiences the world. At the same time, the body's encounter with the world influences and shapes the consciousness. Perception, however, is not influenced by the fact that the body is a physical object in the world but rather by the body being a "living body," in the sense that it exists in the world and experiences it as part of it, rather than as something external.[29] Likewise, a person, present in the world and perceiving it from within his body, is a "bodily being."[30] Dualistic Cartesian thought does not describe human existence but rather an unnatural situation in which a person engages in philosophical reflection and excludes the objects from the dialogue.[31]

27 To a certain degree, the term "intention" replaces the term "cogito." Common to both is self-reflection. Nevertheless, while "cogito" expresses the definition of a person, "intention" expresses a certain aspect of a person whereby he is in a state of self-reflection.

28 Cf. Merleau-Ponty, *The Phenomenology of Perception*, 157–167.

29 Cf. Merleau-Ponty, *The Phenomenology of Perception*, 85.

30 Cf. Merleau-Ponty, *The Phenomenology of Perception*, 239.

31 Cf. Merleau-Ponty, *The Phenomenology of Perception*, 278.

2 A Test Case for the Inability to Ignore the Workings of the Body: The Norms of Modesty

The fact that the body acts in the world is two-directional. The body acts on the world in the sense that it is the vehicle via which a person's conscious decisions are transformed into action. At the same time, the data received by the body is dependent on the world that conveys the stimuli to the person. The world around us is loaded with so many stimuli that a person can only absorb a small fraction of them. Data is absorbed via the body. The choice as to which data the body will absorb and which it will consider "background" to be ignored, depends on the physical and cultural domain within which the body exists: which data is in a familiar domain, and which isn't, and on social values, etc. For example, one of the most contentious arguments in Israeli society is about the visibility of women in the public domain. Among other things, the discussion centers on the way in which ultra-Orthodox (*Haredi*) society (that consists of both men and women) demands that women dress in the public domain,[32] i.e., in a manner it considers modest and not as this would be viewed by many secular women. Ultra-Orthodox (*Haredi*) society also claims that women who do not dress modestly according to this definition harm *Haredi* men. Non-*Haredi* women feel that *Haredi* men transform them into sexual objects by focusing on the female body and ignoring the fact that women are more than just a physical body. Furthermore, they claim that a *Haredi* man can choose not to look at women he considers to be dressed immodestly. Instead, he compels women to dress in a way that not only conceals their sexuality but also their body. An analysis of this tension from the perspective of Merleau-Ponty's phenomenology can shed new light on the discussion.[33] According to this view, the way in which a reasonable *Haredi* man experiences a reasonable secular woman differs fundamentally from the way in which a reasonable secular man experiences the same secular woman. For the reasonable secular man, the encounter between him-

---

32 This reading follows the work of Gibson and Romdenh-Romluc. See Gibson, James J., "The Theory of Affordances," in: Robert Shaw / John Bransford (eds.), *Perceiving, Acting and Knowing. Toward an Ecological Psychology*, Hillsdale, NJ: Erlbaum, 1977, 67–82; Romdenh-Romluc, Komarine, "Habit and Attention," in: Rasmus Thybo Jensen / Dermot Moran (eds.), *The Phenomenology of Embodied Subjectivity*, Contributions to Phenomenology 71, Cham et al.: Springer, 2013, 3–19. On the way in which *Haredi* society shapes the public domain, see Englander, Yakir, "The Image of the Male Body in Lithuanian Ultra-Orthodox Thought in Israel and Corresponding Strategies for Forging an A-Feminine Public Sphere," *Journal of Contemporary Religion* 29, 3 (2014), 457–470.
33 The discussion here is through male eyes and does not relate at all to a secular woman's view of the *Haredi* demand of her, or to the *Haredi* woman's view of a secular woman.

self and the secular woman is a substantive meeting that embodies various possibilities: the woman is a potential "date" or friend, i.e., she represents the potential for a substantive encounter, and not merely an imaginary one. Moreover, the fact that she wears, for example, a sleeveless shirt is, for him, only a kind of background, because the female members of his family and people he meets in the different spheres of his life all dress similarly. The secular man also naturally views the woman through the sexual domain in his life, but this is part of his routine daily life, one that is not isolated or reserved for specific times. The daily domain also contains sexual characteristics.

In contrast, a *Haredi* man is taught that he will be matched for marriage with a young *Haredi* woman who covers her arms. For him, a secular woman does not represent potential for a "date," romantic relationship or, indeed, even potential friend, and the meeting between them is imaginary much more than it is substantive. Moreover, his female relatives, i.e., the women located in the background of his life, do not dress like them. For him, that secular woman is thus a potential for temptation and, consequently, constitutes a danger. Sexuality in *Haredi* society is designed to appear exclusively in the private and not in the public domain. It is thus unsurprising that the meeting between a *Haredi* man and a secular woman leads the Haredi man to sense a physical sexual experience, and that this sensation is experienced as harmful to him. According to Merleau-Ponty, the *Haredi* man has no control over the manifestation of these bodily-sexual experiences; the only choice he has is how to respond to it.[34] The difference between the *Haredi* man and his secular counterpart is not merely in the data that appears before him, but also in the interpretation he gives it in his intention. Unlike the secular man, for whom an experience of sexual sensations does not constitute a moral failing but, rather, evidence of sexual soundness, the dimensions of which he encounters throughout the entire day, for the *Haredi* man, the manifestation of an uncontrolled sexual experience in public domains is experienced as a moral failure and a halakhic problem.

I have no interest here in judging any particular way of life but rather, in using Merleau-Ponty, to clarify the various experiences of people living in different domains, that stem from the different habits of the body there. The difference between the secular and the *Haredi* man is not only in the relation of the culture in which each of them grows to the female body. The difference between them is also in the physical experience itself. In other words, a person is limited in the

34 The discussion here is solely from Merleau-Ponty's research viewpoint. The work of Austin and Althusser raise the need for more in-depth examination of this subject. See Butler, Judith, *Excitable Speech: A Politics of the Performative*, London / New York: Routledge, 1997.

amount of data he can absorb and the choice as to which data materializes in front of him is an involuntary choice that depends on the relation between the body and surrounding domain. This description is important for two reasons: first, it can be assumed that the data absorbed by a halakhist will, to a certain degree, differ from that of a non-halakhic person. The halakha therefore determines not just a person's actions but also the experiences and data he will experience; second, a person does not choose which data he is interested or not in absorbing. He is not a "cogito" who chooses how to exist in the world. The correct way to describe a person's life is that he understands that his body experiences a certain experience, and that he can, to some extent, choose what he wants to do within that experience. If this description is indeed correct, it is much easier to understand the struggle of certain halakhic groups over the visibility of the public domain. If, according to society's translation, the public domain abounds with sexual stimuli, a person cannot choose when he is interested in looking at them, and what his body will experience. He can choose, after seeing something that causes sexual stimulation, whether to look at it again, and what to do with the sexual experience his body has already experienced. The argument between halakhic societies that are considered conservative, and societies regarded as liberal is not only over the freedom of choice of women and men in relation to the way in which they should be seen in the public domain, but also over their freedom of choice regarding the data that their body will absorb in the public domain, in accordance with the background of their lives.

Following Merleau-Ponty's work, other theoreticians (who are not necessarily phenomenologists) attempted to examine the role of the body in the world. Merleau-Ponty did not offer in-depth social conclusions on the body's existence within a cultural domain and the body's influence on the experience itself. Judith Butler, in her work *Gender Trouble*, building on the research of different anthropologists, challenged the familiar distinction between nature and nurture (or, in gender jargon, between sex and gender) in the context of the body.[35] According to that distinction, the term "nature" expresses the natural and therefore, immutable, human domains. Unlike nature, the term "nurture" expresses the human domains which are created by society and can therefore be changed. According to Butler, the very distinction between nature and nurture expresses a social ideology that seeks to create an illusion whereby parts of a person are "clean," natural, devoid of social impact. She opines that one cannot talk of realms within a person as natural without viewing them as a product of the cultural discourse.

---

35 Cf. Butler, Judith, *Gender Trouble: Feminism and the Subversion of Identity*, London / New York: Routledge, 1990.

According to this reasoning, biology, which is perceived as natural and supposedly prior to any cultural influence, is shaped and familiar to us from within language and culture. Butler adopted this claim and also applied it to a person's basic primordial experiences – our physical experiences. Butler's claim is radical, not just because it challenges the ability to talk about the concept of nature outside cultural language but also because it exposes the difficulty to change what is perceived as social and cultural. According to Butler, we acquire familiarity with our body via social influence. The definition of self and our experience of ourselves, of our body, are a product of the society in which we took shape. Butler's work is profoundly influenced by Merleau-Ponty.[36] As mentioned, Merleau-Ponty emphasized the connection between the bodily experience and the domain outside a person with which the body is in constant dialogue. In accordance with the phenomenological description, Butler was correct in claiming that a person's recognition of himself is achieved via mediation of the surrounding society, because a person (with his body) chooses, according to social-cultural contexts, which data to absorb and which to leave in the background.

According to Merleau-Ponty's approach, for as long as a society operates in the way it does, without any change in the social background encountered by the body, certain physical domains will continue to be experienced by a person as "natural" (habitual).[37] Unlike Merleau-Ponty, Butler emphasized an additional characteristic – the need to reconstruct some of the actions, specifically because they are unnatural to a person. She revealed how, for a person to take shape in a socially desired manner, society must demand from him expressions of performance and repeated actions that reconstruct and create the desired social self. Society's demands from a person to repeatedly perform those acts that define him, indicates that there is no "true primordial" self but rather only one that is reconstructed again and again. For example, in the halakhic context, for a male to feel like a man and to create his masculinity in the social-halakhic sense, society demands that, throughout his life, he observes certain Jewish laws (halakhot) from which women are exempt. There is a constant movement between the habit acquired by a man who wakes up in the morning and lays tefillin,[38] and certain unachievable halakhic demands which I will examine below.[39]

---

36 Cf. Butler, *Gender Trouble*, 207–208; Butler, Judith, "Performative Acts and Gender Constitution: An Essay in Phenomenology and Feminist Theory," *Theatre Journal* 40, 4 (1988), 519–531.

37 See Romdenh-Romluc, "Habit and Attention," 3–19.

38 Tefillin (Phylacteries) are a set of small black leather boxes with leather straps containing scrolls of parchment inscribed with verses from the Torah. Tefillin are worn by adult Jewish men during weekday morning prayers.

39 Cf. Butler, Judith, *Bodies that Matter*, London / New York: Routledge, 1993, 223–242.

3 Creating the Halakhic Domain

The phenomenological description of a person as a "bodily being" and the reciprocal relations between a person's body and the surrounding domain can help us understand the relation between a halakhic-cultural living space and a non-halakhic cultural domain. Some attempt to create an image whereby there is a natural non-halakhic domain, a sterile realm in which the "normal" person grows. In contrast, the halakhist adopts a further, halakhic, living space that constitutes a kind of bonus and increment in addition to the natural domain. An expression of this way of thinking can be found for example in the description of the meeting between one of the leaders of the *Haredi* (ultra-Orthodox) community, Rabbi Yeshaya Karelitz (1878–1953), known as the "Chazon Ish," and the State of Israel's first Prime Minister David Ben-Gurion. According to Karelitz, secular Israeli society resembles an empty cart while *Haredi* society, that adheres to the halakha, resembles a full cart. In other words, the halakhist is laden with tradition (culture) that does not belong to the secular Israeli. Among others, this view lies at the heart of religious-Zionist philosophy. Religious-Zionist society is based on the assumption whereby most of its members maintain a lifestyle that includes adoption of liberal values found in secular Israeli society while, at the same time, embodying halakhic values.[40]

Research has already shown that statements such as these are incorrect, simply because there is no practice without theory and no theory without practice. In other words, no society lacks values relative to others or contains a smaller number of values than any other society. Every society has values, and an individual's practice is built through a dialogue with the society in which he grew and is, in turn, what influences society. Merleau-Ponty's novelty is in the emphasis given to the place of the body in that dialogue. Society creates values that cause the body's senses to focus on certain characteristics in the world around it and to relegate the others to the background. Some societies stress with extreme clarity the values they identify as positive and those they view as negative. Other societies outline more vaguely the values to be adhered to or that are underappreciated, and those they do not respect. According to this claim, a society that claims that it has several frameworks of values which, in the eyes of other societies, contradict each other, will discover that, in reality, it lacks specific values they proclaim to be the core of its belief system or that these can be found in a different language or receive differing expression. For example, religious-Zionist society frequently

40 Cf. Englander, Yakir / Sagi, Avi, *Sexuality and the Body in New Religious Zionist Discourse*, trans. Batya Stein, Boston: Academic Press, 2015.

claims that it exists in a state of tension between different cultures – both secular-Zionist and *Haredi*-halakhic. Its claim is that the choice to do so enables it to incorporate values that, for other societies, seem contradictory.

Nevertheless, an in-depth examination of religious-Zionist discourse reveals that it did not maintain values that it supposedly received from *Haredi* society and from secular-Zionist society in similar fashion. In fact, these values changed once they entered religious-Zionist discourse. For example, the discourse pertaining to the body in religious-Zionism differs fundamentally from the secular-western discourse on the same issue. Religious-Zionist halakha abandons the attempt to balance different values (the western perception of the body and the halakhic tradition) and creates a unique perception of the body. Many religious-Zionist halakhic authorities use the fact that the body is frequently used as a halakhic tool to shape the experience of the religious-Zionist halakhist. They demand from halakhic adherents not to heed the bodily experiences they have and not to act on them (similar to secular-western discourse). Instead, they create a semi-halakhic discourse about the "proper body," a discourse that frequently objects to physical experience and categorizes them as improper inclinational experiences.[41] The authors of halakhic literature operate alongside a cultural domain laden with content and ways of shaping the encounter between a person and the world and seek to form a different encounter that is controlled, among others, by halakhic literature. As noted above, the advantage of halakhic literature is that it is directed at the body and therefore has the capacity to intensively shape the encounter between the human body and the space external to it.

One of the ways that halakhic literature creates its halakhic ideal in relation to the non-halakhic cultural domain of the general majority within which it exists is by breaking down a natural physical act into several acts that are divided and controlled by mental reflection. As noted, Merleau-Ponty emphasized a natural physical act as one that does not need a person's intention. Breaking down the naturalness of the act creates interruptions. During these interruptions of the natural body movement, halakhic literature requires a person to think about certain values it is interested in, thereby impressing religious ideology upon the halakhist, and shaping a different cultural environment, containing different values and content from those of the surrounding society. For example, the "Ben Ish Chai" wrote about the laws pertaining to wearing a tallit that:

> This is the manner in which we are to wrap ourselves in our tallit (prayer-shawl): When the blessing has been said, place the tallit at first only upon your head. Don't imitate those who

---

41 Cf. Englander / Sagi, *Sexuality and the Body in New Religious Zionist Discourse.*

> think themselves clever, wrapping the tallit around their whole body from the very outset. Rather, we should all follow the practice of our teacher the "Ari," of blessed memory.
>
> Once you have covered your head with your tallit, its four corners will naturally drape over your shoulders toward the front, two on your right side and two on the left. Then, take hold of the two corners that are on your right side and swing them across in front of you. Pause then, waiting for the time it takes for someone to take four strides, or a bit less. Only then, grasp the opposite tallit corners, on your left side, and toss them up and over your left shoulder . . . Again, pause for the space of four strides. Only then, bring down the tallit that is now around your neck, to cover your entire body. As the verse (in Genesis) says: "Each flock moving separately, with a generous space kept between the flocks."[42]

Wrapping oneself in the tallit is a physical act of putting on a garment. Even a western person unaccustomed to the halakhic domain gets dressed in the morning. Moreover, the "Ben Ish Chai" acknowledges that for some halakhists, wearing a tallit is an act similar to that of a non-halakhist getting dressed: "Don't imitate those who think themselves clever, wrapping the tallit around their whole body from the very outset." In my opinion, the "Ben Ish Chai" has a deliberate interest in dividing the wearing of the tallit into several non-sequential actions in order to disrupt the naturalness of the physical act and, in so doing, to instill religious values. As mentioned, the uniqueness of his book is that it begins each chapter (section) with a kabbalistic metaphysical explanation about the meaning of a halakhic act. In his opinion, wearing the tallit and the tzitzit fringes are part of a halakhist's struggle against evil metaphysical forces. By wrapping himself in the tallit, a Jew remedies the corruption of the serpent that caused the spiritual garment of light worn by the first man Adam to be replaced with a garment of skins. If so, the halakhist wrapping himself in the tallit is not just operating in his immediate physical-social domain (similar to his friends in the synagogue and unlike the surrounding non-Jewish and non-halakhic Jewish society), but rather is also operating in upper heavenly worlds, invisible to a person who is not part of the halakhic domain created by the "Ben Ish Chai." However, for the reasonable halakhist to experience the act of wrapping himself in the tallit as one that also takes place in hidden worlds, the *posek* (halakhic authority) must create the same experience. The "Ben Ish Chai" did so by disrupting the sequence of the natural bodily movement, performed without reflection. He transformed the natural act into an unnatural physical act (similar to that performed in a lab) that is divided into three parts, between each of which the halakhist must pause for the time it takes to walk four strides. This disruption of the physical act causes the halakhist to pause, a period which creates an invitation to connect with the struggle between good and evil – forces that are invisible to a non-

42 Yosef Chaim of Baghdad, *Ben Ish Chai*, Parshat Breishit, §1,5.

halakhic person. The new world that surrounds the "Ben Ish Chai's" halakhist differs from that of the surrounding society, a world in which human physical acts generate a tikkun (a remediation) in concealed, upper worlds. Each morning, as he wraps himself in the tallit, the halakhist reconstructs and creates these heavenly worlds, transforming them to be part of his own, and the subject becomes a warrior in divine struggles, even in the most mundane physical act.

A further example of the disruption of action occurring every morning appears in the halakhot pertaining to washing the hands. A halakhist washes his hands upon awakening each morning, a physical act also performed by a secular person who washes his hands and face in the morning. A careful look at the halakhot pertaining to washing the hands leads us to understand that whereas a secular person cleans his hands, the halakhic person purifies them:

> The order of the washing of the hands for the dawn prayer: First, fill the vessel with water while holding it in your right hand, then transfer the vessel to your left hand, after which use the left hand to pour the water over your right. Next, take the vessel with your right hand, and pour water over your left, thus completing one ablution. And then do the same, repeating the movements a second and third time. [. . .] And do not simply wash each hand separately, three times in a row – for the spirit of evil will not be uprooted thus, but only by washing the two hands in alternation, first one and then the other, as written here, and as also spelled out in the book called *Sha'ar HaKavanot* by our Teacher, the "Ari."[43]

While a secular person cleans his hands – a habitual physical act that requires no special intent –, a halakhist is required to perform a more complex act. He passes the vessel containing the water from the right hand to the left hand which pours the water on his right hand and vice versa 3 times. The significance of the right and left hands and of washing the hands is explained at the beginning of the chapter, with the right hand symbolizing the attribute of *chesed* (kindness) as opposed to the left hand which symbolizes the attribute of judgment. Taking the vessel in the right hand, even if it is immediately transferred to the left hand, magnifies the forces of kindness over those of judgment. Consequently, the vessel should be transferred to the left hand so that the left hand will be subservient to the right hand. The halakhist thereby magnifies the force of kindness in the world over that of judgment.

Further to Merleau-Ponty, the hands being washed and doing the washing are not only the person's body. They themselves symbolize spiritual forces – *chesed* (kindness) and judgment. The hands serve as tools in the struggle over the way the world is run, i.e., whether the force of *chesed* or that of judgment will hold sway over the world. This is how the "Ben Ish Chai" shapes the body and,

43 Yosef Chaim of Baghdad, *Ben Ish Chai*, Parshat Breishit, Parshat Toldot, §1.

hence, the personality of the halakhist – to also be tools in heavenly influences between kindness and judgment. A person is no longer a private subject whose life is conducted in the familiar physical and social domain but rather a permanent warrior among the heavenly forces, his hands themselves acting as the forces of kindness and judgment. Friend and foe are thus also both located in his body. Moreover, even if he refuses to "play" the heavenly game, he still influences it. Even if a halakhist ignores the laws of washing hands and merely cleans them, not only is he not observing the halakha, but he is harming the entire world by magnifying the forces of judgment at the expense of those of kindness.

It is fascinating to note that the "Ben Ish Chai" did not stop at formulating a precise method for washing hands. It can be assumed that this unique method of washing each hand three times could also easily become a sequential and natural physical act. A halakhist who is accustomed, from a young age, to washing his hands in this prescribed manner does so out of habit.[44] Once this act becomes a habit and, consequently, natural for the halakhist's body, it is highly probable that he will forget that he is engaged in a struggle between the forces of kindness and judgment and the "Ben Ish Chai" therefore sought to disrupt the body's physical movements while wrapping oneself in the tallit:

> The right hand must not receive the vessel from the left hand but rather, after pouring water on the right hand, one should lay the vessel on the ground and only then take it from the ground with the right hand to pour onto the left. But each time, the right hand should pass the vessel to the left hand to pour water over it, to show subservience to the left by the right, like the master imposing his authority over a slave.[45]

Laying the vessel on the ground between washing each hand reinforces the disruption of the natural physical act which, in turn, enables the introduction of values.

My emphasis on the places in which the "Ben Ish Chai" disrupted the naturalness of a physical act is not intended to claim that halakhic literature is interested in disrupting physical movement entirely. In my opinion, there is a tension between the desire to disrupt physical movement, thereby enabling the creation of a living space that differs from that of non-halakhic society, and the wish to create halakhists who allow their body to operate naturally within the halakhic living space. This tension can be felt in halakha's attitude towards the concept of experience. Theoretically, the halakhist is required to experience his halakhic actions. However, focusing on the experience impedes the possibility to create a halakhic community which works together even when some of its members do not

44 Cf. Romdenh-Romluc, "Habit and Attention," 4.
45 Rabbi Yosef Chaim of Baghdad, *Ben Ish Chai*, Parshat Toldot, §1.

share the same experiences when performing the halakhic act. For example, a structured tension can be found in the Talmud and, later, in halakhic literature between the shaping of prayer as voluntary, as stemming from within a person, and prayer as a ready-made product that a Jew receives externally. Halakhists are interested in ensuring that Jews pray and in creating a community that prays together. Consequently, they determined set times for prayer and formulated a fixed wording.[46] At the same time, these choices of halakhists shape the halakhist whose prayer is experienced as obligatory, thereby distancing the connection between prayer and the internal fervor that arises within a person. It can be assumed that a person who is obligated to pray in the synagogue three times a day, for approximately two hours a day and while reading dozens of pages of text, will find it hard to experience a desire to pray, even voluntarily. In his *Hilkhot Tefilla* (*The Laws of Prayer*), the Rambam (Maimonides) claimed that the ideal situation is when "a person who was eloquent would offer many prayers and requests. Conversely, a person who was inarticulate would speak as well as he could and whenever he desired. Similarly, the number of prayers was dependent on each person's ability. Some would pray once daily; others, several times."[47] In his opinion, the situation whereby Jews pray three times a day using a fixed wording arose as the result of a post factum reality. Moreover, the Rambam himself cited cases in which a person should not pray. Moreover, until the end of the *Rishonim* period (rabbinic authorities who operated between the 11th and 15th centuries), the question of the prayers' composition remained open, and the tension around it persisted. From the period of the *Acharonim* (rabbis and halakhic authorities who operated from the 16th century onwards), it was decided that every person should pray, regardless of his emotional state, using a fixed wording.

Following Merleau-Ponty, it is important to note that the advantage of prayers with a fixed prayer wording which is recited at fixed times is not just that a Jew will remember to pray to God. The advantage is that at various times throughout the day, his body is part of the prayer – not just the arm on which the tefillin is wrapped, but the entire body prays three times a day. Shaping the body as a tool in service of the halakha enables to create, among others, a halakhic society that differs from a non-halakhic society.

I will present a further example of the tension between the wish to disrupt the physical-halakhic act and compel a person to have intent, and the desire of

---

46 Cf. *b. Ber.* 26b.

47 Maimonides, *Mishneh Torah*, Hilkhot Tefilla U'Virkat Cohanim §1,3 (Warsaw-Vilna Edition, 21).

the creators of halakha to form a halakhic habit.[48] This tension appears when halakhists from birth meet *Ba'alei Teshuva* (newly religious Jews). A halakhist is frequently envious of a *Ba'al Teshuva* when observing him at prayer. The latter's fervor when reciting every prayer and blessing, the initial meeting with the words of the prayers, and the slower recitation all cause the born halakhist a sense of inferiority both vis-à-vis the *Ba'al Teshuva* himself and in relation to his own prayer experience that has an element of the banal.[49]

On the other hand, the born halakhist has an advantage precisely because prayer and the halakhic act are a bodily habit. Moreover, and further to Merleau-Ponty, it is not at all clear that a comparison between the halakhic act of the born halakhist and that of a *Ba'al Teshuva* is at all accurate. The halakhic act of a born halakhist is part of his natural living space, a habit that becomes second nature.[50] This differs from the halakhic act of the *Ba'al Teshuva* which constitutes an act that is still unnatural and is performed within a familiar living space but one where this act is not performed.[51]

The prayer of a born halakhist has characteristics that a *Ba'al Teshuva* cannot achieve, even if they both observe all the halakhic details. This is because the first prays reflexively while the latter prays with his body. For example, knowing the prayers by heart enables the born halakhist to pray in ways that the *Ba'al Teshuva* cannot. Many of those born into the halakhic world know some of the Shabbat songs and large sections of the prayers by heart. What does it mean to know a song by heart and recite it aloud? The author of the *Arukh HaShulchan* wrote that: "Happy is the person whose eyes are always closed while praying [. . .] because closing the eyes is very beneficial for having intention."[52] As I noted above, the first chapter of *Arukh HaShulchan* features a halakhic stance that is similar in its approach to the dualistic approach, although it views a person as also consisting of the emotional experience and not being confined exclusively to intellectual thought. Closing the eyes therefore enables us to restrict the data reaching our bodily senses and to focus on thought and emotional experience. According to this approach,

48 This example is based on the article by Edgar, Orion, "Attention and Habit: Praying the Psalms with Simone Weil," published as a paper presented at the conference of the Society for the Study of Theology, Nottingham, 6–8 April, 2013. Available at http://cambridge.academia.edu/OrionEdgar/Conference-Papers (June 26, 2023).

49 "It should be remembered that religious society sometimes envies or admires *Ba'alei Teshuva* (newly religious people). [. . .] for a person who is religious from birth, the performance of mitzvot is, at times, mechanic, automatic. This contrasts to a newly religious person who performs mitzvot in a deliberate, conscious manner." Excerpt from an unpublished rabbi's letter.

50 Cf. Romdenh-Romluc, "Habit and Attention," 3–19.

51 Cf. Romdenh-Romluc, "Habit and Attention," 3–19.

52 *Arukh HaShulchan*, Hilkhot Tefilla.

knowing the prayers by heart means that the soul (that defines a person) knows the meaning of the prayer and commands the mouth to recite it. But does this mean he really knows the prayer by heart? Further to Merleau-Ponty, I will claim that knowing the words of the prayer does not constitute a guarantee that a person understands them all. Knowing Shabbat songs by heart is a physical familiarity connected to bodily knowledge of reciting the words but not necessarily to intellectual acquaintance with them. For example, it can be assumed that if a halakhist is asked to recite the words of the Shabbat songs he will struggle to do so unless he can recite them together with the accompanying music. This represents a physical knowledge of the Shabbat songs – he only knows the songs when praying and singing them aloud with his mouth, with his body. This physical knowledge enables him to pray in ways that a *Ba'al Teshuva* cannot. For example, someone born as a halakhist can sing the Shabbat songs with his eyes closed and observe, via intention, the words of the prayer which are recited by his body as a habit. This is a different experience of prayer, one connected to the meeting between physical prayer and the emotional domain in which the halakhist is currently present.

4 Halakhic Literature and the Creation of an Imaginary "Cogito"

I showed above how characteristics of halakhic literature can be understood in light of Merleau-Ponty's phenomenological description in relation to the body and indicated the relation between the body and the domain (the world) in which the body operates. Below, I will claim that some parts of halakhic literature refuse to recognize a person as a "bodily being" but rather attempt to shape his image as an "intellectual cogito" that does not depend on the physical domain (but rather merely instructs the body how to act).[53] Historically, the body has been associated with those attributes that are considered socially negative, whereas the soul was associated with positive qualities. According to this model, human uniqueness is identified with the soul while the body is regarded as a hindrance to be contended with. The ideal objective is to arrive at an existential situation whereby each act occurs only after mental reflection and a conscious choice that this is

53 As noted, this attempt is not unique to halakhic literature but rather was, for many generations, also the central approach of significant parts of western culture.

how a person should act. Rabbi Moses Isserles, known as the "Rema" (1520–1572), began his commentary on Rabbi Yosef Karo's *Shulchan Arukh* with the following words:

> "I have set the Lord before me constantly" (Psalms 16:8); this is a major principle in the Torah and amongst the virtues of the righteous who walk before God. For a person's way of sitting, his movements, and his dealings while he is alone in his house are not like his way of sitting, his movements, and his dealings when he is before a great king; nor are his speech and free expression as much as he wants when he is with his household members and his relatives like his speech when in a royal audience. All the more so when one takes to heart that the Great King, the Holy One, Blessed Is He, Whose glory fills the earth, is standing over him and watching his actions, as it is stated: "'Will a man hide in concealment and I will not see him?' – the word of God" (Jeremiah 23:24), he immediately acquires fear and submission in dread of God, May He Be Blessed, and is ashamed of Him constantly (Guide for the Perplexed 3, 52).[54]

Opening this halakhic opus with a meta-halakhic statement testifies to the intention of the author throughout the book. The "Rema" defined the role of halakha as an attempt to create a person in constant reflection. In his opinion, a person who finds himself in a non-halakhic domain walks through the world without reflection, except when in the presence of someone who wields power over him. In such cases, he engages in reflection and carefully considers his body's movements and his speech. In contrast, the halakhist must internalize the character of the person wielding power such that he does not need his actual physical presence. The halakhist internalizes God's gaze constantly scrutinizing his conduct in all places, a gaze assimilated in his body. Internalizing the gaze prevents the creation of the discrepancy between the public and private domains with which we are familiar in modern western society. The Divine gaze requires the halakhic person to monitor his body's movements which must not be devoid of intellectual-emotional reflection and should only be done with intent. This way of life itself reinforces and reconstructs the ideology behind it. A halakhic way of life infuses the halakhist's consciousness with the image of the king constantly overseeing a person who thereby becomes not only a person observing the mitzvot but also one whose personality is shaped as someone for whom the emotion of guilt (related for him to halakha) guides his way of life.[55]

The book's opening is surprising because it contrasts with most of what follows: the author of the *Shulchan Arukh* (Rabbi Karo) focused on the physical act, and not on emotional experience. The "Rema's" introduction can therefore be re-

54 Commentary of Rabbi Moses Isserles (the "Rema") on the *Shulchan Arukh*, Orach Chaim 1:1.
55 Cf. Althusser, Louis, "Ideology and Ideological State Apparatuses," in: id., *Lenin and Philosophy*, trans. Ben Brewster, New York / London: Monthly Review Press, 1971, 170–186.

lated to as a kind of lip service, a sort of rigid and unequivocal statement which enables Rabbi Karo to ignore intention throughout the remainder of the book. Another possibility is to view the "Rema's" remarks as stage instructions and designing of the halakhic "play." According to this approach, even if the remainder of the book focuses primarily on the body and on the technical manner in which the halakhic act should be performed, the shaping of the body is also part of the stage instructions of the halakhic life performance. Whatever the case may be, the "Rema's" statement proclaims his creed, represents his attempt to create a "cogito" that controls the body, and dictates its function.

Lithuanian-*Haredi* Musar (ethical) literature contains other statements that correspond with the "Rema's" remarks. For example, after quoting the "Rema," Rabbi Chaim Friedlander wrote:[56]

> The whole purpose of the divine commandments (the mitzvot) is to give every [Jewish] man the opportunity to be fully aware, that every detail of every halakhic action, and even every one of his voluntary movements, has meaning. [. . .] Certainly, then, a man should think long and hard about each of his actions. [. . .] Not only during the action itself, but even before he begins, he should consider, and plan each movement in advance, that all may be done in a way that is most fitting and good, and most pleasing to Him (God).[57]

According to Merleau-Ponty, the attempt to live in constant reflection of the mind over the body is futile, because the body has knowledge that does not depend on reflection. In other words, according to the phenomenological description, the approach of the "Rema" and Rabbi Chaim Friedlander, whether consciously or not, is one that is predestined to fail. As noted, the "Rema" bases his approach on the emotion of guilt. The emotion of guilt should be formed and, in continuance of Butler's words, be repeatedly reconstructed by the "Rema's" halakhic society. A person's inability to exist with his body as if in the constant presence of a king reinforces the feeling of guilt of not fulfilling the necessary requirement, an emotion that causes him to adhere with even greater vigor to the principles he faces (the halakhic minutiae featured throughout the entire book), and which are supposed to bring him to this utopic situation of absolute control over his body. In this way, the mechanism of power is preserved and repeatedly reconstructed. Despite the similarity between the endeavor of the "Rema" and that of Rabbi Friedlander, it is also important to highlight their differences. The "Rema" only emphasized a person's physical actions whereas Friedlander also included thoughts: "not just at the

56 Rabbi Chaim Friedlander (1923–1986) learned at Ponevezh Yeshiva, was a student of Rabbi Dessler, and served as a spiritual supervisor at both the Ponevezh and Azata Yeshivot (ultra-Orthodox institutes of religious learning).

57 Friedlander, Chaim, *Siftei Chaim*, vol. 1, 405–6.

time of the act itself, but even before he goes to perform it, he considers and plans how to perform each and every movement in the proper way . . ."[58] The discrepancy between the reflective control over actions and control over thoughts is qualitative, not quantitative.

In his book *History of Sexuality*, Michel Foucault pointed out the change in the discourse on sexuality since the seventeenth century. Since then, people have confessed to their pastor, not only forbidden acts, as was previously accepted in Christian tradition, but also passions and desires, pleasures, sensual thoughts, and imaginations, and combined movements of body and mind.[59] On a profound level, the center of gravity moved from the moment of the act itself to the moment that is so difficult to discern and define, of the materialization of the passion.[60] Generally, the halakha as a normative system does not address the halakhist's emotional experiences but rather stipulates a person's obligations in this world. Halakhic literature addresses the outlining of the set of norms imposed on a person, the actions he should perform or refrain from, but not the delineation of feelings, thoughts, and passions. An examination of the standard responsa literature reveals a distinct halakhic argumentation, an occupation with halakhic sources, and comparisons with precedents, all in order to ascertain "the practices they are to follow."[61]

Friedlander's progression from the halakhic act to thought indicates that he sought to alter the balance of power between the body and the "cogito." As mentioned, Jewish Orthodoxy's choice of halakha as the center of a Jew's world simultaneously strengthened the status of the body via which the halakha is performed. Post-Holocaust Musar literature internalized western culture's higher regard for the body vis-à-vis that of the "cogito," a change that also impacted *Haredi* society. In response, members of the Musar Movement attempted to undermine the standing of halakha and the body in favor of other spheres in a Jew's life. Rabbi Friedlander was one of the leading Musar personalities in this effort. His reference to the words of the "Rema" is but one example of this endeavor. Friedlander seemingly reinforces the stance of the "Rema," however, in practice, he distorted it and transferred the center of power from the body and halakha to moral contemplation and the "cogito."

Whereas many halakhic books try to portray a picture of a world in which man is symbolized by the "cogito," there are also other voices. According to these,

58 Friedlander, *Siftei Chaim*, vol. 1, 410–11.

59 Cf. Foucault, Michel, *History of Sexuality*, vol. 1, trans. Robert Hurley, NY: Vintage Books, 1990.

60 Cf. Foucault, *History of Sexuality*, vol. 1.

61 Exod 18:20. See also Leibowitz, Yeshayahu, *Judaism, the Jewish People and the State of Israel*, Jerusalem: Schocken Publishing House, 1975, 13–36 (Heb.); Goldman, Eliezer, *Expositions and Inquiries: Jewish Thought in Past and Present*, Jerusalem: Magnes Press, 1996, 306–15 (Heb.).

the halakhist is a "bodily being," similar to Merleau-Ponty's approach. For example, the Yerushalmi Talmud states that: "Rabbi Matanya said: 'I am thankful to my head, for whenever I come to the *Modim* blessing, it bows down of its own accord.'"[62] According to a worldview whereby man is identified with the "cogito," when the halakhist reaches the *Modim*[63] blessing in the *Amida* prayer, the "cogito" instructs the head to bow down. This approach will concede that man is occasionally not himself, i.e., not reflective and that he "forgets himself." However, according to this approach, the same person who prays the Amida prayer while his thoughts are not on the words of the prayer will simply forget to bow down. The fact that the head bowed down at the right moment is evidence that he possesses a certain level of awareness, even if his prayer lacked intent.

The Talmudic statement appears in a sequence of stories-testimonies about rabbis who acknowledged that they fail to have proper intent and that various passing thoughts from daily life intrude during prayer. The Talmud's statement has also permeated the halakhic writings of certain *poskim*. For example, Rabbi Joseph Messas (1892–1974) used this Talmudic passage to revoke the custom of *Chazarat HaShatz* (public repetition of the *Amida*). According to Rabbi Messas, this custom evolved out of an assumption that a halakhist who fails to have proper intent while reciting the silent *Amida* prayer will succeed in doing so during the cantor's public repetition of it. He opines that if the rabbis of the Talmud, considered a spiritual model, admit that even they fail to have proper intent throughout the *Amida* prayer, we must certainly accept this reality and not attempt to alter it.[64]

This option was perceived by others as bold and inconceivable. Certain commentators provided a 'religious' explanation as to how these Amoraic sages failed to have proper intent during prayer, but they too accepted the phenomenological description found in the Yerushalmi.[65] One such example is the last Lubavitcher Rebbe (Rabbi Menachem Mendel Schneerson, 1902–1994) who wrote that:

> Now concerning something we find in the Yerushalmi Talmud: "Rabbi Matanya said, 'I am thankful for my head, for whenever I come to the *Modim* blessing, my head bows of its own accord'". This reference to "bowing of its own accord" could be understood, you might say, on the simplest level – as meaning that the rabbi might be unaware that he had reached the

62 *y. Ber.* 2,4.
63 The *Amida* is the central prayer of the Jewish liturgy. Observant Jews recite the *Amida* at each of the three daily prayer services in a typical weekday. The *Amida* includes eighteen blessings – one of them called: *Modim*.
64 Cf. Messas, Joseph, *Responsa Mayim Chayim* 1, §41, Fez: Sharvit-Chazan Press, 1934, 25.
65 For example, the Yerushalmi commentator who wrote *Pnei Moshe* explained that Rabbi Matanya did not have intention during prayer because he was engaged in Torah study while praying.

> *Modim* blessing, perhaps because he was distracted by some thought or other, and still, when the time came, his head would always bow of its own accord, simply because it was his habit to bow his head at the *Modim* blessing. However, surely here the reference to "the head bowing of its own accord" is meant in a loftier sense, since this matter is cited in the Yerushalmi in the context of describing Jewish sages who were possessed of the highest virtues.[66]

While accepting the reality whereby a person is not just his thoughts, at the same time the Rebbe preserved the hierarchy between mind and body. He created a different interpretation to the passage in the Yerushalmi according to which a person should negate himself (i.e., his thoughts and experience) while praying and immerse himself absolutely in the prayer itself. The primary element of a person is missing in such a reality: "That is to say, it is not about the way he bows, inasmuch as when one is in a state of negation and lack of reality, no-one makes a decision but rather, 'it bows of its own accord,' because this is the natural necessity of prayer."[67] If so, the lofty level of the Amoraic sages enabled their body to bow down in prayer even without the reflexive existence that defines them as human. The Lubavitcher Rebbe expressed a similar sentiment elsewhere when he wrote that:

> That is to say, we are speaking here not so much about the soul as about the body. The rabbi is saying that he is grateful for his actual, physical head, which bows of its own accord at the recitation of the *Modim* blessing. In other words, he is grateful that his soul does not need to think about giving commands to the body how to act. The soul is entirely free to focus on other things (as the text goes on to clarify, that those engaged in prayer are thinking about the heavenly kingdom) – and, even so, what does the earthly body do? It "bows down of its own accord."[68]

In line with Merleau-Ponty, I will claim that the Lubavitcher Rebbe is aware that the body possesses knowledge of its own. Nevertheless, instead of accepting this fact and identifying the body as equal in value to reflective contemplation, he preserves a disconnection between reflection and the body. While in the classical Talmudic commentaries, reflection is directed at the prayer arrangement we are familiar with, according to the Rebbe's interpretation, prayer itself is not the essence. The main facet of prayer takes place in upper worlds. Prayer is a mystical act that enables the soul of the *tzaddik* (a righteous person) to enter and act in the upper worlds. The *tzaddik* wants the words of the prayer to be recited automatically, without thought, and uses his body to this end. A person can negate himself (at least in his experience) and assimilate into the prayer precisely because his

---

66 Torat Menachem, *Sichot Parshat Shavua* 16 (1956), 78.
67 Torat Menachem, *Sichot Parshat Shavua* 16 (1956), 78.
68 Torat Menachem, *Sichot Parshat Shavua* 21 (1961), 86.

body knows how to pray, even without intention and reflection. The body's habit of prayer liberates a person from thinking (just as he knows how to drive without thinking), enabling the soul to ascend to the upper worlds.[69]

Bibliography

Afterman, Adam, "Letter Permutation Techniques, Kavannah and Prayer in Jewish Mysticism," *Journal for the Study of Religions and Ideologies* 6 (2007), 52–78.

Althusser, Louis, *Lenin and Philosophy*, trans. Ben Brewster, New York / London: Monthly Review Press, 1971.

Baker, Gordon / Morris, Katherine, *Descartes' Dualism*, London / New York: Routledge, 1996.

Baumgarten, Albert I. / Assmann, Jan / Stroumsa, Guy G. (eds.), *Self, Soul and Body in Religious Experience*, Leiden: Brill, 1998.

Butler, Judith, *Bodies that Matter*, London / New York: Routledge, 1993.

Butler, Judith, *Excitable Speech: A Politics of the Performative*, London / New York: Routledge, 1997.

Butler, Judith, *Gender Trouble: Feminism and the Subversion of Identity*, London / New York: Routledge, 1990.

Butler, Judith, "Performative Acts and Gender Constitution: An Essay in Phenomenology and Feminist Theory," *Theatre Journal* 40, 4 (1988), 519–531

Carlisle, Clare / Sinclair, Mark, "Editor's Introduction," in: Félix Ravaisson, *Of Habit*, London: Continuum, 2008, 1–21.

Carman, Taylor, *Merleau-Ponty*, London / New York: Routledge, 2008.

Corcoran, Kevin (ed.), *Soul, Body, and Survival: Essays on the Metaphysics of Human Persons*, New York: Cornell University Press, 2000.

Ehrlich, Uri, *"All My Bones Shall Say": The Non-Verbal Language of Jewish Prayer*, Jerusalem: Magnes Press, 1999 (Heb.).

Englander, Yakir, "The Image of the Male Body in Lithuanian Ultra-Orthodox Thought in Israel and Corresponding Strategies for Forging an A-Feminine Public Sphere," *Journal of Contemporary Religion* 29, 3 (2014), 457–470.

Englander, Yakir, *The Male Body in Ultra-Orthodox Jewish Theology*, Eugene, OR: Pickwick Publications, 2021.

Englander, Yakir / Sagi, Avi, *Sexuality and the Body in New Religious Zionist Discourse*, trans. Batya Stein, Boston: Academic Press, 2015.

Foucault, Michel, *History of Sexuality*, vol. 1, trans. Robert Hurley, New York: Vintage Books, 1990.

Gibson, James J., "The Theory of Affordances," in: Robert Shaw / John Bransford (eds.), *Perceiving, Acting and Knowing. Toward an Ecological Psychology*, Hillsdale, NJ: Erlbaum, 1977, 67–82.

Goetz, Stewart / Taliaferro, Charles, *A Brief History of the Soul*, London: Blackwell, 2011.

Goldman, Eliezer, *Expositions and Inquiries: Jewish Thought in Past and Present*, Jerusalem: Magnes Press, 1996 (Heb.).

Heidegger, Martin, *Being and Time*, trans. John MacQuarrie / Edward Robinson, New York: Harper and Row, 1962.

69 Cf. Edgar, "Attention and Habit." See also Carlisle, Clare / Sinclair, Mark, "Editor's Introduction," in: Félix Ravaisson, *Of Habit*, London: Continuum, 2008, 1–21.

Henry, Michel, *I am the Truth: Toward a Philosophy of Christianity*, trans. Susan Emanuel, Stanford: Stanford University Press, 2003.
Kearney, Richard, *Modern Movements in European Philosophy*, New York: Manchester University Press, 1994.
Kearney, Richard, *Anatheism*, New York: Columbia University Press, 2010.
Leibowitz, Yeshayahu, *Judaism, the Jewish People and the State of Israel*, Jerusalem: Schocken Publishing House, 1975 (Heb.).
Merleau-Ponty, Maurice, *The Phenomenology of Perception*, trans. Colin Smith, London: Routledge, 1962.
Naeh, Shlomo, "Creates the Fruit of the Lips: A Phenomenological Study of Prayer According to Berakhot 4:3, 5:5," *Tarbits* 63 (1994), 185–218 (Heb.).
Romdenh-Romluc, Komarine, "Habit and Attention," in: Rasmus Thybo Jensen / Dermot Moran (eds.), *The Phenomenology of Embodied Subjectivity*, Contributions to Phenomenology 71, Cham et al.: Springer, 2013, 3–19.

Suggestions for Further Reading

Adler, Rachel, *Engendering Judaism: An Inclusive Theology and Ethics*, Boston: Beacon Press, 1999.
Balberg, Mira, *Purity, Body, and Self in Early Rabbinic Literature*, Berkely: University of California Press, 2014.
Biale, David, *Eros and the Jews: From Biblical Israel to Contemporary America*, Berkely: University of California Press, 1997.
Greenberg, Blu, *How to Run a Traditional Jewish Household*, Boston: Touchstone, 2011.
Greenberg, Steve, *Wrestling with God and Men: Homosexuality in the Jewish Tradition*, Madison: University of Wisconsin Press, 2004.
Imhoff, Sarah, *Masculinity and the Making of American Judaism*, Indianapolis: Indiana University Press, 2017.
Irshai, Ronit, *Fertility and Jewish Law*, Waltham, MA: Brandeis University Press, 2012.
Kamir, Orit, *Betraying Dignity: The Toxic Seduction of Social Media, shaming, and Radicalization*, Vancouver: Fairleigh Dickinson University Press, 2019.
Levitt, Laura, *Jews and Feminism: The Ambivalent Search for Home*, New York: Routledge, 1997.
Marienberg, Evyatar, *Traditional Jewish Sex Guidance: A History*, Leiden / Boston: Brill, 2022.
Plaskow, Judith, *The Coming of Lilith: Essays on Feminism, Judaism, and Sexual Ethics*, Boston: Beacon Press, 1995.
Presner, Todd, *Muscular Judaism: The Jewish Body and the Politics of Regeneration*, New York: Taylor&Francis, 2007.
Ross, Tamar, *Expanding the Palace of Torah*, Boston: Brandies University Press, 2004.
Segol, Marla, *Kabbalah and Sex Magic: A Mythical-Ritual Genealogy*, Philadelphia: Penn University Press, 2021.
Sztokman, Elana, *When Rabbis Abuse: Power, Gender and Status in the Dynamics of Sexual Abuse in Jewish Culture*, Minneapolis: Indiana University Press, 2022.

Gregor Etzelmüller

The Concept of Body in Christianity

It is no exaggeration to say: The body is at the center of Christian theology. God has revealed himself in Jesus Christ in body and flesh; thus, the body of Christ belongs to God from all eternity. Martin Luther rightly said: "No, comrade, wherever you place God for me, you must also place the humanity for me."[1]

The doctrine of incarnation, thus, implies a theological affirmation of the body: "the human body not only reveals God, it is the privileged medium of divine self-disclosure."[2] The body is intended to be the place of God's revelation. This is not only true with regard to Jesus Christ and the Church as his body, but also with regard to the individual bodies of the faithful (cf. 2Cor 6:19). Despite the fact that the human flesh is in danger of being subjected to the power of sin, Paul emphasizes that even this mortal flesh can and will be the place of the epiphany of Christ (cf. 2Cor 3:3; 4:1).[3]

In the Gospel of John, incarnation is described as the Logos becoming flesh (see John 1:14: "And the Word was made flesh"). This implies that human beings, in general, are flesh, *sarx*. The ecclesial tradition has rejected a possible dualistic interpretation of this passage. Instead, the ancient church has emphasized that flesh, according to John 1:14, refers to the whole human being, the entire person, including body, soul, and reason.[4] The human being is always embodied.

While the Gospel of John emphasizes the carnality of the logos, Paul stresses the bodily existence of Christ. A contemplation on the biblical notion of *sarx* (flesh) will be able to demonstrate the connection between the concept of "flesh" in the Gospel of John and the Pauline conception of the "body."

First, in the Bible, the flesh of animals and the flesh of humans are described with the same term both in Hebrew and in Ancient Greek (cf. Gen 6:12–13, 17; 1Cor 15:39).[5] The term 'flesh' applied to humans puts them in an evolutionary continuity to animals and implies that human beings in some way *are* animals. This

---

1 Luther, Martin, "Confession Concerning Christ's Supper," in: Robert H. Fischer (ed.), *Luther's Works*, vol. 37: *Word and Sacrament III*, Philadelphia: Fortress Press, 1961, 219.

2 Johnson, Luke Timothy, *The Revelatory Body: Theology as Inductive Art*, Grand Rapids / Cambridge: Eerdmans, 2015, 57.

3 Cf. Theißen, Gerd, *Erleben und Verhalten der ersten Christen: Eine Psychologie des Urchristentums*, Gütersloh: Gütersloher Verlagshaus, ^{2}2007, 89–90.

4 Cf. Beutel, Albrecht, *In dem Anfang war das Wort: Studien zu Luthers Sprachverständnis*, HUTh 27, Tübingen: Mohr Siebeck, 1991, 427.

5 Cf. Sand, Alexander, "sarx," in: Horst Balz / Gerhard Schneider (eds.), *EWNT* III, Stuttgart / Berlin / Cologne: Kohlhammer, ^{2}1992, 549.

https://doi.org/10.1515/9783110748246-002

strong connection between humans and animals is also expressed in Gen 1, when it is said that God created land-living animals and humans on the same day (cf. Gen 1:24–31).

Furthermore, the strong connection between animals and humans is emphasized in the Bible because both creatures are described as "living beings." Both the Hebrew Bible and its Greek translation – the Septuagint – use the term "living beings" to describe animals (cf. Gen 1:20, 24) and human beings (cf. Gen 2:7; 1Cor 15:45). On the sixth day of creation, God says: "Let the earth bring forth living creatures" (BHS: nefesh ḥajjāh; LXX: psychēn zōsan; Gen 1:24).

Following these textual observations, it can be argued that the biblical notion of flesh implies that animals and humans share the same living materiality. Flesh is associated with living beings. Accordingly, Paul refers to the living heart as flesh in contrast to a heart of stone (cf. 2Cor 3:3). Carnality, thus, represents liveliness.

If we notice that in the Bible plants and trees are not perceived as "living beings,"[6] it becomes clear that the Bible conceives living beings – just as the 'common sense' – in such a way that living beings are self-moved. Self-moved living beings are not just moved by pressure from outside, but they move themselves and – while moving – perceive themselves as moving. Thus, when human beings move, they simultaneously perceive themselves as both subject and object.[7] So, in every self-movement, subjectivity is "present and effective [. . .]. In all their actions living beings appear both as physical and as psychic,"[8] as *sōma psychikon*, as Paul writes (cf. 1Cor 15:44), as a psychosomatic unity. To be flesh means to be a *sōma psychikon*.

Flesh biblically refers to the materiality of the flesh of the whole person, which also includes subjectivity. The words "flesh" and "body" can be used synonymously (as Paul does in 1Cor 15:35–49). The statement in the Gospel of John: "And the Word was made flesh" is to be translated in Pauline terms as follows: "And the Word was made *sōma psychikon*."

In continuity with the Old Testament, the New Testament has emphasized the bodily and carnal nature of all human actions. Furthermore, the New Testament has perceived the body as the privileged medium of God's self-revelation. Despite these clear tendencies, Christianity and its theologies have supported and culti-

---

6 Löning, Karl / Zenger, Erich, *Als Anfang schuf Gott: Biblische Schöpfungstheologie*, Düsseldorf: Patmos Verlag, 1997, 144.

7 Cf. Merleau-Ponty, Maurice, *Phenomenology of Perception* (1945), New York: Routledge, 2012, 96.

8 Fuchs, Thomas, *Das Gehirn – ein Beziehungsorgan: Eine phänomenologisch-ökologische Konzeption*, Stuttgart: Kohlhammer, ^{4}2013, 120.

vated dualistic ideas of humankind for centuries. What is more, body-hostile traditions have shaped Christianity from the patristics right down to the present.

1 The Basic Terminology and the Sources of the Concept in the Bible

At the beginning of the Bible, humanity is presented as the image of God. This was often interpreted as man having reason and, thus, mirroring God. However, this interpretation ignores the fact that the Hebrew term for "image," *tselem*, means "well-crafted, generally three-dimensional statues."[9] "God created humankind as his statue. As God's statue he created him" (Gen 1:27).[10] Thus, the human being represents God precisely in and through its body.

Accordingly, the Hebrew Bible does not contain any dualism between body and soul, but perceives human beings as fundamentally embodied. Hans Walter Wolff has demonstrated that the Hebrew term *nefesh*, which, so far, has often been translated as "soul," in the Hebrew Bible means "the organ for the vital human needs, which have to be met to ensure existence."[11] If a person is described as *nefesh*, he or she is not understood as a pure spiritual being, but is described in his or her embodied vitality and embodied needs.[12] There is no "indestructible core of the self [. . .] that could exist without the body with its vital needs."[13]

Therefore, in the Hebrew Bible, emotional and cognitive functions are understood as embodied functions.[14] In Ps 84:2, longing is attributed to the throat, joy is

9 Wagner, Andreas, "Verkörpertes Herrschen: Zum Gebrauch von 'treten'/'herrschen' in Gen 1,26–28," in: Gregor Etzelmüller / Annette Weissenrieder (eds.), *Verkörperung als Paradigma theologischer Anthropologie*, TBT 172, Berlin / Boston: de Gruyter, 2016, 132; cf. Johnson, *The Revelatory Body*, 54.

10 The translation is inspired by Lohfink, Norbert, "Die Gottesstatue. Kreatur und Kunst nach Genesis 1," in: id., *Im Schatten deiner Flügel. Große Bibeltexte neu erschlossen*, Freiburg et al.: Herder, ²1999, 29.

11 Wolff, Hans Walter, *Anthropology of the Old Testament*, trans. Margaret Kohl, Philadelphia: Fortress, 1974, 18 (trans. altered).

12 Cf. Janowski, Bernd, "Die lebendige naepaes: Das Alte Testament und die Frage nach der 'Seele'," in: Gregor Etzelmüller / Annette Weissenrieder (eds.), *Verkörperung als Paradigma theologischer Anthropologie*, TBT 172, Berlin / Boston: de Gruyter, 2016.

13 Wolff, *Anthropology of the Old Testament*, 20.

14 Cf. Smith, Mark S., "The Heart and innards in Israelite Emotional Expressions: Notes from Anthropology and Psychobiology," *JBL* 117 (1998), 431: "emotions are associated with the heart and innards because they are physically experienced there. [. . .] Israelites associated emotions with the internal organs where the emotions were perceived to be felt physically."

attributed to the heart and to the flesh: "My throat longeth, yea, even fainteth for the courts of the LORD: my heart and my flesh crieth out for the living God." In the Proverbs, it says: "The heart of him that hath understanding seeketh knowledge" (Prov 15:14) and: "The heart of the wise teacheth his mouth, and addeth learning to his lips" (Prov 16:23). Even though the heart receives a special position in the Old Testament, no unilateral hierarchy of the body is intended.[15] For one thing, in different situations different organs are emphasized, for example the kidneys are mentioned in moral or relationship conflicts. What is more, different organs can stand in for each other.

It is striking that the term "body" does not even appear in the Hebrew Bible.[16] Embodiment is thought of in such a concrete way and in such concrete acts and situations that even the conception of the body itself is an abstraction. Basic bodily functions and needs such as eating and breathing, but also emotional and cognitive abilities are not attributed to the body, but to single organs, which then, in turn, represent the whole person.[17]

The Hebrew Bible's consistency in how it describes the relationship with God as embodied deserves particular attention: Throat and flesh thirst and yearn for God (cf. Ps 63:1), heart and flesh rejoice in the living God (cf. Ps 84:2), throat and belly praise God's holy name (cf. Ps 103:1), and the bones rejoice when God hears the worshipper (cf. Ps 10). The commandments of the Lord are preserved in the heart (cf. Ps 37:31), but also in the belly (Ps 40:9). God judges "hearts and reins" (Ps 7:9; 26:2; Jer 11:20; 17:10; 20:12). But also the inner parts of the belly with their digestive processes (cf. Prov 18:8) are shown through by God the judge (cf. Prov 20:27).[18] In accordance with this, the promised New Covenant with God is thought of as an embodied, even a fleshly covenant: The new heart is explicitly called a "heart of flesh" (Ezek 11:19). In all these statements the whole person is addressed, but this whole person is understood in such a way that the human being can neither be distinguished nor separated from his or her own body. "To see [. . .] the bodily as a mere expression of the soul and, therefore, what is said about the bodily as mere description of what are proper processes of the soul, is to interpret

15 Cf. Di Vito, Robert A., "Old Testament Anthropology and the Construction of Personal Identity," *CBQ* 61 (1992), 229.

16 Cf. Krieg, Matthias, "Leiblichkeit im Alten Testament," in: id. / Hans Weder (eds.), *Leiblichkeit*, ThSt 128, Zürich: Theologischer Verlag, 1983, 9.

17 Cf. Janowski, Bernd, "Der Mensch im Alten Israel: Grundfragen Alttestamentlicher Anthropologie," *ZThK* 102 (2005), 148–49.

18 Cf. Wolff, *Anthropology of the Old Testament*, 63.

the statements on the basis of a very different understanding of man from that presented in the texts, and, therefore, to misunderstand them."[19]

The New Testament, too, understands the relationship between God and the human being as embodied. In the following, I will concentrate on Paul. He asks the faithful in Corinth: "What? know ye not that your body is the temple of the Holy Ghost which is in you, which ye have of God, and ye are not your own? For ye are bought with a price: therefore glorify God in your body" (1Cor 6:19–20). Human beings are related to God only in and through their body and God himself is related to the body of human beings: "Now the body is [. . .] for the Lord; and the Lord for the body" (1Cor 6:13).

Paul is fascinated by the human body. This fascination becomes especially obvious when Paul uses the term "body" as a metaphor for the congregation to describe a new eschatic reality. Paul was the first to use the term "body" to describe the Christian congregation.[20] What fascinates Paul about the human body is "the mutual dependence"[21] of its limbs, but also the consideration for the supposedly weakest parts of the body, which is necessary in order for the whole body to work.

The distinctive feature of the Pauline perception of the body becomes clear when compared to pagan texts of his environment and to the Deutero-Pauline letters. Antiquity knows the metaphor of the body as a reflection of an ideal society. But this metaphor usually supports the existing social hierarchies. The human body is understood as hierarchically organized – and this perception supports the socially constructed, contingent constitution of the society.[22] In opposition to such a conception, Paul emphasizes that no member is of lesser value than any other. Rather, the supposedly weakest members are treated with the greatest respect (cf. 1Cor 12:22–23[23]).

Paul understands the whole congregation as the body of Christ. However, the Deutero-Pauline Letters distinguish between the head and the rest of the

---

19 Barth, Karl, *The Church Dogmatics*, vol. III/2, Edinburgh: T&T Clark, 1960, 436.

20 Cf. Wolter, Michael, *Paulus: Ein Grundriss seiner Theologie*, Neukirchen: Vandenhoeck & Ruprecht, 2011, 291; Walter, Matthias, *Gemeinde als Leib Christi: Untersuchungen zum Corpus Paulinum und zu den Apostolischen Vätern*, NTOA 49, Freiburg / Göttingen: Vandenhoeck & Ruprecht, 2001, 105–164.

21 Sigurdson, Ola, *Heavenly Bodies: Incarnation, the Gaze, and Embodiment in Christian Theology*, Grand Rapids: Eerdmans, 2016, 377.

22 Cf. Horell, David G., "Σῶμα as a Basis for Ethics in Paul," in: Friedrich W. Horn et al. (eds.), *Ethische Normen des frühen Christentums: Gut – Leben – Leib – Tugend*, Kontexte und Normen neutestamentlicher Ethik IV, Tübingen: Mohr Siebeck, 2013, 352–362.

23 Cf. Sigurdson, *Heavenly Bodies*, 377: "Verses 14–20 warn against all inferiority complexes, while 21–25 warn against ideas of superiority."

body (cf. Eph 1:22–23; 4:15–16; 5:23; Col 1:18; 2:19): In Col 2:19, Christ is understood as "the Head, from which all the body by joints and bands having nourishment ministered, and knit together, increaseth with the increase of God." Unlike Paul, Col 2:19 describes a hierarchy that is drawn into the metaphor of the body. The antique imagination of the ruler as head of the body is transferred to Christian ecclesiology and changes the perception of the human body. According to Paul, however, the head cannot tell the feet: "I have no need of you" (1Cor 12:21). Here, Paul appears as a pioneer of the current paradigm of embodiment. In direct opposition to dualistic tendencies to separate the brain from the body, the philosophy of embodiment states that the brain cannot say to other organs: "I have no need of you!"[24]

It is exciting that Paul does not only refer to the congregation as a body. Furthermore, he assumes that this body is constituted via bodily interactions: first, through baptism (cf. 1Cor 12:12–13), and second, through the Lord's Supper. Through bodily interactions, a mutual incorporation (*Einleibung*) occurs and something like a new body is formed.

As an embodied person, a human being is always shaped by certain practices and traditions, by memories and expectations. Paul expresses this fact by saying that the body does not belong to itself (cf. 1Cor 6:19), but it is always defined by others. There is no body which has not already been shaped socially and culturally (in Pauline terms: the body is brought under the power of something else).[25] This insight, for Paul, is connected with the hope that the body can become new and begin anew. This hope is guaranteed by baptism. In baptism, human beings have died to existing social norms, in order to "walk in newness of life" (cf. Rom 6:3–4). When people let themselves be baptized, they confess that they are dead to the policies and rules of their environments. Instead, they live in a new community. They enter "a liminal status in the *communitas*, where the social rules of the ordinary *societas* are annulled."[26]

The liberation from social norms and hierarchies has consequences for the concrete bodies of the baptized: Those differences that had oriented actions until now are dissolved. For example, the difference between men and women, free men and slaves as well as Jews and pagans are dissolved in favor of an orientation along the needs and gifts of the concrete individual. "There is neither Jew

24 Cf. Fuchs, *Das Gehirn*, 21: "The brain by itself would only be a dead organ. It only becomes alive in connection with our muscles, intestines, nerves and senses, with our skin, our environment and with other people." (Transl. by the editor.)

25 Cf. the inspiring ideas of Marquardt, Friedrich-Wilhelm, *Was dürfen wir hoffen, wenn wir hoffen dürften? Eine Eschatologie*, vol. 3, Gütersloh: Gütersloher Verlagshaus, 1996, 446–456.

26 Theißen, *Erleben und Verhalten der ersten Christen*, 362.

nor Greek, there is neither bond nor free, there is neither male nor female: for ye are all one in Christ Jesus" (Gal 3:28).

The differences between men and women, free men and slaves as well as Jews and pagans were not just cognitive distinctions. Rather, they were inscribed into the body. For example, through circumcision, the difference between Jews and pagans was inscribed into the body.[27] Dietary rules and the Jewish festival calendar, too, shaped the bodily conduct. Similarly, social differences shaped the behavior of each individual: "The body is influenced through the social class from which he comes. The body reveals the social origin of its carrier up to the smallest gestures."[28] Additionally, the difference between men and women, which Paul mentions, is culturally constructed and, thus, creates the male and female body.[29]

Paul describes how the baptized, by being embedded into a new bodily community, are taken away from the influence of existing social and cultural practices. Bodily inscribed differences, which were effective in antique society but harmful to the life of the individual, are overcome. Baptism, thus, represents a reconfiguration of an embodied person. A body, which has so far been shaped by harmful social rules and differences, through baptism, becomes a temple of the Holy Spirit (cf. 1Cor 6:19), in other words, the body becomes a place of God's presence for others.

In baptism, people experience the ability to start anew – and that is why Paul admonishes them to take part in the fight over who or what shapes our bodies: "Neither yield ye your members as instruments of unrighteousness unto sin: but yield yourselves unto God, as those that are alive from the dead, and your members *as* instruments of righteousness unto God" (Rom 6:13).

Paul understands baptism as a change in sovereignty because he knows that the human body is always shaped by social and cultural practices. He does not proclaim the end of the fact that every body is inevitably shaped by social and cultural norms. Rather, he proclaims the liberation from those harmful social and cultural norms that, according to Paul, belong to the realm of sin. Because the body is always already shaped by exterior influences, the body cannot be thought of as a self-contained entity. In order to start anew, the body itself must be integrated into a new community of other bodies, where new social and cultural practices can be learned. Concretely, Paul deals with the question whether bodies

---

27 Cf. Boyarin, Daniel, *A Radical Jew: Paul and the Politics of Identity*, Berkeley: University of California Press, 1994.

28 So, following Pierre Bourdieu, Schroer, Markus, "Zur Soziologie des Körpers," in: id. (ed.), *Soziologie des Körpers*, stw 1740, Frankfurt: Suhrkamp, [3]2005, 37.

29 Cf. Butler, Judith, *Bodies That Matter: On the Discursive Limits of "Sex"* [1993], Routledge Classics, London / New York: Routledge 2011.

are shaped by powers that enslave them and make them agents of death or whether bodies are shaped by a spirit who liberates them and frees them to be there for others.

In the early church, the baptized were integrated into a community which, on the one hand, held certain convictions, but which, on the other hand, also expressed these convictions in an embodied form in the celebration of the Lord's Supper. The spirit of the community cannot be separated from the bread that is broken and eaten together.

At the center of the Lord's Supper stands the crucified body of Jesus Christ. The community at the table serves to remember and to proclaim Jesus' death (cf. 1Cor 11:24–26). But the community at the table not only remembers the one who was crucified by the Romans, it also confesses Jesus Christ as living and returning. Thus, the community at the table exposes the Roman Empire in its body-hostility and also makes clear that the power of the Roman Empire is transient.

> The remembrance of Jesus' death gave Rome's imperial oppression the name that unmasked it. It did not bring peace, but rather death. [. . ..] Proclaiming the death of the Messiah means telling the truth about human violence and, at the same time, seeing beforehand how it will come to an end. [. . .] It is no accident that 1Cor. 11:26 links the meal, as a proclamation of Christ's death, with the expectation of his coming. When the Messiah comes, he will put an end to 'every ruler and every authority and power' (1Cor. 15:24) [. . .] It is the very proclamation of the death of Jesus in the common meal that announces the end of violence that kills and oppresses human beings. The simple fact that people, through their common meal, bring a crucified body into their midst, already meant at that time the naming of that violence as an injustice and anticipating its end.[30]

In this way, it becomes clear how the body of the crucified Christ permanently transforms existing rules on how to interact with one another. In the congregation, people are exposed in bodily form to God's suffering from this world. This suffering becomes manifest in the crucifixion of Jesus Christ. By taking part in God's suffering, the congregation gains a new perspective on and a new behavior towards the existing society.

Simultaneously, the believers experience themselves as integrated into a living environment that has its origins in Jesus Christ. This means, in a very concrete sense, that faith, charity, and hope of each and everyone in the congregation are strengthened because faith, charity, and hope find resonance with other people, thus, transforming social interactions.

30 Bieler, Andrea / Schottroff, Luise, *The Eucharist: Bodies, Bread & Resurrection*, Minneapolis: Fortress Press, 2007, 58.

> Faith, hope, and charity do not symbolize their general meaning in dry words. Instead, they search for lively forms of communication that encompass the human being as a whole in his living contexts and his multi-dimensional ways of life [. . .]. They transform our psychological status, our cognitive attitudes and perspectives as well as our bodily forms of existence and community. Thus, they are catalysts for a transformation of the world.[31]

The concrete bodily forms of interaction are not without consequences for the character of the community. Paul admonishes the congregation in 1Cor 11 that they do not celebrate the Lord's Supper in an appropriate way. The rich members of the congregation consume their own food at the Lord's Supper and, thus, humiliate those members who have no food and remain hungry. Paul blames them for violating the unity of the congregation. The strong and rich, whom Paul addresses, might have rejected Paul's admonition saying that a unity includes differences and hierarchies and is not threatened by them. Implicitly, the strong and the rich, thus, resume the values of Roman antiquity. Here it becomes clear that social transformations presuppose a changed behavior, more concretely: changed bodily interactions. The bodily interaction participates in the transformation of social communication. That is why Paul demands to supply God with the members of the body as weapons for justice (cf. Rom 6:13).

2 The Theological and Philosophical Principles of the Concept in Christianity

The biblical and, thus, Christian understanding of personhood as radically embodied and the appreciation of the human body as a place of God's self-revelation are unfamiliar in pagan antiquity as well as in modernity. In cultures where the body appears only as place of impurity, sin, and suffering, the biblical appreciation of the body cannot but confuse. To the ancient and to the modern ideal of "the rule of reason over the body (or the rule of spirit over nature),"[32] the biblical appreciation of the body must appear absurd and dangerous. In antiquity, partic-

---

31 Brandt, Sigrid, "Sünde: Ein Definitionsversuch," in: ead. et al. (eds.), *Sünde: Ein unverständlich gewordenes Thema*, Neukirchen: Neukirchener Theologie, 1997, 24.

32 Moxter, Michael, "Anthropologie in systematisch-theologischer Perspektive," in: Jürgen van Oorschot (ed.), *Mensch*, TdT 11, Tübingen: Mohr Siebeck, 2018, 179; cf. Brown, Peter, *The Body and Society: Men, Women and Sexual Renunciation in Early Christianity*, New York: Columbia University Press, 1988, 27–28.

ularly to Celsus, Christians appear as a "body-loving community."[33] From the perspective of Celsus, the Christian appreciation of the body misjudges the role of reason as the ability that distinguishes human beings from animals. Thus, a rational ethics is made impossible.

The biblical and, thus, Christian conception of the body contradicts the separation of body and mind that is a characteristic of modernity. René Descartes distinguishes between body and mind, between *res extensa* and *res cogitans.* According to Descartes, the modern human being gains certainty about himself precisely by reflecting himself out of this world (and, thus, out of his body). By doubting all material and sensual, I become aware of myself: Cogito ergo sum.[34]

The modern anthropology is, thus, characterized by a dualism. This dualism is also reflected in Immanuel Kant's separation between a physiological and a pragmatic anthropology. "A systematic treatise comprising our knowledge of man (anthropology) can adopt either a physiological or a pragmatic point of view. – Physiological knowledge of man investigates what nature makes of him: pragmatic, what man as a free agent makes, or can and should make, of himself."[35] The scientific anthropology works with the principle of causality and does not know human freedom, whereas philosophical anthropology presumes precisely this freedom.

So, Kant distinguishes between two epistemological approaches towards anthropology: Human beings could either be understood as beings that simply appear in the world or as beings that act in the world.[36] Human beings, thus, can be seen from either a physiological or a pragmatic perspective. Kant then claims the right of the second perspective over the first – and, thus, renounces an anthropology that is the result of a mathematical natural science only.

The separation between scientific and philosophical anthropology has, during the last decades – especially as a result of progress in neurobiology – led to attempts by scientists to take over the tasks of a philosophical anthropology: Since Descartes, modernity has hypostasized the bodily subject to a transcendental self-

33 Volp, Ulrich, "Der Mensch: Kirchen- und theologiegeschichtliche Perspektive," in: Jürgen van Oorschot (ed.), *Mensch*, ThTh 11, Tübingen: Mohr Siebeck, 2018, 114: "Für Celsos waren die Christen [. . .] ein 'leibverliebtes Geschlecht' (φιλοσώματον γένος, Origenes, Contra Celsum 7,36 und 7,39)."

34 Cf. Link, Christian, *Schöpfung: Ein theologischer Entwurf im Gegenüber von Naturwissenschaft und Ökologie*, Neukirchen: Neukirchener, 2002, 177.

35 Kant, Immanuel, *Anthropology from a Pragmatic Point of View*, trans. Mary J. Gregor, The Hague: Martinus Nijhoff, 1974, 3.

36 On this distinction, see Hampe, Michael, "Anthropology," in: *Religion Past and Present*, vol. 1, H. D. Betz et al. (eds.), Leiden: Brill, 2006, 258 (article wrongly attributed to C. Auffarth).

consciousness. In late modernity, this self-consciousness is identified with an objectified brain. Thus, the last field of activity for the spirit is naturalized.[37]

In late modernity, the human spirit is subject to a mathematical, scientific thinking. Interestingly, this development is itself the result of a process, in which the modern spirit had subordinated the world, including its own body, as inferior and second-class and, by doing so, had defined itself as spirit. The existing naturalistic reductionism is, thus, the consequence of the modern reduction of the living body to a lifeless object.

In order to counter the existing naturalistic reductionism, it is not advisable to reactivate the modern dualism between body and mind or body and soul. Instead, phenomenological insights and experiences, which are made in daily life, should be taken up. They demonstrate that the human body, but also the world in which we live, are much more complex and ingenious than in their reconstruction through science alone. It is, therefore, necessary to detect a creativity and spontaneity of the spirit within the body. This is precisely the concern of the *Embodied Cognitive Science* and the *Philosophy of Embodiment*. The first originates from neurosciences, the second from phenomenology. However, both disciplines are concerned with a non-reductionist perception of the (human) body, with a new concept of the relation between *res cogitans* and *res extensa*, that is the realm of nature and the realm of freedom. Instead of setting nature and freedom against each other as in modernity, the question is posed as to how – within nature – a realm of freedom could emerge and has emerged.

In my opinion, there is a close proximity between the biblical concept of a human being and the current paradigm of embodiment.[38] Both perspectives assume that a human being is always already embodied, that is: a person does not just have a body, but that a person also is the concrete body that he or she has. "The body is not the prison, the shell, the exterior, of a human being; instead a human being is a human body. A human being does not 'have' a body or 'have' a soul; instead a human being 'is' body and soul."[39] Yet, biblical traditions and the paradigm of embodiment both indicate that the (human) body is much more complex than the body as described by natural science because subjectivity, freedom and communicability are inscribed into the human body. Therefore, the human body cannot be understood without the dimension of inwardness.

---

37 Cf. Fuchs, *Das Gehirn*, 99.

38 Cf. Etzelmüller, Gregor, *Gottes verkörpertes Ebenbild: Eine theologische Anthropologie*, Tübingen: Mohr Siebeck, 2021, ch. 3 and 4.

39 Bonhoeffer, Dietrich, *Creation and fall: A Theological Exposition of Genesis 1–3*, DBWE 3, Minneapolis: Fortress Press, 1997, 76–77.

In the following, I would like to illustrate this point with the help of the categories of natality and vulnerability. I will draw on both these categories because the Christian tradition, which is deeply rooted in the belief of the incarnation of the Son of God, understands embodied beings as born and compassionate beings: Christians confess that the Son of God was born and suffered.

2.1 Natality. Human Beings as Born Beings

The phenomenon of natality, the fact that human beings are born, first refers to the intercorporeality through which all life takes place. That the human being grows in another person (the mother's womb), experiences his or her body for the first time in that womb, and that every person is born from a womb, these are elementary experiences in every human life. Therefore, the idea of incarnation implies that Christ did not suddenly descend from heaven but was born of a woman.

In a biblical perspective, the birth of Jesus can be understood without procreation. But the Bible cannot think of Jesus as descending immediately from Heaven: thus, biblically speaking, there is no person Jesus of Nazareth without birth. That is the reason why Jesus' mother and the birth of Jesus are mentioned even in those traditions of the New Testament which do not know anything of a virgin birth. The biblical canon and with it the tradition of the Early Church preserve the doctrine of the humanity of Jesus Christ in such a way that they emphasize that every human being – and, thus, also Jesus of Nazareth – always already lives in spheres of intercorporeality.

This insight is of fundamental importance for anthropology: Every human being – as is shown by his or her birth – comes from a sphere of intercorporeality. Not subjectivity but intercorporeality is antecedent.

Having been born implies (secondly) that every human is a unique person that has not existed before and that will never exist again. This fact was strongly emphasized by Hannah Arendt, who introduced the concept of natality into philosophy in critical opposition to Martin Heidegger. "Because they are *initium*, newcomers and beginners by virtue of birth, men take initiatives, are prompted into action."[40]

By reminding us that through the birth of Jesus something new begins, the Christian faith also sensitizes for the hope that arises in life together with every

40 Arendt, Hannah, *The Human Condition: Second Edition*, with a new foreword by D. Allen, introduction by M. Canovan, Chicago: The University of Chicago Press, [16]2018, 178.

new birth. Arendt says: "It is this faith in and hope for the world that found perhaps its most glorious and most succinct expression in the few words with which the Gospels announced their 'glad tidings': 'A child has been born unto us.'"[41]

As a bodily being, the human being is not autonomous but free to repeatedly present himself/herself in new ways. The Gospel of Luke makes this clear when it lets Jesus react in a unique way even during his suffering on the cross. During his crucifixion, Christ says: "Father, forgive them; for they know not what they do" (Luke 23:34). As a bodily being, the human being can contribute to and engage in the world in surprising ways – and, thus, human beings are not doomed to repeat again and again what has always been.

Being-born is (thirdly) an experience that all humans share. Every human being must be born of his or her mother. The Jewish-Christian traditions embed the dignity and the rights of every human being in the phenomenon of natality. Thus, they annul a distinction that had so far shaped the thinking in antiquity, that is: the idea of a natural inequality. In the Hebrew Bible, this connection is evident in the Book of Job: "If I have rejected the cause of my manservant or my maidservant, when they brought a complaint against me, what then shall I do when God rises up? When he makes inquiry, what shall I answer him? Did not he who made me in the womb make him? And did not one fashion us in the womb?" (Job 31:13–15). This insight of Job finds resonance in Article One of the Universal Declaration of Human Rights from 1948: "All human beings are born free and equal in dignity and rights."

The phenomenon of natality shows (fourthly) that the life of every born individual results from a kept promise of a woman, to carry a child to full term. "Without the willingness of others to carry me before my own conscious existence, this my existence would not be."[42] The single human being does not need to be immediately intended in the act of procreation by his parents, but every person owes his existence to the willingness (and ability) of the mother to carry the child to full term. In this way, Jesus of Nazareth would not exist without Mary.

The experience of having been carried to full term has consequences for the freedom of a person to commit himself or herself and make oneself reliable for others. According to Arendt, this ability is grounded in the experience that others, too, have kept their promises.[43] The phenomenon of natality refers to a basic experience of a kept promise. It gives hope because it demonstrates that even in a world under the power of sin, others keep their promises to me.

---

41 Arendt, *The Human Condition*, 247.

42 Sandherr, Susanne, *Die heimliche Geburt des Subjekts: Das Subjekt und sein Werden im Denken Emmanuel Lévinas'*, PThH 34, Stuttgart / Berlin / Cologne: Kohlhammer, 1998, 162.

43 Cf. Arendt, *The Human Condition*, 304.

As born beings, humans owe their life (fifthly) not only to the kept promise of their respective mother, but also to the creative powers of the earth that bring forth a free human being. The human freedom is already preformed in the freedom that appears already during the history of nature.

According to the Priestly account of Creation in Gen 1:1–2:4, God does not only grant humans a share in his creative power. The pre-human creatures, too, are included in the emergence of life. God equips the earth with creative potential (cf. Gen 1:11–12, 24), in a way that the earth produces plants and animals. Like humans, animals are able to multiply on their own and, thus, fill their environments with life and co-design their environments (cf. Gen 1:22).

Because the Israelites knew about the creative power of the earth, it does not come as a surprise that in wisdom texts the idea of earth as the mother of all living things appears. In Psalm 139, it is said: "My frame was not hidden from you, when I was being made in secret, intricately woven in the depths of the earth" (Ps 139:15). God's acting is limited here to the role of a father during a pregnancy. To perceive God in this way simultaneously allows to perceive the creative inherent activity of the earth. With reference to the phenomenon of natality, it is striking that womb and earth can mutually represent each other: "Naked came I out of my mother's womb, and naked shall I return thither" (Job 1:21; cf. Eccl 5:14).

If we suppose that these traditions have the potential to disclose reality, the following can be stated: The fact that we are born not only means that we can act as free beings in the world, but it also implies that we are already created by the earth as such free beings.

In analogy to the human birth, which stands in evolutionary continuity with birth in the animal world, human freedom, too, stands in evolutionary continuity with forms of freedom that emerge in the history of nature.

The behavior of organisms is always characterized by the freedom to act in different ways: "Animal life is distinguished [. . .] from machines by the unpredictability of its behavior. Stimulus and reaction [. . .] are only weakly coupled; that is, stimuli do not trigger a fixed behavior, but modulate an existing intrinsic activity, so that only the probability of a certain behavior of the living being is modified."[44] Under laboratory conditions, it can be shown that even fruit flies can consider different possibilities and that they can reflect their behavior, even though this reflection is quite simple. Thus, it is not possible to deny animals inwardness. "If man was the relative of animals, then animals were the relatives of

44 Fuchs, *Das Gehirn*, 113–114.

man, and in degrees bearers of that inwardness of which man, the most advanced of their kin, is conscious in himself."[45]

If we take seriously the evolutionary continuity in which every human being stands, then the strict distinction between nature and freedom is dissolved: The human freedom to bring forth new things has continuities in our history of nature. The phenomenon of natality, thus, reminds us that the human being has evolved out of the history of nature, which is always already characterized by an interplay of freedom and necessity and which opens up a scope of freedom.

Due to the physiological prematurity of human beings, the phenomenon of natality reminds us (sixthly) that a human being is an organism with reduced instincts. As such, it is able to behave relatively independently towards his or her instincts. "Thus, in man, even the most instinctual part of behavior, the sexual sphere, is open to a far-reaching freedom of personal choice."[46] Humans can set aims for their behavior, which do not result from their immediate environment and their immediate desires. A human being "can replace the loosened connection to present things and their demands with a freely chosen attachment to an imagined unconditionality and its demands. He can posit transcendent goals for his *conduct* and actually does so in such things as faith, devotion to an absolute ideal [. . .] or even a delusory construct of his fallible understanding of values, of a misguided eros."[47]

This relative freedom of the human being from the natural conditions of his or her existence is presupposed by Jesus of Nazareth when he says: "Therefore do not be anxious, saying, 'What shall we eat?' or 'What shall we drink?' or 'What shall we wear?' For the Gentiles seek after all these things, and your heavenly Father knows that you need them all. But seek first the kingdom of God and his righteousness, and all these things will be added to you" (Matt 6:31–33).

2.2 Vulnerability and Empathy

In and through our bodies we always experience ourselves in dependence on others, but also in an openness towards others.

---

45 Jonas, Hans, *The Phenomenon of Life: Toward a Philosophical Biology*, Chicago: University of Chicago Press, 1982, 57.

46 Portmann, Adolf, *Biologische Fragmente. Zu einer Lehre vom Menschen*, Basel: Schwabe, 1944, 59.

47 Jonas, Hans, "Matter, Mind, and Creation: Cosmological Evidence and Cosmogonic Speculation," in: id., *Mortality and Morality: A Search for the Good after Auschwitz*, Lawrence Vogel (ed.), Evanston, IL: Northwestern University Press, 1996, 175.

> As soon as we make contact with another person, our bodies interact with each other. They sense each other and provoke subtle emotions in each other. We enter into something like a force field, an autonomous sphere of correlation and interdependencies, which we can scarcely regulate or control. Our bodies understand each other, but we are unable to define precisely why and how this happens.[48]

From a biblical perspective, the phenomenon of intercorporeality is expressed in such a way that what others do is inscribed into one's own body. Because the human being is an embodied being, the Old Testament can characterize him right up to his inner self (heart, kidneys) as open towards others: "[M]y inmost being will rejoice when your lips speak what is right" (Prov 23:16). Because human beings are open to others, they are also vulnerable: "My eyes grow weak with sorrow; they fail because of all my foes" (Ps 6:7).

The fact that a human being is always dependent on the mercy of other human beings and influenced by them makes Paul state that "you are not your own" (1Cor 6:19). As bodily beings, we live in relationships that influence us. Paul illustrates this through the example of man and woman: "The wife does not have authority over her own body but yields it to her husband. In the same way, the husband does not have authority over his own body but yields it to his wife" (1Cor 7:4). That means: What a person becomes in a relationship does not lie in that person's own hands because everybody is shaped by his or her counterpart. According to Paul, in a relationship every human being gives up his sovereignty, his *exousia*, his (presumed) power over his own life. To prevent misunderstandings, I would like to distinguish here between sovereignty and freedom: Though every human being is part of a story whose outcome he or she does not know and, thus, is not sovereign about, he or she is still free to present him- or herself in a relationship anew again and again.[49]

Paul realizes that human relationships influence the human body much more than non-living objects can do. That is why Paul can grant the consumption of certain foods to the congregation in Corinth (cf. 1Cor 6:13; 10:25–26), but prohibits sexual contact with a prostitute: "Shun fornication! Every sin that a person commits is outside the body; but the fornicator sins against the body itself" (1Cor 6:18). With regard to metabolism, the human being can consume something without being made similar to it. Relationships between living bodies, however, leave traces within a person. They possess a special power to influence bodily life.

---

48 Fuchs, Thomas, "Non-verbale Kommunikation: Phänomenologische, entwicklungspsychologische und therapeutische Aspekte," in: Hermann Lang (ed.), *Was ist Psychotherapie und wodurch wirkt sie?*, Würzburg: Königshausen & Neumann, 2004, 87.

49 Cf. Arendt, *The Human Condition*, 223–236.

What Paul explains with regard to sexual relationships is also true with regard to all intercorporeal relationships. As bodily beings, we are always co-shaped by others. Even the ascetic cannot escape from it. No one is an island over which he or she can rule with complete power, with *exousia*. Paul puts it even more bluntly when he says that the body always belongs either to sin or to God. According to Paul, before baptism, the body belongs to sin (cf. Rom 6:4), through baptism we have died to sin so that the body now belongs to the Lord: "The body is meant [. . .] for the Lord, and the Lord for the body" (1Cor 6:13). In the "body we are always connected with others, it can even be said: In the body we belong to others, this is the fundamental social dimension of bodily living."[50] That is why, for Paul, everything depends on the question in which relationships we live and by whom we allow our bodies to be shaped.

Drawing on the example of Jesus, Paul realizes that bodily life is always related to others: Jesus Christ is the human being who lives for God (cf. Rom 6:10). But Christ realizes this living-for-God by living for others as "body that is for you" (1Cor 11:24). According to Paul, this bodily pro-existence of Jesus is an expression of real humanity and real human existence. Through the body, a human being always exists in relation to others.

As bodily beings, we are vulnerable – but this vulnerability can be understood as a good gift from God. "Christians should see vulnerability as a created fact; we were created as vulnerable, we did not fall into it. [. . .] Vulnerability [. . .] bespeaks a fundamental truth about the nature of human being, namely, that we are not meant to be autarkic selves, we are not ideally invulnerable."[51] Without taking into account this specific vulnerability, the specific sociality and humanity of a person cannot be explained: "Bodily needs necessitate that human beings form social relationships and institutions, which range from the family to the nation-state and beyond. In other words, functioning and responsive social units are the only (although only partial) antidote for human vulnerability. In other words, we are beings dependent on the care of others."[52]

Because of our intercorporeality, the suffering of one person affects another person in such a way that this other person aims at overcoming and ending the suffering. The vulnerability of the human being, thus, makes him sensitive to the

---

50 Marquardt, *Was dürfen wir hoffen, wenn wir hoffen dürften?*, 451.

51 Mathewes, Charles, "Vulnerabilty and Political Theology," in: Heike Springhart / Günter Thomas (eds.), *Exploring Vulnerability*, Göttingen: Vandenhoeck & Ruprecht, 2017, 170.

52 Fineman, Martha Alberton / Allard, Silas W., "Vulnerability, the Responsive State, and the Role of Religion," in: Heike Springhart / Günter Thomas (eds.), *Exploring Vulnerability*, Göttingen: Vandenhoeck & Ruprecht, 2017, 192–193.

suffering of others. This is precisely what we can see in the specific vulnerability of Jesus Christ.

The Apostles' Creed reduces the life of Jesus Christ to specific key data – "born of the Virgin Mary, [. . .] suffered under Pontius Pilate" – and, thus, seems to ignore the life of the earthly Jesus. This focus on Jesus' birth and death has had a lasting influence on the iconography of the Western World and the Christian theology in general. Even in current dogmatics, the life of the earthly Jesus often plays only a marginal role.

However, it is possible to read the Apostles' Creed from a different angle: Jesus was "born of the Virgin Mary. He suffered. Under Pontius Pilate he was crucified, died, and was buried." Read from this perspective, the Apostles' Creed emphasizes that it is possible to subsume "the whole life of Jesus [. . .] under the heading 'suffered'."[53] When one understands the life of Jesus as a suffering existence, then one can perceive Jesus Christ as "the fellow-sufferer who understands,"[54] as a human being who lets himself be moved by the suffering of others – by their illnesses as well as by their social exclusion. Jesus lets himself be (bodily) touched by a bleeding woman and he lets himself be anointed by a prostitute.

The New Testament uses a specific term in order to express this passion, and compassion, of Jesus: *splagchnizomai* (cf. Mark 1:41; 6:34; 8:2; 9:22; Matt 9:36; 14:14; 15:32; 20:34; Luke 7:13). The noun *splagchnon*, which in general is used in the plural, refers to the inner organs. It is used in Acts 1:18 with a purely physical meaning: When Judas commits suicide, it is said that "all his bowels gushed out." That means: The (com)passion of Christ, his empathy, the fact that he is moved by the suffering of others, has to be understood as a bodily process.

That the New Testament assumes a connection between the inner organs and empathy becomes especially clear in the Pauline letters. Here, it becomes apparent that the feeling of empathy and helping others is a behavior that has been provoked and co-shaped by one's own body (cf. 2Cor 7:15; Phlm 1:7). By sending the slave, Onesimus, back to his master, Paul also sends back his own "bowels" (Phlm 1:12). That means: What Philemon does to Onesimus affects Paul in a bodily way – and even his inner organs. Crises and relationships (even between other people) are inscribed into one's own body. That is why Paul asks Philemon at the end of his letter: "[R]efresh my bowels in the Lord" (V. 20) by interacting with Onesimus in a friendly and brotherly way. How people interact with each other,

53 Barth, Karl, *Dogmatics in outline*, transl. G.T. Thomson, New York: Harper, 1959, 102.
54 Whitehead, Alfred North, *Process and Reality: An Essay in Cosmology*, Corrected Edition, David Ray Griffin and Donald W. Sherburne (eds.), New York: Free Press, 1978 [1929], 351.

what becomes of people who have grown close to one's own heart, affects a person in a bodily way into the depths of his or her inner self. The inner self is, thereby, not conceived of as separate from the body but as embodied.

Accordingly, for Paul, the bowels are the location of the desire for others (cf. Phil 1:8), but also the place of mercy (cf. Phil 2:1; cf. Col 3:12). Of course, a person can shut down his inner feelings (cf. 1John 3:17), so that he becomes restricted towards himself and towards others (cf. 2Cor 6:12). However, the inner organs are organs of relations. As such, their well-being depends on others. In this sense, the example of the slave, Onesimus, who ran away from his master, shows that Paul's well-being relies on what Philemon does to Onesimus. As bodily being, as the body that I am, I find myself at the mercy of other human beings, I am affected and shaped by their actions, their sufferings, and their needs.

It is precisely this passivity that enables human life (in the qualitative sense, thus, differing not from an animal, but from an unhuman life). The fact that the suffering of others touches me in a bodily way is the precondition for empathy. This is illustrated by the parable of the Good Samaritan: "But a Samaritan, as he journeyed, came to where he was, and when he saw him, he had compassion. He went to him and bound up his wounds, pouring on oil and wine. Then he set him on his own animal and brought him to an inn and took care of him" (Luke 10:33–34).

The parable of the Good Samaritan illustrates the following: Helping someone requires that the helping person is sensitive to her bodily, inward consternation, which is evoked by the suffering of the other. In this sense, the parable tells us about two other people – who, of course, have bowels as well – but who are not moved by their bowels to act and to help the person who fell among the robbers. So, it can be concluded that you have to be sensitive to what your own body wants to tell you. When you do not understand your body and its wisdom, the body may fall silent in the end, so that you then can pass a beaten person without being affected by it in a bodily and inward way.[55]

2.3 The Embodiment of Empathy in the Fact of Being Born

The description in the New Testament of the embodied empathy of Jesus Christ has a multilayered parallel in the Hebrew Bible. On the one hand, Hebrew Bible texts connect mercy (*raḥ^{a}mîm*) with the womb (*reḥem*): Here, mercy is understood as embodied, though not in the inner organs but in the womb. On the other

55 Cf. Böhme, Gernot, *Ethik leiblicher Existenz*, Frankfurt: Suhrkamp, 2008, 198–199.

hand, the Old Testament speaks of God's "womb love."[56] From the perspective of the Bible as a whole, it can be said that Jesus lets himself be moved by the needs and sufferings of human beings. Thus, he reveals the "womb love" of God, which has been described in the Old Testament. God's "womb love" helps people in their needs and refuses to turn away from them despite their failure and guilt.

From an anthropological perspective, the embodiment of mercy in the womb must be considered more carefully. Magdalene Frettlöh has rightfully pointed out in her exegesis of two biblical texts that embodiment should not be misunderstood as a purely naturalistic process. On the one hand, it becomes clear in the narration of the Salomonic judgment in 1Kgs 3 that "the mere fact of having a womb (and to have given birth) does not guarantee mercy."[57] In this respect, one of the two women is willing to let the child be killed. On the other hand, mercy is "a strong emotion in favor of life [. . .] which is also hoped for and expected from men. Similarly to women's bodies, men's bodies, too, can burn or groan from the emotion of mercy."[58] Joseph can be mentioned as one example. When he meets his youngest brother, Benjamin – still unrecognized by him and his other brothers – Joseph blesses Benjamin and is, thereby, overwhelmed by his feelings: "With that, Joseph hurried out, because he was overcome with affection for his brother, and he was about to weep. So he went into a private room and wept there" (Gen 43:30). Similar to Jesus and the Good Samaritan, Joseph, too, is bodily-inwardly moved by another person. He is overcome with feelings so that he cries.

On the one hand, biblical texts connect mercy with the womb; on the other hand, they illustrate that mercy is expected of men, too. Because the biblical texts describe both aspects, it is wrong to interpret the separation of mercy from the womb as a separation of feelings from the body. As in the New Testament, the Hebrew Bible, too, describes the merciful behavior of men as embodied. The specific connection of mercy with the womb is nevertheless meaningful because it refers back to the place where every person emerges as an intercorporeal being: that is the womb. That the human being always comes from others is true not only in a metaphorical, but also in a physical sense. When we ask for the reason why the human body lets itself be moved by others, we are drawn to the intercorporeality of every person. Every person comes from a female other. Before I adopt a certain behavior towards her, she has embraced me already. This intercorporeality, which precedes all consciousness, is the precondition and basis for the human capacity for mercy, for empathy.

---

56 Trible, Phylis, *God and the Rhetoric of Sexuality*, Philadelphia: Fortress Press, 1978, 51.

57 Frettlöh, Magdalene L., *Gott Gewicht geben: Bausteine einer geschlechtergerechten Gotteslehre*, Neukirchen: Neukirchener, ^{2}2009, 288; see also Trible, *God and the Rhetoric of Sexuality*, 31–59.

58 Frettlöh, *Gott Gewicht geben*, 289.

This is also illustrated by developmental psychology: Because a newborn has lived in relation to another person already in the uterus, it is no surprise that a newborn is able to take part in communication immediately after birth. Even newborns imitate the behavior of others. Coming from a sphere of intercorporeality, they are immediately open for communication. Coming from intercorporeality, human beings naturally are communicative beings open for others.[59]

Similar to the New Testament, the Apostles' Creed is sensitive to the relation between natality and empathy: The compassionate, who understands, has to be born from a woman. He is only conceivable as someone who comes from the specific intercorporeality, from the womb. This is why in the Apostles' Creed the description of Jesus' birth through the Virgin Mary precedes the description of Jesus' suffering.

3 The Historical Development of the Concept of the Body in the History of Christianity

The biblical and, thus, Christian view on humans conceives them as embodied and understands the human body as the privileged medium of God's self-revelation. Nevertheless, the history of the Church and the history of theology are both characterized by a strong hostility towards the body. In the following, I will outline how this shift happened and how Christianity, for its part, has contributed to a lifestyle that forgets and despises the body. However, simultaneously it must be argued that the biblical insight that being human also means being a body has always reappeared in the history of the Church and in the history of theology.

3.1 Starting Points for the Christian Contempt for the Body in Pauline Texts

In my view, there are three starting points in New Testament texts to which later Christian traditions of body critique and contempt of the body could refer.

First, Paul could appreciate the body on the one hand, but he could also define a life according to the flesh as a life in sin. Second, early Christianity generally was an ascetic movement. Jesus and Paul were celibates. Thirdly, despite the overall

59 Cf. Meltzoff, Andrew N. / Moore, M. Keith, "Newborn Infants Imitate Adult Facial Gestures," *Child Development* 54 (1983), 702–709.

trend in both testaments to view human beings as a whole, both the Septuagint and the New Testament show traces of a dualistic or tripartite anthropology.

3.1.1 Living in the Flesh

According to Paul, the human being lives his or her life in and through the body. But this bodily life can be lived in two different ways: either as a life "in the flesh" or "in newness of spirit" (cf. Rom 7:5–6). Here, it must be emphasized that, according to Paul, the life in the spirit is lived in the body, too – even beyond death (cf. 1Cor 15). But Paul also describes a connection between living in the flesh and living in sin: "but I am carnal, sold under sin" (Rom 7:14). Due to his fleshly-bodily constitution, the human being is prone to sin. Thus, it can be interpreted: Because a human being is flesh, he knows about his finite nature. By knowing about his finite nature, the human being wants to satisfy his greed for life at all costs. Because human beings are flesh, according to Paul, they tend to idolatry, hatred, emulation, wrath, strife, seditions, heresies, envyings, murders, drunkenness, revelings (cf. Gal 5:20–21). The human being who lives according to the flesh becomes a slave to the natural tendencies of his or her body, that is: he or she cares primarily for himself and his and her survival. By not rising above this tendency of his body, the human being, who lives according to the flesh, misses his or her better opportunities. Those opportunities, which are themselves enabled by the body, include being there for others, being a body for others and, thus, to contribute to a communication of love, joy, peace, longsuffering, gentleness, goodness, faith, meekness, and temperance (cf. Gal 5:22–23).

Instead of promoting an attitude that accepts human's finite nature, sin tempts human beings to understand their own finitude as a problem. Thus, human beings are tempted to put all their vital energies in the fight against finitude in order to raise their own vitality, instead of using their limited and finite possibilities in the spirit of Jesus Christ.

In Rom 7, Paul goes even further: It is not only the awareness of one's own finite nature that makes human beings vulnerable to the promises of sin. What is more, there is a tendency within the human body, Paul calls it "the law in my members," which is at war with the desire of the inward man and reason to do good (cf. Rom 7:21–23). Sin dwells in one's own "fleshly body" (Rom 7:20). There is an essential feature of the fleshly body to subordinate everything else to one's own self-preservation and one's own well-being.

This Pauline insight has its parallels in the results of modern evolutionary psychology. The evolutionary psychology calls attention to the fact that human beings are evolutionarily socialized.[60] Human beings are influenced by a long evolutionary history of violence: Violence begins with the evolution of predators, through which envy and cruelty are formed. Also, violence is used to establish hierarchies and to foster predictability. Rapacity, drive for "dominance, and revenge" have proven successful during the course of evolution – and, thus, belong to our biological heritage.[61]

By locating desires in the flesh, Paul indicates that these desires belong to the biological heritage of human beings: This becomes clear because the term *flesh/ sarx* in Pauline writings can have the meaning of inheritance and heritage. Thus, Christ is a Davidian "according to the flesh" (Rom 1:3), Abraham is the ancestor of the Jews "pertaining to the flesh" (Rom 4:1) and the Israelites are Paul's brothers according to the flesh (cf. Rom 9:3–4). Accordingly, those works of the flesh that must be overcome are quite predominantly "biologically based behaviors."[62] To live according to the flesh describes a way of existence in which humans succumb to the tendency of their biological existence, which aims for self-assertion and self-enforcement.

So, both evolutionary psychology and Paul believe that the natural life of a human being, his biological body, has a tendency to violently pursue his own interests – including the interest of the group to which he belongs – at the expense of others.[63]

Paul understands the human being as a bodily being through and through – and until eternity (cf. Phil 3:21; 1Cor 15). As body, the human being can become a temple of the Holy Spirit, a body which radiates faith, love, and hope. As a fleshly body, which knows about its finitude, the human being is also endangered to succumb to the tendency of his or her natural life to pursue his or her interests and the interests of his or her group at the expense of others. If a human being lives according to the flesh, he or she uses his or her options in life just for his or her own self-interest, and, thus, succumbs to sin.

The Pauline appreciation of the body is countered by Paul's realistic perception of the power of sin. By contrasting an inner will, an inward person who wants the good, with the law of the human body that aims for the implementation

60 See as an introduction Buss, David M., *Evolutionary Psychology: The New Science of the Mind*, New York / London: Routledge, ^{6}2019.

61 Pinker, Steven, *The Better Angels of Our Nature: The Decline of Violence in History and its Causes*, London: Lane / Penguin Books, 2011, 483; see also Wrangham, Richard / Peterson, Dale, *Demonic Males: Apes and the Origins of Human Violence*, Boston / New York: Mariner Books, 1996.

62 Theißen, Gerd, *Biblischer Glaube in evolutionärer Sicht*, Munich: Kaiser, 1984, 166.

63 See also Peters, Ted, "The Evolution of Evil," in: Gaymon Bennett et al. (eds.), *The Evolution of Evil*, RThN 8, Göttingen: Vandenhoeck & Ruprecht, 2008, 52.

of one's self-interest, Paul has set the scene for a later interpretation that conceives of the fight between sin and spirit in such a way that this fight becomes a battle between the human body and the human mind. "In all later Christian writing, the notion of 'the flesh' suffused the body with disturbing associations."[64]

3.1.2 The Ascetic and Sexuality

The second reason for the Christian uneasiness about the inherent activity of the body and the contempt for the body was that Paul – as an ascetic – was critical towards the sexual desires of the body. Paul makes it clear that he wants everybody to be like him, that is a celibate (cf. 1Cor 7:7). "It is good for a man not to touch a woman" (1Cor 7:1). Only in order to prevent fornication, he grants the members of the Christian congregations to have a wife, or a husband respectively, and to sleep with one's partner. The danger of *porneia* is so paramount to Paul that he does not even consider the possibility of a legitimate enjoyment of sexuality (even within marriage).[65] "Marriage, like household slavery, was a 'calling' devoid of glamor."[66]

On the other hand, both Paul's own way of living as an ascetic and his line of argument in his first letter to the Corinthians indicate his appreciation of the body. Precisely because the body is the "temple of the Holy Ghost" (1Cor 6:19), bodily action is of utmost importance to Paul. Consequently, the distinction between right bodily conduct and a bodily conduct that is deemed unworthy is necessary. Paul's line of argumentation is quite ambiguous here: On the one hand, the body is appreciated as a place of God's indwelling. On the other hand, sexuality, a natural expression of life, is believed to be so dangerous that it has to be controlled via marriage or, even better, has to be overcome through asceticism.

In order to understand the Pauline distrust towards human sexuality, this distrust must be put in the historical context. In Antiquity, sexuality was no playful celebration of human intercorporeality, but was staged as a power discourse. Antiquity understands "the sexual act first and foremost as a game of superiority and inferiority: penetration places two partners in a relationship of domination and submission. It is victory on the one hand, defeat on the other; it is a right that is exercised for one of the partners, a necessity that is imposed on the other."[67]

64 Brown, *The Body and Society*, 48.
65 Cf. Brown, *The Body and Society*, 54–57.
66 Brown, *The Body and Society*, 57; cf. 1Cor 7:33–34.
67 Foucault, Michel, *The Care of the Self*, The History of Sexuality 3, trans. Robert Hurley, New York: Vintage Books, 1988, 30.

The connection between sexuality and violence is shown in the correlation of prostitution and the bloody fights in the arenas, "the raging sexuality of the arena came to a focus in the gladiator's scarred body, and Rome's prostitutes gathered at the arena exits, where they did a brisk trade."[68] All this shapes the attitude of the apostle: "Undoubtedly, Paul perceives the realm of human sexual relations as a field in which very much wrong is done."[69]

Paul himself cannot conceive of sexuality other than in terms of hierarchy, of superiority, and inferiority. "The wife hath not power of her own body, but the husband: and likewise also the husband hath not power of his own body, but the wife" (1Cor 7:4). This verse is revolutionary because Paul speaks of a relationship of mutual superiority and inferiority. However, in his understanding of sexuality as a relationship in hierarchies, Paul remains committed to ancient patterns of thinking.[70]

What points forward in Pauline thinking on sexuality, although this argument was of little impact in the course of Church history, seems to be another aspect. Paul recognizes the danger that lies in sexuality, but he does not condemn sexuality itself. This becomes apparent in Gal 5 where Paul contrasts fornication – not with sexual abstinence or marriage, but with love. Thus, Paul contrasts a world that stages even sexuality as a power discourse with a way of life that is characterized by *agape*, i.e.: that is shaped by voluntary self-restraint for the benefit of others.[71] Instead of asserting their own power in sexuality, human beings are inspired by the Spirit to mutual self-restraint. This voluntary self-restraint can be lived in many different ways according to Paul: either in the way of asceticism, which Paul himself prefers, or in the way of a mutual subordination. The difference between asceticism and sexuality is not the central category for Paul. Rather, Paul emphasizes that the difference between selfishness and love is decisive. In this way, it becomes possible to think a praxis of sexuality which is shaped by love and not by power. This concept is really a revolution in antiquity – a concept that, granted, to a large extent, has not been successful in Christianity, either.

---

68 Nell, Victor, "Cruelity's rewards: The gratification of perpetrators and spectators," *Behavioral and Brain Sciences 29* (August 2006), 220.

69 Berger, Klaus, *Historische Psychologie des Neuen Testaments*, SBS 146/147, Stuttgart: Katholisches Bibelwerk, 1991, 283.

70 See also Theißen, *Erleben und Verhalten der ersten Christen*, 443.

71 On the understanding of love as a "power of free, creative self-restraint for the benefit of others," see Welker, Michael, "Romantic Love, Covenantal Love, Kenotic Love," in: John Polkinghorne (ed.), *The Work of Love: Creation as Kenosis*, Grand Rapids / London: Eerdmans / SPCK, 2001, 127–136.

3.1.3 Tripartite Concepts of the Human Being

As early as in the Septuagint, a tendency can be observed to dissolve the Hebrew perception of the embodiment of the human being in favor of the exclusive perception of the human being as cognitive being. According to the translation of the Schma Israel in the Septuagint, the Israelite shall love JHWH no longer "with all thine heart" (MT), but "with all thy mind" (Deut 6:5). Accordingly, the words that God commands to his people not only "shall be in thine heart" (Deut 6:6), but "in thy heart and in thy soul" (LXX). The bodily heart is supplemented by the spiritual soul.[72] The Hebrew imagery of the human being as an embodied person is, in many places, suspended and replaced by more abstract concepts.[73] For example, in the Greek translation, the "link between a mother's womb and compassion" is lost.[74] Therefore, a tendency to disembodiment can be rightfully diagnosed. This tendency made it possible for the Early Church "to connect Platonic thinking with the Christian traditions and thus to help Platonic thinking to its importance in the theology of the Fathers of the Church."[75]

There are some passages in Paul which could be interpreted as expressions of a dualistic or tripartite anthropology. For example, Paul distinguishes body and spirit in 1Cor 7:34, and he distinguishes spirit, soul, and body in 1Thess 5:23. However, the term 'spirit' refers here to the human relationship with God, the term 'soul' to human vitality. So, Paul asks God not to preserve three different parts of the human, but to preserve faith, vitality, and the body of the Christians in Thessaloniki.

3.2 A Dualistic Anthropology and the Resurrection of the Flesh

Incorporating the little evidence of a tripartite view of the human being in the New Testament and corresponding tendencies in the Septuagint, the early Church has adopted the dualistic anthropology of Greek philosophy.[76] However, a continuous reception of this anthropology was hindered by the Christian hope for a bodily resurrection. This hope did not allow to identify the human being exclu-

---

72 Cf. Rösel, Martin, "Den Herrn aus ganzem Denken lieben (Dtn 6,5 LXX): 'Entkörperung' in der griechischen Übersetzung des Alten Testaments?," in: Gregor Etzelmüller / Annette Weissenrieder (eds.), *Verkörperung als Paradigma theologischer Anthropologie*, TBT 172, Berlin / Boston: de Gruyter, 2016, 143.

73 Cf. Rösel, "Den Herrn aus ganzem Denken lieben," 147.

74 Rösel, "Den Herrn aus ganzem Denken lieben," 156.

75 Rösel, "Den Herrn aus ganzem Denken lieben," 158.

76 Cf. Volp, "Der Mensch," 110.

sively with his soul, as it was possible in Platonic traditions. For example, Socrates defines the human being as soul in the *First Alcibiades*, a dialogue that was originally attributed to Plato but probably originated in the wider milieu of the academy: "Since then neither the Body, nor the Compound of Soul and Body together, is the Man, it remains, I think, either that a Man's Self is nothing at all, or, if it be any thing, it must be concluded, that the Man is no other Thing than Soul."[77]

Due to the challenge by Docetistic and Gnostic positions, orthodox theologians intensified the expectation of a bodily resurrection. In contradiction to Paul (cf. 1Cor 15:50), they claimed the doctrine of the resurrection of the flesh, occasionally they claimed even the resurrection of this flesh – "*huius carnis resurrectionem*" (Tyrannius Rufinus).[78]

The expectation of the resurrection of the flesh was founded in the doctrine of the incarnation of the Logos. "The confession of the incarnation of the saviour (Barn, Herm, II Clem, Justin; EvPhil) and the confession of his fleshly constitution became the basis for the defense of the resurrection of the flesh (Ps.Justin, 3 Cor, Irenaeus, Rheg)."[79] The Word was made flesh – and was resurrected (cf. Luke 24:36–43, esp. 39; John 20:19–29) as flesh (cf. IgnSm 7:1[80]). As a consequence, the believers were promised the resurrection in the flesh.

The confession of the resurrection of the flesh evokes a holistic anthropology. For example, according to Justin (100–165), the human being is created as body, so that he cannot be perceived without his body. Consequently, Justin argues: "as a man does not live always, and the soul is not for ever conjoined with the body, since, whenever this harmony must be broken up, the soul leaves the body, and the man exists no longer."[81] Even though the life of a human being depends "on the life-giving presence of the soul in the body [. . .]. The soul alone, however, is not the human being."[82] For the theologians of the early Church, "being human relies on the unity of body and soul."[83]

77 Plato, "The First Alcibiades," in: *Dialogues of Plato*, vol. 2, London: W. Sandby, 1767, 285.

78 Denzinger, Heinrich, *Enchiridion symbolorum definitionum et declarationum de rebus fidei et morum: Quod emendavit, in linguam germanica transtulit et adiuvante Helmuto Hoping editit Petrus Hünermann*, Editio XLIII, Freiburg et al.: Herder, 2010, 16; see also Angenendt, Arnold, "Corpus incorruptum: Eine Leitidee der mittelalterlichen Reliquienverehrung," *Saeculum* 42 (1991), 338–339.

79 Lona, Horacio E., *Über die Auferstehung des Fleisches: Studien zur frühchristlichen Eschatologie*, BZNW 66, Berlin / New York: de Gruyter, 1993, 257.

80 See Lona, *Über die Auferstehung des Fleisches*, 33–40.

81 Justin the Martyr, *Dialogue with Trypho, a Jew*, 6:2, ANF 2 (1867), 95.

82 Lona, *Über die Auferstehung des Fleisches*, 98.

83 Kretschmar, Georg, "Auferstehung des Fleisches: Zur Frühgeschichte einer theologischen Lehrformel," in: *Leben angesichts des Todes. Beiträge zum theologischen Problem des Todes. Hel-*

Irenaeus of Lyon (~135–200) says:

> For that flesh which has been moulded is not a perfect man in itself, but the body of a man, and part of a man. Neither is the soul itself, considered apart by itself, the man; but it is the soul of a man, and part of a man. Neither is the spirit a man, for it is called the spirit, and not a man; but the commingling and union of all these constitutes the perfect man.[84]

The orthodox theologians connected the doctrine of creation and eschatology. Thus, they confessed "the faithfulness of God to his creation, which is expressed in the resurrection of the 'carnis substantia'. The separation of a creator God and a redeeming God in the dualistic gnosis [in contrast] involves the fundamental devaluation of the body."[85]

3.3 The Unease about Sexuality

Living as a celibate, Paul had a critical attitude towards marriage (cf. 1Cor 7). However, he granted the possibility that the body of a married and, thus, sexually active person was a "temple of the Holy Spirit." In contrast, already the *Acts of Paul and Thekla* from the 2nd century draw a different picture: The metaphor of the temple is used as appraisal for those Christians that live sexually abstinent.

> Blessed are they that keep the flesh chaste, for they shall become the temple of God. Blessed are they that abstain [. . .], for unto them shall God speak. Blessed are they that have renounced this world, for they shall be well-pleasing unto God. Blessed are they that possess their wives as though they had them not, for they shall inherit God.[86]

This appraisal of abstinence is not unfamiliar to Paul, but it is strengthened and intensified during the separation of Judaism and Christianity in post-biblical time. While Judaism emerged as "a religion of the book and of the sanctified, married household,"[87] Christianity counted on the ideal of chastity: "The renunciation of marriage laid bare the fragility of a seemingly changeless order. The means by which society was continued could be abandoned. Chastity announced the immi-

mut Thielicke zum 60. Geburtstag, Tübingen: Mohr Siebeck, 1968, 16; cf. Beinert, Wolfgang, *Die Leib-Seele-Problematik in der Theologie*, Cologne: Karl-Rahner-Akademie, 2002, 15.

84 Irenaeus of Lyon, *Adversus haereses* 5:6:1, ANF 9 (1869), 68f.

85 Lona, *Über die Auferstehung des Fleisches*, 266.

86 *The Acts of Paul*, in: The Apocryphal New Testament, trans. James Montague Rhodes, Oxford: Clarendon Press, 1924, 273: The Acts of Paul 3:5.

87 Brown, *The Body and Society*, 61; cf. 61–64.

nent approach of a 'new creation'."[88] The new message of the impending end of the world was embodied – in a celibate body.

The decision to live as an ascetic could be experienced as a gain in freedom. Virginity in early Christian communities was synonymous with an increase in autonomy for women. There was now an alternative to marriage with its subordination to the man and with its risky births.[89] Young people who refused to marry and to have children resisted the expectations of society and, thus, the expectations of their parents, occasionally also those of their spouses. Thus, they questioned the continuation of society, which relied on procreation and descendants. In this way, the body became the place of a bio-political protest and articulated the freedom from that which apparently both nature and society requested.

With extreme clarity, this position can be found with Marcion (~140–180), who built up a church which was characterized by radical asceticism. "Only by rendering men and women utterly unfamiliar to each other, by demanding that they should renounce the marriages that had previously held them together, and even by dissolving the ties that bound children to their parents, could true Christians come together in a freely chosen communion, undetermined by preexisting family bonds, loyalties, and habits."[90] Love and affection should not be limited and controlled through obligations towards the spouse and relatives. By imitating Christ, love and affection should overflow to strangers and socially marginalized persons.[91] Here, asceticism serves to discover new possibilities of bodily action in following Jesus Christ. "Where the Creator had ordered men to shun leapers, Christ had touched them. Where the Creator had decreed menstruating women to be a source of impurity, Christ had let the woman with an issue of blood lay her hand upon him."[92]

Marcion's opponent, Tertullian (160–220), warned his listeners about Marcion's radicality which would destroy family relations. In contradiction to Marcion, Tertullian did not demand lifelong chastity, but demanded only the abstinence of older widows, male and female, who had already produced and raised children. In this way, Tertullian connected a family ethos with the ideal of asceticism. According to Tertullian, it was necessary to beget children and, thus, to preserve the Christian community, but also to live in celibacy at an older age and to open oneself up for

88 Brown, *The Body and Society*, 64.
89 Cf. Seeliger, Hans Reinhard, "Lehre und Lebensform: Über die 'Hellenisierung' und 'Enkratisierung' des antiken Christentums," *ThQ* 196 (2016), 127–138.
90 Brown, *The Body and Society*, 89.
91 Cf. Brown, *The Body and Society*, 89.
92 Brown, *The Body and Society*, 89; see Tertullian, *Adversus Marcionem*, Ernest Evans (ed.), Oxford: Oxford University Press, 1972, 288.366–368 [IV: 9,3. 20,9].

God's spirit: "For continence will be a mean whereby you will traffic in a mighty substance of sanctity; by parsimony of the flesh you will gain the Spirit."[93]

Tertullian was not a dualist. He could ask his opponent Marcion, *quid est autem homo aliud quam caro.*[94] The embodied soul and the visible body, to him, formed a unity, so that

> it was directly through the body and its sensations that the soul was tuned to the high pitch required for it to vibrate to the Spirit of God. [. . .] Yet the doctrine had its shadow-side. The instinctual life of the body, the random, distressing fantasies of the heart, made themselves felt in the soul with unbuffered, gripping intensity. [. . .] With Tertullian, we have the first consequential statement, written for educated Christians and destined to enjoy a long future in the Latin world, of the belief that abstinence from sex was the most effective technique with which to achieve clarity of soul.[95]

Tertullian writes: "For let us ponder over our conscience itself, (to see) how different a man feels himself when he chances to be deprived of his wife. He savours spiritually. If he is making prayer to the Lord, he is near heaven. If he is bending over the Scriptures, he is 'wholly in them.' If he is singing a psalm, he satisfies himself."[96]

3.4 Forgetfulness and Contempt of the Body

An ascetic Christianity could get close to the Platonic understanding of the body as dungeon of the soul. Origen (185–254), for example, praises martyrdom as a possibility to reach God. The reason for this lies in the fact that in martyrdom the body is killed and in this way that which prevents humans from the clear vision of God is eliminated.

> Why do we still hesitate and doubt to remove the obstructive, transient body which complains the soul, the earthly dwelling which burdens the anxious spirit, to free us from the fetters and to release it from the waves which are given with flesh and blood? Let us take away this dwelling to enjoy with Christ Jesus the peace inherent in bliss, looking at Himself

93 Tertullian, *De exhortatione castitatis*, X:1, ANF 4 (1885), 56.
94 Tertullian, *Adversus Marcionem*, 66 [I:24,5], cf. Greschat, Katharina, "'Teilweise auferstehen wäre eine Strafe, keine Erlösung': Tertullians Verteidigung der fleischlichen Auferstehung und des göttlichen Gerichts als Beginn des ewigen Lebens," in: Günter Thomas / Markus Höfner (eds.), *Ewiges Leben: Ende oder Umbau einer Erlösungsreligion?*, DoMo 21, Tübingen: Mohr Siebeck, 2018, 57–71.
95 Brown, *The Body and Society*, 77–78.
96 Tertullian, *De exhortatione castitatis*, X:2–3; ANF 4 (1885), 56.

as the Word that completely brings life to life. Then we will be nourished by him and grasp the very diverse wisdom that lives in him.[97]

According to Origen, it is imperative "to reduce the bodily needs to a minimum" until martyrdom, and to live dispassionate and angelic (that is: disembodied). Consequently, Origen connected the fact that humans were created in the image of God solely with the inner being. To the body he granted only "an honor derived from the divine dignity of man."[98] Even in the 4th century, Epiphanios of Salamis (315–403) could protest against such a position with reference to the Bible. Epiphanios of Salamis criticized Origen for denying that the human body was made in the image of God.

Gregory of Nyssa (335/340–394 or later) ended the anthropological disputes within the Eastern Church by distinguishing between "a first creation of the godly nature of humans and then a second creation of a sexual and passionate human nature."[99] Along with this distinction went a devaluation of the body, as is shown by Gregory's appraisal of virginity:

> Nature's inevitable changes are many; they agonize him whose love is passionate. One way of escape is open: it is, to be attached to none of these things, and to get as far away as possible from the society of this emotional and sensual world; or rather, for a man to go outside the feelings which his own body gives rise to. Then, as he does not live for the flesh, he will not be subject to the troubles of the flesh. But this amounts to living for the spirit only, and imitating all we can the employment of the world of spirits. There they neither marry, nor are given in marriage. Their work and their excellence is to contemplate the Father of all purity, and to beautify the lines of their own character from the Source of all beauty, so far as imitation of It is possible.[100]

To Gregory of Nyssa, the appraisal of virginity corresponds with eschatological expectations: In death, man sheds all that strange appearance which he has assumed through passionate inclinations, and this is sexual intercourse, conception, giving

97 Origen, *Schriften vom Gebet und Ermahnung zum Martyrium*, trans. Paul Koetschau, BKV I/48, Munich: Kösel 1926, 207f.: "Warum also zögern und schwanken wir (noch), abzulegen den hinderlichen 'vergänglichen' Leib, der die Seele beschwert, das 'den vielsinnenden Geist' belastende 'irdische Zelt', und uns loszulösen von den Fesseln und abzufahren aus den Wogen des irdischen Seins? Können wir doch dann mit Christus Jesus die der Seligkeit eigene Ruhe genießen, indem wir dasselbe durch das Weltall hindurch (wirkende) lebendige Wort ganz anschauen und von ihm genährt werden und die [in] ihm (wohnende) überaus mannigfaltige Weisheit erfassen."

98 Volp, "Der Mensch," 115.

99 Volp, "Der Mensch," 117.

100 Gregory of Nyssa, *On Virginity*, IV:8, NPNF II/5 (1888), 350–51; see also Karras, Valerie A., "A Re-Evaluation of Marriage, Celibacy, and Irony in Gregory of Nyssa's On Virginity," *JECS* 13 (2005), 111–121.

birth, impurity, suckling, feeding, defecation, old age, illness, and death. Here, not only sexuality is questioned but also all (life-creating and life-preserving) activity and initiative of the body. This initiative of the body, which keeps us alive day after day and night after night, can only be despised when the desire to die and to be with the Lord completely shapes one's own life.

3.5 The Augustinian Heritage

In his *Soliloquies*, one of his early philosophical writings, Augustine answered the question, posed by his reason, what it was that he wanted to know or understand. "I want to know God and the soul" – and when asked again by his reason, if there was nothing else that he wanted to know, he answered briefly: "Nothing whatever."[101] The body is excluded from those things that Augustine wants to understand. Accordingly, Augustine can define the human being as soul: The human being, "as viewed by his fellow-man, is a rational soul with a mortal and earthly body in its service."[102] The human being is soul and uses a body. Consequently, the anthropological epistemic interests of the early Augustine focused exclusively on the soul. Thus, his theology can be described as characterized by an oblivion of the body (*Körpervergessenheit*).

When Augustine becomes aware of the body, the body appears as danger to the knowledge of the soul. For example, Augustine could read in Cicero's *Hortensius*, a writing that motivated his turn to philosophy: "For a violent lust of the body can not harmonize with rational thinking. Who is able, when he enjoys the pleasure, which is greater than any other, to concentrate his mind on something else? [. . .] Who, equipped with good sense, will not prefer that we would have been given no desire by nature at all?"[103] Even in Neoplatonic works, Augustine could read that the desires and passions that derive from the body prevent the soul from the vision of the spiritual being.[104] Against this neoplatonic backdrop,

101 Augustine, *Soliloquia*, I:7, NPNF I/7 (1888), 539.

102 Augustine, *Morals of the Catholic Church* [Mor 1:52]: "*homo igitur ut homini apparet, anima rationalis est mortali atque terreno utens corpore*"; NPNF I/7 (1888), 55.

103 Cicero, Marcus Tullius, "Hortensius," in: id., *Hortensius – Lucullus – Academici libri: Lateinisch-deutsch*, Laila Straume-Zimmermann et al. (eds.), Düsseldorf / Zürich: Artemis & Winkler, ^{2}1997, 88: "congruere enim cum cogitatione magna voluptas corporis non potest, quis enim cum utatur voluptate ea, qua nulla possit maior esse, attendere animo, inire rationem, cogitare omnino quidquam potest? [. . .] quis autem bona mente praeditus non mallet nulla omnino nobis a natura voluptates datas?" (Cicero, Hort. Frg. 84 I).

104 Cf. Plotinus, *Ennead IV*, trans. A.H. Armstrong, Loeb Classical Library 443, Cambridge, MA: Harvard University Press, 1989, eighth tractate.

Augustine interpreted the Pauline opposition of flesh and spirit as an opposition between sinful nature and God's spirit.

The conversion of Augustine occurs with reference to the biblical word of the apostle Paul: "Let us live honorably as in the day, not in reveling and drunkenness, not in debauchery and licentiousness, not in quarreling and jealousy. Instead, put on the Lord Jesus Christ, and make no provision for the flesh, to gratify its desires" (Rom 13:13–14).[105]

For Augustine, this quote makes clear that the desires and passions of the body are concentrated in the field of sexuality. In Augustine's description of his confession, the topics of sexual desire and asceticism are paramount.[106] The libido

> not only takes possession of the whole body and outward members, but also makes itself felt within, and moves the whole man with a passion in which mental emotion is mingled with bodily appetite, so that the pleasure which results is the greatest of all bodily pleasures. So possessing indeed is this pleasure, that at the moment of time in which it is consummated, all mental activity is suspended.[107]

Although the sexual desire is just one of many possible desires that human beings can succumb to, for Augustine the sexual desire became the clearest symptom for the human condition as such.[108]

Cicero's rhetorical question, who would not prefer to live a life without any passion or desires, is echoed in *De civitate*, when Augustine asks: "What friend of wisdom and holy joys, who, being married, but knowing, as the apostle says, 'how to possess his vessel in sanctification and honor, not in the disease of desire, as the Gentiles who know not God,' would not prefer, if this were possible, to beget children without this lust?"[109] As a consequence, Augustine claims that Adam, if he had not been expelled from paradise, would have begotten children without sexual arousal.[110] "Augustine never found a way, any more than did any of his Christian contemporaries, of articulating the possibility that sexual pleasure might, in itself, enrich the relations between husband and wife."[111]

To Augustine, every human being feels lust, even though – as a friend of wisdom – he does not want to feel it and so, the body resists the will. According

105 Cf. Augustine, *Confessiones*, VIII:12,29, NPNF I/1 (1886), 127.
106 Cf. Augustine, *Confessiones*, VIII:11,26–27, NPNF I/1 (1886), 126–127.
107 Augustine, *De civitate Dei*, 14:16, NPNF I/2 (1887), 275.
108 Cf. Brown, *The Body and Society*, 406–407.
109 Augustine, *De civitate Dei*, 14:16, NPNF I/2 (1887), 275f.
110 Cf. Augustine, *De civitate Dei*, 14:23–24, NPNF I/2 (1887), 279–281.
111 Brown, *The Body and Society*, 402.

to Augustine, this behavior is a consequence of Adam's Fall.[112] Because humanity had not been obedient to God in paradise, God has punished humankind with a body that was disobedient to the soul.

This punishment does not only become apparent when human beings get sexually aroused despite their conscious will,[113] but also in the phenomenon that the body sometimes withstands the lust:

> But even those who delight in this pleasure are not moved to it at their own will, whether they confine themselves to lawful or transgress to unlawful pleasures; but sometimes this lust importunes them in spite of themselves, and sometimes fails them when they desire to feel it, so that though lust rages in the mind, it stirs not in the body. Thus, strangely enough, this emotion not only fails to obey the legitimate desire to beget offspring, but also refuses to serve lascivious lust; and though it often opposes its whole combined energy to the soul that resists it, sometimes also it is divided against itself, and while it moves the soul, leaves the body unmoved.[114]

Here, it becomes apparent that for Augustine, the real problem of the body lies in its lack of restraint;[115] the body does not completely obey our conscious will. Augustine cannot integrate the resistance of our body into his self-image, but only interprets it as punishment and downfall. Augustine cannot perceive that even where my body resists my will, the wisdom of the body is at work.

The body's resistance to the human will becomes not only visible in sexuality, but also in the phenomenon of illness.[116] Consequently, Augustine teaches that both the body before the Fall (in paradise) but also the bodies of the resurrected righteous men are free from illness and desires.[117] Following Paul, Augustine describes such a body as a "spiritual body" (*corpus spiritale).*[118] For Augustine, such

---

112 Cf. Augustine, *De civitate Dei*, 14:15, NPNF I/2 (1887), 274–275.

113 Augustine interprets Adam's shame as sexual shame; he assumes that Adam had a short erection, which demonstrated him the own activity of his body, which is no longer exclusively obeying his will (cf. Brown, *The Body and Society*, 417).

114 Augustine, *De civitate Dei*, 14:165, NPNF I/2 (1887), 276.

115 Augustine speaks of a "weakness of flesh that cannot be curbed" (Augustine, *De bono coniugali*, 5, NPNF I/3 (1887), 401).

116 In his *De beata vita*, Augustine offers a positive appreciation of the wisdom of the ill body. According to the description of his conversion there, it was a lung disease that made the further practice of his work as a rhetorician impossible and thus led Augustine to a new way of life (cf. Drecoll, Volker Henning, "Die 'Bekehrung' in Mailand," in: id. (ed.), *Augustin Handbuch*, Tübingen: Mohr Siebeck, 2014, 154).

117 Cf. Fuhrer, Therese, "Körperlichkeit und Sexualität in Augustins autobiographischen und moraltheoretischen Schriften," in: Barbara Feichtinger / Helmut Seng (eds.), *Die Christen und der Körper: Aspekte der Körperlichkeit in der christlichen Literatur der Spätantike*, BzA 184, Munich / Leipzig: Saur, 2004, 185.

118 Augustine, *Gen. ad litt.*, 6:24; see Fuhrer, "Körperlichkeit und Sexualität," 185.

a body is characterized by its complete subordination to the human will. Therefore, a spiritual body cannot hinder the vision of God that comes through the soul[119] and so Augustine can think of an embodied blissful vision of God.[120]

However, this expectation of a sensual body, which does not hinder the vision of God that comes through the soul, only strengthens Augustine's distrust towards the existing body: "Let me put it to you yet more intimately. Your flesh is like your wife [. . .]. Love it, rebuke it [. . .]. Learn now to master what you will receive as a united whole. Let it now go short, so that it will then enjoy abundance."[121]

Augustine's distrust towards the ill body, towards the lust of the body, and towards the inherent activity and self-initiative of the body is inherited by the Middle Ages. The contempt for the body that was characteristic for the Middle Ages (cf. 3.6.) is based here.

This practical contempt for the body comes along with a theoretical ignorance of the body. Although Augustine suffered from the activity and initiative of his body, this was hardly the real problem for him. Staying true to his early agenda – to know God and the soul – his real question deals with the perversion of the will, the experience of a split will within the soul itself: "Whence is this monstrous thing? and why is it? The mind commands the body, and it obeys forthwith; the mind commands itself, and is resisted."[122] There is a defect in the soul which involuntarily bends low to the flesh, the *concupiscentia carnis*. The term "flesh," as Augustine repeatedly declares, does not mean body, but all that, which tempts human beings to prefer their own will over God's will. This *concupiscentia carnis* becomes visible in sexuality, but does not lie primarily in the body but

> in a lasting distortion of the soul itself. With Adam's Fall, the soul lost the ability to summon up all of itself, in an undivided act of will, to love and praise God in all created things. Concupiscence was a dark drive to control, to appropriate, and to turn to one's private ends, all the good things that had been created by God to be accepted with gratitude and shared with others. It lay at the root of the inescapable misery that afflicted mankind.[123]

---

119 Cf. Fuhrer, "Körperlichkeit und Sexualität," 185.

120 Cf. Augustine, *De civitate Dei*, 10:29: The bodies of the resurrected "shall be absolutely incorruptible and immortal, and shall offer no hindrance to the soul's contemplation" (NPNF I/2 (1887), 200). According to Augustine, of course, only the bodies of the redeemed are freed from their pains, the damned suffer "in the fire of hell, which Augustine does not understand like Origen metaphorically but materially, pain without end" (Fuhrer, "Körperlichkeit und Sexualität," 177; cf. Augustine, *De civitate Dei*, 21).

121 Augustine, *Enarrationes in psalmos*, 140:16: "Et ut aliquid coniunctius eloquamur, caro tua tanquam coniux tua est. [. . .] ama et castiga [. . .] modo doma quod postea recipias; modo deficiat, ut tunc sufficit" (MPL 37, 1825–26); as cited in Brown, *The Body and Society*, 426.

122 Augustine, *Confessions*, 8:21, NPNF I/1 (1886), 127.

123 Brown, *The Body and Society*, 418.

This understanding of the *concupiscentia carnis* is similar to the Pauline understanding of the desires of the flesh. Following recent exegetical insights, the desires of the flesh can be understood as "the sin of asserting oneself and one's group at the expense of others."[124] By illustrating the *concupiscentia carnis* as sexual desires, Augustine contributes to the hostility towards the body within Christian traditions. What is more, by understanding the *concupiscentia carnis* as a distortion of the soul, Augustine deflects the anthropological interest away from the body. Not the body, but the soul and the will become central categories in later theology.

Excursus: The Christianity of the Majority and the Moral Teaching of the Elites

Theologians of the early Church remained dubious about the bodiliness of human existence and especially about human sexuality despite the expectations of a resurrection of the flesh. Granted, the attitude illustrated here was that of the elites. This attitude of the elite should not conceal the fact that the majority of Christians lived in marriage and could arrange a Christian existence with a (joyous) sexuality.[125] Vis-a-vis the strict ascetic movements, theologians such as Tertullian and Augustine could accept the fact that the majority of Christians lived their sexuality. Augustine could warn African nuns to look down on married women.[126] As an allowance, in order to prevent licentious behavior, Augustine could even grant couples sexual activity, which does not happen under the control of the will to the effect of posterity, but through the victory of pleasure for the sake of pleasure.[127]

In this way, Christianity took shape as a religion of two ways, as already described by Eusebius of Ceasarea (260/64–339/340).[128]

---

124 Jewett, Robert, "The Anthropological Implications of the Revelation of Wrath in Romans," in: Kathy Ehrensperger / J. Brian Tucker (eds.), *Reading Paul in Context: Explorations in Identity Formation: Essays in Honour of William S. Campbell*, London / New York: T&T Clark, 2010, 33.

125 Cf. Brown, *The Body and Society*, 401–2. As an expression of the self-image of this "silent majority" (401), according to which God created people for marriage and birth, Adam and Eve reach out their right hands on Roman sarcophagi of the time as a sign of the unity and harmony of a Roman marriage.

126 Cf. Brown, *The Body and Society*, 397.

127 Cf. Augustine, *De nuptiis et concupiscentia*, 1:16 [XIV]; 1:27[XXIV], NPNF I/5 (1887), 270.274–275; see also id., *De bono coniugali*, 11, NPNF I/3 (1887), 404; see also id., *De bono coniugali and De sancta virginitate*, ed./trans. P.G. Walsh, Oxford Early Christian Texts, Oxford: Clarendon Press, 2001, 1–61.

128 Cf. Brown, *The Body and Society*, 205.

> Two ways of life were thus given by the law of Christ to His Church. The one is above nature, and beyond common human living; it admits not marriage, child-bearing, property nor the possession of wealth, but wholly and permanently separate from the common customary life of mankind, it devotes itself to the service of God alone in its wealth of heavenly love! And they who enter on this course, appear to die to the life of mortals, to bear with them nothing earthly but their body, and in mind and spirit to have passed to heaven. Like some celestial beings they gaze upon human life, performing the duty of a priesthood to Almighty God for the whole race [. . .]. And the other more humble, more human, permits men to join in pure nuptials and to produce children.[129]

Without people who took this second way, the early Church would not have survived in antiquity. However, the Christian elites did not consider this second way as equal to the first way, as became clear in the aforementioned quote. The ideal of the chastity of the elites cast a shadow on the actions of the majority of Christians: "To beget children with a certain, medically approved zest, as a duty to the earthly city, was no longer enough. The Christian married couple must 'descend with a certain sadness' to that particular task: for in the act of married intercourse itself, their very bodies spoke to them of Adam's fall."[130] Marriage is "the good use of a malum (an evil), namely the evil of *concupiscentia.*"[131]

3.6 Devaluation of the Body in the Middle Ages

> There is no epoch in European history that has uplifted the soul more and devalued the body more deeply than the Middle Ages. In all clarity, a maxim of St. Bartholomew of Farne (died 1194) says: "We must do everything harmful to our bodies, if we want to lead them to the perfect splendor of the soul!" (Vita 9, in: Rolls Series 75/1, 1882, 302) Even Francis of Assisi who was known as a worshipper of the material world, which he regarded as God's creation, and who wrote the famous 'Canticle of the Sun' [. . .] taught this antagonism: "I have no greater enemy than my body: *maiorem inimicum non habeam corpore*" (2 Cel 2,86). "Let us hate our body with its vices and sins," the saint specifically recommends in his letter to all believers, "for the Lord says in the Gospel: all evils, vices, and sins are from the body" [. . .]. Francis not only preached this in theory, but also lived it out in practice: with fasting and self-flagellation, he sufficiently disciplined the "brother donkey" (2Cel 2:92). He explains that animal metaphor, which is so popular among ascetics, saying

129 Eusebius of Caesarea, *The Proof of the Gospel. Volume 1*, trans. W. J. Ferrar, London: SPCK, 1920, 48f [Demonstratio Evangelica 1,8].
130 Brown, *The Body and Society*, 426–427, quoting sermons of Augustine.
131 Löhr, Winrich, "Sündenlehre," in: Volker Henning Drecoll (ed.), *Augustin Handbuch*, Tübingen: Mohr Siebeck, 2014, 504.

> that the body "should be subjected to heavy work like a pack animal, often whipped and fed on bad fodder" (Bonaventura, Legenda maior 5,6,2).[132]

Only the body that is subjected to asceticism and mortification is good. Consequently, asceticism reached a "hardness and sophistication that had not been achieved since the time of the Desert Fathers."[133] Peter Dinzelbacher reminds us of the "self-flagellation that started in the 2nd half of the 11th century [. . .], which was practiced extensively not only in the flagellations of 1216 and 1348, but also in everyday life of the monasteries and brotherhoods."[134]

In another way, chastity and sensuality were connected in female mysticism. Close to heresy, women who lived in celibacy developed a sensual love-life. It is said about Saint Gertrude (died 1302): "She felt how her innermost heart let enter her lover and embraced him, rejoicing that the gracious presence of the bridegroom's tenderness was bestowed upon her [. . .]. Oh true power of the insuperable right of the Most High, that a vessel of clay sufficed [. . .] for the pouring of such precious fluid!"[135]

Here, the body becomes the place where communion with God is experienced in a sensual way – thus, the dignity of the human body and of sensuality in this world is discovered. Salvation is experienced in bodily form.

3.7 Scholasticism

The theological tendency to forget the body becomes apparent in scholasticism, where the epistemic interests focus primarily on the soul and not on the body of the human being. Thomas Aquinas (1224/25–1274) emphasizes the *intellectualis natura*, the human reason, which is the connecting element between God and humans. "Now among all others, the rational creature is subject to Divine providence in the most excellent way, in so far as it partakes of a share of providence, by being provident both for itself and for others. Wherefore it has a share of the Eternal Rea-

---

132 Dinzelbacher, Peter, *Körper und Frömmigkeit in der mittelalterlichen Mentalitätsgeschichte*, Paderborn: Schöningh, 2007, 14–15.

133 Dinzelbacher, *Körper und Frömmigkeit*, 109.

134 Dinzelbacher, *Körper und Frömmigkeit*, 109.

135 Gertrude of Helfta, *Legatus divinae pietatis*, 2,6; as cited in Dinzelbacher, *Körper und Frömmigkeit*, 95: "Sie spürte, wie ihr Innerstes den Geliebten eingelassen hatte und ihn umschloß, und freute sich, daß die gnadenhafte Anwesenheit der Zärtlichkeit des Bräutigams ihr herrlichst gewährt wurde . . . Oh wahre Kraft der unüberwindlichen Rechten des Höchsten, daß ein Gefäß aus Lehm . . . der Eingießung so kostbarer Flüssigkeit genügte!".

son, whereby it has a natural inclination to its proper act and end."[136] "For Bonaventure (1221–1274), human reason constitutes the *imago dei.*"[137]

The theology of the early Church has left medieval theology with the problem of how to harmonize the confession of the resurrection of the body with the platonic dualism – and, thus, how to solve the mind-body problem. Thomas Aquinas tried to solve it by reverting to Aristotle.

> He had seen in the body the principle of matter, in the soul he saw that [. . .] of form and regarded man as a unity of both principles, thus no longer consisting of two subsisting entities, as his teacher assumed. The problem was, of course, the mind: Aristotle lets him enter the human being from the outside. Thomas improves Aristotle by letting the soul subsist, but then he assumes his fundamental statement that man is a unity of two principles, of the body as matter, of the subsistent soul as '*unica forma corporis*'. So the soul can do nothing without the body; in the body she also expresses her relationship with God. After death, the soul lives as an indestructible subsistent spiritual being – that is, after all, again thought of as Platonic – further, but no longer as an actuating form of the body: death is now really a human death, not just death of the body. What remains is something that is no longer really the *body* but the *corpse of the X*. The only thing that can continue living is something fragmentary, not an actual, personal person, although this remains the carrier of human existence beyond death. Aquinas expressly says that the *anima separata* is in an unnatural state (see ScG IV, 79). But then he falls into inconsistencies. He insists on the perfect bliss of this *anima*. But how can a fragment be happy? He continues to insist on the selfsameness of the resurrection body, although this selfsameness does not have to be postulated when the soul alone is the identity subject of man.[138]

The recourse to Aristotle has consequences on the perception and evaluation of sexuality. According to Thomas, not only the human as a whole has a teleological orientation, but also all parts of the body. Consequently, the use of the genitals for their purpose, that is sexual intercourse, "cannot be evil in itself, because things that exist naturally are ordered to their end by divine providence [. . .]. Therefore, it is impossible for carnal union to be evil in itself."[139] Thus, according to Thomas, every use of the genitals can be called good which serves a wider purpose, namely the preservation of humankind. Sexual intercourse ultimately serves procreation – and should be embedded in a context that allows the best possible upbringing of children. For Thomas, this context is marriage. Since sexual intercourse within marriage for the purpose of procreation can be called good, the same can be said

---

136 Thomas Aquinas, *Summa Theologiae*, http://www.logicmuseum.com/wiki/Authors/Thomas_Aquinas/Summa_Theologiae/Part_IIa/Q91#q91a2arg1: S.Th. I-II q. 91 a. 2 co.

137 Volp, "Der Mensch," 122.

138 Beinert, *Die Leib-Seele-Problematik*, 17.

139 Thomas Aquinas, *Contra Gentiles. Book three: Providence Part II*, trans. Vernon J. Bourke, Notre Dame: University of Notre Dame Press, 1975, https://isidore.co/aquinas/english/ContraGentiles3b.htm: ScG III, 126, explicitly with reference to the genitals.

for the lust that comes with it. "Within theology, Thomas entered uncharted territory with this decision. He is the first medieval theologian ever who does not condemn sexual pleasure and can even consider it a good."[140] Unlike Augustine, Thomas does not assume that the procreation of children would have happened without lust in paradise. Instead, he argues that "the sensual pleasure [in paradise] would have been not less, as some think. For the purer the nature was and the more tender the sensual part of the body were, the greater the sensual pleasure would have been."[141]

3.8 Reformation

Martin Luther's understanding of the body includes both contempt for the body and an appreciation of the body. His contempt for the body is rooted in his monastic heritage. "It is no surprise that a man from the 16th century, who became a monk at the age of 21, shows contempt for the body."[142] In the monastery of the Augustinian hermits, Luther had become familiar with the ideal of renunciation. Renouncing the world and one's own body was, thereby, understood as a preparation for one's death as the true entrance to life. Because death was understood as "dissolution of the body,"[143] all investments into the body were seen as transient and in vain; thus, it was only logical to emphasize the eternal things and not the transient already in this life. The monastic ideal of renunciation still appears in the early reformatory texts written by Martin Luther. Thus, Luther says in his writing on Christian freedom:

> Although [. . .] a man is abundantly and sufficiently justified by faith inwardly, in his spirit, and so has all that he needs, except insofar as this faith and these riches must grow from day to day even to the future life; yet he remains in this mortal life on earth. In this life he must control his own body and have dealings with men. Here the works begin; here

140 Fuchs, Josef, *Die Sexualethik des heiligen Thomas von Aquin*, Köln: Bachem, 1949, 23.
141 Thomas Aquinas, *Summa Theologiae*, http://www.logicmuseum.com/wiki/Authors/Thomas_Aquinas/Summa_Theologiae/Part_I/Q98: S.Th. I q. 98 a. 2 ad 3: "Sed in statu innocentiae nihil huiusmodi fuisset quod ratione non moderaretur, non quia esset minor delectatio secundum sensum, ut quidam dicunt (fuisset enim tanto maior delectatio sensibilis, quanto esset purior natura, et corpus magis sensibile); sed quia vis concupiscibilis non ita inordinate se effudisset super huiusmodi delectatione, regulata per rationem, ad quam non pertinet ut sit minor delectatio in sensu, sed ut vis concupiscibilis non immoderate delectationi inhaereat."
142 Leppin, Volker, "Madensack und Tempel des Heiligen Geistes: Leiblichkeit bei Martin Luther," in: Bernd Janowski / Christoph Schwöbel (eds.), *Dimensionen der Leiblichkeit: Theologische Zugänge*, Neukirchen-Vluyn: Neukirchener Verlag, 2015, 86.
143 Leppin, "Madensack und Tempel des Heiligen Geistes," 87.

> a man cannot enjoy leisure; here he must indeed take care to discipline his body by fastings, watchings, labors, and other reasonable discipline and to subject it to the Spirit so that it will obey and conform to the inner man and faith and not revolt against faith and hinder the inner man, as it is the nature of the body to do if it is not held in check.[144]

It is important for Luther – both before and after his reformatory insight – to discipline the body. However, "with his wedding on June 13th, 1525, Luther discovered a completely new world of bodily experiences."[145] The world of sexuality and the world of bodily joys opened up to him – not only through his relationship with Katharina von Bora, but also through the joy he experienced at the play and the growth of his children.

Additionally, Luther's theology, with its focus on the Word that became flesh,[146] the incarnation of God, led to a new appreciation of the body. In fact, Luther emphasized the role of the incarnation so strongly that he was unwilling to conceive the presence of Christ other than as a presence in the flesh. According to Luther, the human being recognizes God only when he perceives God in his bodiliness.[147] Therefore, in the controversy over the meaning of the Lord's Supper, Luther says: "No, comrade, wherever you place God for me, you must also place the humanity for me."[148]

Because Luther interprets the Christian faith unanimously in light of the incarnation of God, he also regards the human body from a new perspective. The human body is able to have a share in the divine attributes, so that Luther can use the term "spiritual flesh" with regard to Christ (cf. WA 23,203:15; 205:10: "geistlich Fleisch"). Because body and flesh can become the place of God's presence, the body no longer has to be denounced, but the bodily life can be appreciated in its own right.

Because Luther realizes God's appreciation of the body, he is also able to understand how encompassingly God cares for the human body. In his interpretation of the first article of the Apostles' Creed, Luther confesses

144 Luther, Martin, "The Freedom of a Christian," in: Martin Luther, *Three Treatises*, trans. W.A. Lambert, 265–316, Minneapolis: Fortress Press, ^{2}1970, 294.

145 Leppin, "Madensack und Tempel des Heiligen Geistes," 93.

146 Cf. Bayer, Oswald, *Leibliches Wort: Reformation und Neuzeit im Konflikt*, Tübingen: Mohr, 1992.

147 Cf. Gräb-Schmidt, Elisabeth, "Leiblichkeit – das Ende der Werke Gottes? Materialität und Kommunikation als Dimensionen theologischer Anthropologie," in: Bernd Janowski / Christoph Schwöbel (eds.), *Dimensionen der Leiblichkeit: Theologische Zugänge*, Neukirchen-Vluyn: Neukirchener Verlag, 2015, 98.

148 Luther, "Confession Concerning Christ's Supper," 219.

> that God has created me and all that exists; that he has given me and still sustains my body and soul, all my limbs and senses, my reason and all the faculties of my mind, together with food and clothing, house and home, family and property; that he provides me daily and abundantly with all the necessities of life, protects me from all danger, and preserves me from all evil.[149]

So, the christological appreciation of the body in the context of the second article of the Apostles' Creed leads Luther to a new appreciation of the body in the context of creaturely life that is described in the first article.

The close connection between the divine and human nature of Jesus Christ rightly corresponds to Luther's interpretation of the close connection between the Holy Spirit and the Word in the third article of the Apostles' Creed. Luther explicitly refutes the doctrine of the enthusiasts, "*dass uns Gott ohn Mittel und ohn sein Wort im Herzen tröste*" (WA 31/I, 99), that God comforts us in our hearts without means and without His Word. The comforting work of the Spirit is instead bound to the oral, vivid preaching, to the intercorporeal communication of the word. Belief and faith arise where Christ appears as embodied in the congregation in order to inspire belief and to assure the congregation of their faith through bodily actions. The christologically reasoned appreciation of the body in the second article of the Apostles' Creed, thus, leads to a new appreciation of the intercorporeality in the third article of the Apostles' Creed.

With regard to the appreciation of the body, the reformed tradition is more cautious. However, it has to be taken into account that Calvin himself spent his bodily life in much tribulation: He first had to mourn the death of his children and then the death of his wife. Besides, he suffered from chronical pain and illnesses. Seen in this context, it is remarkable that Calvin was able to create an enormously comprehensive theological work and at the same time built up the city of Geneva as a place of refuge for the persecuted and as an inspiring center of the international, global reformation. The experience of transcending suffering and bodily pain and still creating new things by trusting in God is also reflected in Calvin's understanding of the relationship between body and soul. As Calvin has experienced first-hand, the human being "consists of a body and a soul," but, according to Calvin, the soul is the "nobler part."[150] Consequently, Calvin attributes mortality to the human body, but rationality to the soul of the human being: "For though the whole man is called mortal, the soul is not therefore liable

149 Luther, Martin, "Der kleine Katechismus," in: Irene Dingel (ed.), *Die Bekenntnisschriften der Evangelisch-Lutherischen Kirche. Vollständige Neuedition*, Göttingen: Vandenhoeck & Ruprecht, 2014, 870; cf. https://www.ekd.de/en/Small-Catechism-298.htm (June 06, 2023).

150 Calvin, John, *The Institutes of the Christian Religion*, trans. Henry Beveridge, Edinburgh: Calvin Translation Society, 1846, 160: Inst. 1:15:2.

to death, nor when he is called a rational animal is reason or intelligence thereby attributed to the body."[151]

A unique perspective within the reformed tradition is taken by the Heidelberg Catechism. Starting from the first question, the Heidelberg Catechism always understands and addresses the human being as a unified whole, which consists in time and eternity as body and soul. The Catechism points out that "I am not my own, but belong with body and soul, [. . .] to my faithful Saviour Jesus Christ." Because God provides for body and soul "without the will of my heavenly Father not a hair can fall from my head" (Answer to Question 1). Because Christ ascended to heaven in bodily form, we can be certain that "we have our flesh in heaven as a sure pledge that He, our Head, will also take us, His members, up to Himself" (Answer to Question 49: How does Christ's ascension into heaven benefit us?). This is why the faithful can await their judge *with uplifted head* (cf. Answer to Question 52) – the certainty of salvation lifts up the body. The Heidelberg Catechism conceives of salvation as thoroughly embodied: The faithful are already here and now "united more and more to His sacred body," so that they are "flesh of His flesh and bone of His bones" (Answer to Question 76). What is more, one day "this my flesh [. . .] shall be [. . .] made like Christ's glorious body" (Answer to Question 57).[152]

4 The Perception of the Concept within Different Christian Schools of Thought

4.1 Friedrich Schleiermacher

Friedrich Schleiermacher's perception of the body is pervaded by an interesting tension: On the one hand, he asks to concentrate on "the inner life";[153] on the other hand, he clearly recognizes that the human being is always a psychosomatic being.

151 Calvin, *The Institutes of the Christian Religion*, 163: Inst. 1:15:3.
152 Neuser, Wilhelm H., "Heidelberger Katechismus von 1563," in: Andreas Mühling / Peter Opitz (eds.), *Reformierte Bekenntnisschriften. Band 2/2: 1562–1569*, Neukirchen-Vluyn: Neukirchener Verlag, 2009, 167–212; cf. http://www.heidelberg-catechism.com/pdf/lords-days/Heidelberg-Catechism.pdf.
153 *Schleiermacher's Soliloquies.* An English Translation of The Monologen. With a Critical Introduction and Appendix by Horace Leland Friess [1926], Eugene, OR: Wipf and Stock, 2002, 20; cf. Schleiermacher, Friedrich Daniel Ernst, "Monologen: Eine Neujahrsgabe," in: id., *Schriften aus der Berliner Zeit 1800–1802*, Günter Meckenstock (ed.), KGA I/3, Berlin: de Gruyter, 1988, 11:27.

In the *Soliloquies*, he says: "To me the spirit is the first and only being, for what I take to be the world, is the fairest creation of spirit, a mirror in which it is reflected."[154] The body has no autonomy, it is just the instrument of the spirit: "Is there indeed a body without a spirit? Does not the body exist only because and insofar as the spirit requires it and is conscious thereof?"[155] Schleiermacher explicitly denies an existing impact of the body on the spirit.[156] The body is just the "material world,"[157] the "rohe Stoff,"[158] which is governed by the spirit. The spirit is "free from every restriction of Necessity," the spirit does not know the "feeling of bondage."[159] Anybody who knew about this freedom of the spirit would not have to fear bodily decay and dementia: "To lament my physical decline is of all things furthest from my mind! Why should that trouble me? Would it be such a misfortune, if I did forget the events of yesterday?"[160] Bodily decay and suffering would not really affect the human being because it is only "an ill that man inflicts upon himself; [. . .] an ugly fruit of the mad delusion that the spirit is dependent on the body!"[161]

However, in his lectures on psychology, Schleiermacher could claim: "The life of human beings is the being together of body and soul, the interaction between body and soul [. . .]. In the 'I' the opposition between soul and body is suspended."[162] Schleiermacher here explicitly stresses that there is both "an influence of the psychic on the pure matter" as well as "an influence of the (biological) organization on the psychic."[163] This insight already influences Schleiermacher's review of Immanuel Kant's anthropology published in 1799. In this review, Schleiermacher fundamentally criticizes Kant's basic distinction between a physiological (scientific)

154 *Schleiermacher's Soliloquies*, 16; cf. Schleiermacher, "Monologen," 9:37–38.
155 *Schleiermacher's Soliloquies*, 17; cf. Schleiermacher, "Monologen," 10:8–10.
156 Cf. *Schleiermacher's Soliloquies*, 17; cf. Schleiermacher, "Monologen," 10:10–13.
157 *Schleiermacher's Soliloquies*, 19.
158 Schleiermacher, "Monologen," 11:26.
159 *Schleiermacher's Soliloquies*, 18 f.; cf. Schleiermacher, "Monologen," 11:3–5.
160 *Schleiermacher's Soliloquies*, 93; cf. Schleiermacher, "Monologen," 55:32–34.
161 *Schleiermacher's Soliloquies*, 92; cf. Schleiermacher, "Monologen," 55:18.
162 Schleiermacher, Friedrich Daniel Ernst, *Vorlesungen über die Psychologie*, Dorothea Meier (ed.), KGA II/13, Berlin / Boston: de Gruyter, 2018, 622:20–21.31–32: "Das Leben des Menschen ist das Zusammensein von Leib und Seele, das aufeinander wirken von Leib und Seele [. . .]. Im Ich ist der Gegensatz zwischen Seele und Leib aufgehoben."
163 Schleiermacher, *Vorlesungen über die Psychologie*, 644:10–13; see as introduction Herms, Eilert, "Leibhafter Geist – Beseelte Organisation: Schleiermachers Psychologie als Anthropologie: Ihre Stellung in seinem theologisch-philosophischen System und ihre Gegenwartsbedeutung," in: Arnulf von Scheliha / Jörg Dierken (eds.), *Der Mensch und seine Seele. Bildung – Frömmigkeit – Ästhetik: Akten des Internationalen Kongresses der Schleiermacher-Gesellschaft in Münster*, Schleiermacher-Archiv 26, Berlin: de Gruyter, 2017.

and a pragmatic (philosophical) anthropology. The fact that in his philosophical anthropology Kant largely ignores the scientific findings[164] makes it clear to Schleiermacher that for Kant "the 'I' has no nature."[165] In contrast to Kant, Schleiermacher demands a "unification" of a physiological and a pragmatic anthropology.[166] "It is not appropriate to divide anthropology into psychology and physiology. Instead, anthropology must always incorporate the physical and the psychological."[167] Schleiermacher criticizes that Kant has lost "the embodied self, the self that is an organic part of the world of experience."[168] "For Schleiermacher, Kant was like an individual who, when questioned about the fundamentals of a building, responded by pointing out the partitions ('Zwischenwände') that separate the rooms from one another."[169] In contrast, Schleiermacher emphasizes: Beyond acting and thinking, when both of these faculties reach their limits and thinking becomes objectless, in the intuition of the universe, the human being experiences himself as an embodiment of life. That is why, to Schleiermacher, the distinction between body, soul, life, and nature is always already an abstraction. In pure feeling, the human being becomes aware of himself as a psychosomatic unity that is embedded in nature, where the psychic and the physical constantly penetrate each other.

> You lie directly on the bosom of the infinite world. In that moment, you are its soul. Through one part of your nature you feel, as your own, all its powers and its endless life. In that moment it is your body, you pervade, as your own, its muscles and members and your thinking and forecasting set its inmost nerves in motion.[170]

The distinction between body and soul is, thus, always already a secondary abstraction from the life that is first and foremost lived and only afterwards reflected upon. Accordingly, Schleiermacher can formulate: "It is already suspicious to speak of a bodily life and an inner life [. . .] because life is only one."[171] This is why, even in his discourse on eschatology, Schleiermacher writes in his *Christian Faith*:

---

164 See Kant, Immanuel, *Anthropologie in pragmatischer Hinsicht*, Hamburg: Meiner, 2000, 3.
165 Schleiermacher, Friedrich Daniel Ernst, "Rezension von Immanuel Kant: Anthropologie (1799)," in: id., *Schriften aus der Berliner Zeit: 1796–1799*, Günter Meckenstock (ed.), KGA I/2, Berlin / New York: de Gruyter, 1984, 366: "das Ich [hat] bei ihm [= Kant] keine Natur."
166 Schleiermacher,"Rezension von Immanuel Kant: Anthropologie (1799)," 366.
167 Schleiermacher, *Vorlesungen über die Psychologie*, 16:23–25.
168 Thandeka, "Schleiermacher's Dialektik: The Discovery of the Self that Kant Lost," *HTR* 85:4 (1992), 434; cf. ead., *The Embodied Self: Friedrich Schleiermacher's Solution to Kant's Problem of the Empirical Self*, Albany: State University of New York Press, 1995.
169 Thandeka, "Schleiermacher's Dialektik," 441.
170 Schleiermacher, Friedrich Daniel Ernst, *On Religion: Speeches to Its Cultural Despisers*, trans. John Oman, New York: Harper & Brothers, 1958, 43.
171 Schleiermacher, *Vorlesungen über die Psychologie*, 5,9–10.

> We are so generally conscious of the interconnection of all the activities of our spirit, even the deepest and innermost ones, with our physical activities that we cannot really manage to get a notion of an individual's finite spiritual life without having a notion of its organic, bodily existence. Indeed, we only imagine the spirit as soul if it is in a body, so that there can be no talk whatsoever of an immortality of the soul in its distinctive meaning without a bodily life.[172]

But in order to be able to think the perfection of the Church, e.g. the complete shaping of nature through the Spirit of Christ, the distinction "between our future and present corporality" has to be taken into account.[173] Following 1Cor 15:42 and Matt 22:30, Schleiermacher emphasizes

> that the resurrection body would be immortal and without distinct gendered functions [. . .]. The first defining qualification, which already presupposes an entirely different constitution of the future world, would push the interest in bodily self-preservation out of the way, an interest that we experience as a rampant seed of strife between flesh and spirit. In addition, the other defining qualification would guard against a mixture of the church consummate with new souls emerging as they are being restored, in that we cannot imagine the latter process without some natural force preceding the development of spirit, consequently without sinfulness.[174]

These statements reveal Schleiermacher's general understanding of human nature, of the body that we are. On the one hand, due to Christ's sinlessness, Schleiermacher can state:

> sin belongs so little to the very nature of human beings that we can never view it except as a disturbance of nature [. . .]. From this it follows that the possibility of a sinless development is not, in and of itself, incompatible with the concept of human nature. Indeed, this possibility is included as something acknowledged in the consciousness of sin as fault, as it is generally understood.[175]

---

172 Schleiermacher, Friedrich Daniel Ernst, *Christian Faith. A New Translation and Critical Edition*, vol. 2, Catherine L. Kelsey / Terrence N. Tice (eds.), Louisville (KY): Westminster John Knox Press, 2016, 406; cf. Schleiermacher, *Vorlesungen über die Psychologie*, 9:11–15: "Immaterialität Freiheit und Unsterblichkeit können wir der Seele gar nicht zuschreiben[.] Denn wir sehn sie nur mit dem materiellen Leibe zugleich werden; wir sehen sie nur im Zustande der Wechselwirkung, und wir sehn sie mit dem materiellen Leibe zugleich verschwinden[,] überall aber uns durch ihn wirken." ["It is impossible to ascribe immateriality, freedom and immortality to the soul because we perceive the soul emerging only together with the material body. We perceive both only in interaction with each other, and we perceive the soul disappearing together with the body; but everywhere we act through the body." Transl. by the author].

173 Schleiermacher, *Christian Faith*, 982.

174 Schleiermacher, *Christian Faith*, 982.

175 Schleiermacher, *Christian Faith*, 575.

On the other hand, however, sin is attached to the bodily constitution of humanity: In the evolution of life and humankind, “flesh has been shown to bear a certain magnitude already before spirit had any magnitude.”[176] This is why the natural inclination towards self-preservation has been inscribed so deeply into the body that this strife inhibits the formation of God-consciousness and, thus, the effects of the spirit.

Having been developed from nature, the human spirit forms itself and then, in turn, is more and more able to shape and define nature. In light of this thought, natural evil (such as illnesses) appear as “stimuli toward an unfolding of the human spirit.”[177] The early Schleiermacher hoped that “the perfecting of sciences and arts” would liberate human beings from the “load of mechanical and unworthy labours” by transforming “the corporeal world, and everything of the spiritual that can be regulated [. . .] into an enchanted castle where the god of the earth only needs to utter a magic word or press a spring, and what he requires will be done. Then for the first time, every man will be free-born.”[178] Because Schleiermacher cherished this hope, he brought to the fore the “animation of human nature through reason”[179] – and the “influence of the organic on the psychic”[180] receded into the background. However, from a systematic perspective, it can be stated: “On the one hand, according to Schleiermacher, reason is thought of as the active part in opposition to nature, while nature appears as ‘mass’ and ‘rough fabric’. On the other hand, however, reason can only act in unity with nature, and the stronger this unity is, the more reason can act effectively.”[181]

This supposed mutual impact that body and spirit have on each other is also expressed by Johann Wolfgang von Goethe in a letter to Wilhelm von Humboldt dated March 17th, 1832: “Animals, we have been told, are taught by their organs. Yes, I would add, and so are men, but men have this further advantage that they can also teach their organs in return.”[182]

---

176 Schleiermacher, *Christian Faith*, 406.
177 Schleiermacher, *Christian Faith*, 481.
178 Schleiermacher, *On Religion*, 178–179.
179 Schleiermacher, Friedrich Daniel Ernst, *Brouillon zur Ethik* (1805/06), Hans-Joachim Birkner (ed.), Hamburg: Meiner, 1981, 11: “Beseelung der menschlichen Natur durch die Vernunft”.
180 Schleiermacher, *Vorlesungen über die Psychologie*, 644:13: “Einfluß der Organisation auf das Psychische”.
181 Hasler, Ueli, *Beherrschte Natur: Die Anpassung der Theologie an die bürgerliche Naturauffassung im 19. Jahrhundert (Schleiermacher, Ritschl, Herrmann)*, BBStHST 49, Bern / Frankfurt: Lang, 1982, 76.
182 Johann Wolfgang von Goethe, “To Wilhelm von Humboldt,” Weimar, 17th of March 1832, in: *Goethes Werke*, Weimarer Ausgabe, IV. Abteilung, vol. 49, Letter 193. http://www.zeno.org/nid/20004860926 (June 06, 2023).

4.2 Karl Barth

In *Church Dogmatics* III/2, in his anthropology, which is grounded in Christology and orientated towards the Bible, Karl Barth supports a "concrete monism,"[183] which, in contrast to an abstract monism, does not dissolve the tension between being a body and having a body in any one direction. According to Barth, "man is the ruling soul of his serving body."[184] The human being is a "subject, who thus or thus rules, determines, stamps and guides himself and with himself his body."[185]

It is surprising that Barth in his interpretation of 1Cor 6:19–20 ("Or do you not know that your body is a temple of the Holy Spirit within you, whom you have from God? You are not your own, for you were bought with a price. So glorify God in your body.") says: "The Holy Spirit is immediate to the soul, but through the soul He is also mediate to the body."[186] The statement that the soul is the temple of the Holy Spirit cannot be found in the New Testament. On the one hand, Barth emphasized the biblically described unity of the human as a living organism as a "besouled body"[187] over and against a Greek dualism, but also against a reductionist materialism. On the other hand, Barth hardly succeeds in his teaching of a "primacy of the soul,"[188] of the superiority of the soul, and the subordination of the body. He is apparently at pains to find a biblical justification for this thesis. His note that soul and body were in the same relation as "man and woman"[189] does not illuminate anything – except the difficulty of his statements.

Barth's confession to a concrete monism shows the biblical orientation of his theology. However, his description of the relation between soul and body is characterized by a dogmatic axiom. Soul and body relate to each other in the same way as the godly and the human nature of Jesus Christ. That relation is described by Barth with the help of the Christological doctrine of anhypostasis.[190] Having in mind that this doctrine was often accused of a subtle Docetism, for example by Adolf Harnack and Dietrich Bonhoeffer,[191] we can argue: This subtle Docetism characterizes Barth's anthropology, too.

---

183 Barth, *Church Dogmatics* III/2, 395.
184 Barth, *Church Dogmatics* III/2, 434.
185 Barth, *Church Dogmatics* III/2, 421.
186 Barth, *Church Dogmatics* III/2, 368.
187 Barth, *Church Dogmatics* III/2, 329.
188 Barth, *Church Dogmatics* III/2, 421.
189 Barth, *Church Dogmatics* III/2, 429.
190 Cf. McCormack, Bruce, *Karl Barth's Critically Realistic Dialectical Theology: Its Genesis and Development 1909–1936*, Oxford: Oxford University Press, 1995, 360–367.
191 See Harnack, Adolf, *Dogmengeschichte*, GThW IV/3, Tübingen: Mohr, 1914, 253; Bonhoeffer, Dietrich, "Vorlesung 'Christologie' (Nachschrift) Sommersemester 1933," in: id., *Berlin 1932–1933*,

This becomes apparent in Barth's understanding of illness. While Barth rejects the strong Docetism of Christian Science, according to which illness is an illusion, he nevertheless shows a fine Docetistic tendency when he formulates the commandment to the ill: "to stand upright and not to fall."[192] Apparently, for Barth there is always a self that, however fragile, can remain master over the illness, a self that is ultimately not affected by the illness. In contrast, the perception of the existence of an illness that can overwhelm the ill person makes it clear that illnesses can be so serious that only others can lead the fight against it.

Barth claims a "freedom [of the human being] over his body."[193] Thus, he fails both to understand the bodily dependence of the human being and the gift that comes with this dependence.[194] This gift can already be seen by the healthy person because the body takes the lead in many spheres of life. But also in the course of a disease the power and wisdom of the body can be recognized. For example, an emotional conflict can be transformed into a physical illness "and the body does the service to him – to continue to live, to recover and to start anew."[195] In addition to that, a disease can make a human being aware of the fact that he or she misses his or her aim in life. In this sense, my body can open up for me a new perspective of my own life.

This insight of the medical anthropology is not alien to the biblical traditions. For example, in 1Cor, Paul explains the increased rate of diseases in the congregation with conflicts and divisions during the celebration of the Lord's Supper: "That is why many of you are weak and ill, and some have died!" (1Cor 11:30). This means: A psycho-social conflict has an impact even on the physical – and it is this (in Corinth misunderstood) wisdom of the body that makes it clear that something in the congregation is wrong. Paul, thus, demonstrates to the Corinthians what was already expressed in the congregation by and through the illness. Like a physician, Paul acts as an interpreter, who explains to the ill person what his or her illness means. Illness can reveal a truth – and could be understood as a crisis in which the possibility of change is given.[196]

DBW 12, Carsten Nicolaisen / Ernst-Albert Scharffenorth (eds.), Gütersloh: Gütersloher Verlagshaus, 1997, 319.

192 Barth, Karl, *Church Dogmatics*, vol. III/4, Edinburgh: T&T Clark, 1961, 362.

193 Barth, *Church Dogmatics* III/2, 426.

194 Cf. Weizsäcker, Viktor von, "Die Medizin im Streit der Fakultäten," in: id., *Grundfragen medizinischer Anthropologie: Allgemeine Medizin*, Frankfurt: Suhrkamp, 1987, 202.

195 Weizsäcker, Viktor von, "Von den seelischen Ursachen der Krankheit," in: id., *Körpergeschehen und Neurose: Psychosomatische Medizin*, Frankfurt: Suhrkamp, 1986, 409.

196 Cf. Etzelmüller, Gregor, "Medical Anthropology and Theology on Human Destiny, " in: Michael Welker et al. (eds.), *The Impact of Health Care on Character Formation, Ethical Education,*

Karl Barth misjudges the human dependence on the body. Thus, he fails to recognize the mercy of this dependence, that is the offering of truth through the illness, the subsequent crisis and, thus, the possibility of a transformation.

Barth's confession to a concrete monism corresponds to his understanding of the death of human beings as an incident that affects the whole person. Thus, Barth understands death as the "division of soul and body."[197] It seems that death really destroys the human existence. But God keeps body and soul together in his healing remembrance. Because in death a gracious God awaits us,[198] Barth says (a quote that is often overlooked):

> Man cannot succeed in making an absolute separation of soul from body, nor can this come upon him. [. . .] Even in death there is only a relative differentiation in man. He can and must die; but even in death he cannot and must not suffer the destruction of this interconnexion. For even in death God watches over him. Their interconnexion and therefore his inner coherence may be powerfully challenged by himself and then by God, but the God whose creature he is has made them indestructible.[199]

5 Possible Dialogical Elements, Differences and Overlaps of the Concept in Relation to the Other Two Monotheistic Religions

In Christianity, the appreciation of the body is grounded in the belief in the incarnation of the Son of God. The Word became flesh – this Christological confession has prevented a continuous reception of the Greek dualism in the early Church. In modernity, it has led to the recognition of the human right for physical integrity and bodily joys. As a comparison one might ask: Which theological symbol systems enable and demand the development of a body-affirmative ethics and perception of the world both in Judaism and in Islam?

The Hebrew Bible portrays the human being as the image of God precisely in and through his or her bodiliness. The human being – as a royal being – should prepare the way for God's justice in this world. Accordingly, in the Qur'ān, the

and the Communication of Values in Late Modern Pluralistic Societies, Leipzig: Evangelische Verlagsanstalt, 2023, 175–195.

197 Barth, *Church Dogmatics* III/2, 372.

198 Cf. Barth, *Church Dogmatics* III/2, 611.

199 Barth, *Church Dogmatics* III/2, 373.

human being is understood as God's caliph. Which meaning does the bodiliness of human beings have for the realization of God's justice on earth?

As a body, every human being is necessarily a sexual being. The so-called hostility towards the body in Christianity is, at its origin, hostility towards sexuality. The historical background from which Christianity emerged can explain this attitude: At a time when sexuality was mainly staged as a power discourse, asceticism promised a gain in freedom and the experience of freedom. A more laid-back coping with sexuality, however, could not be achieved in early Christianity. Even though potentials for a more positive perception of sexuality existed in and through the practices and the self-understanding of the majority of Christians, they were not taken up in theological thinking.

In Christianity, ascetic ideals found their way into the canon and the ideal of virginity shaped the Early Church and, thus, shaped Christianity as a whole. However, Judaism did not include ascetic traditions into the Hebrew Bible and they were not received among the prevailing rabbinic traditions either. How did the ideal of family instead of the ideal of virginity shape the Jewish religion and their attitude towards the body and sexuality? And which answers were found in the Qur'ān as a document of late antiquity on the then dominant aim to discipline the body and especially sexual desires?

As bodily life, human life is vulnerable. The incarnated Son of God must suffer – and, thus, reveals God as "the great companion – the fellow-sufferer who understands."[200] From a Christian perspective, the passions of Christ are prefigured in the vulnerability of Israel. It must be asked: How can vulnerability be conceived and understood as a dimension of human life without glorifying the suffering of humans and without justifying the suffering that humans cause each other?

As bodily life, human life is finite. Even the incarnated Son of God dies. In Christianity, only the theology of the 20th century has re-discovered this radical finitude of the human being – and, thus, has uncovered a common feature of Judaism and Christianity. In dialogue with Judaism and Islam, it now must be discussed how the monotheistic religions can keep loyalty to the earth without abandoning all hope.

200 Whitehead, *Process and Reality*, 351.

6 The Current State of the Concept in the Concrete Religious Community and in Research

The body has never been completely absent in Christianity. The confession of the incarnation of the Son of God hindered a complete theological ignorance of the bodiliness of human beings. The celebration of the Eucharist made the body of Christ present or at least reminded the congregation of the body of Christ. The retaining of the confession of the resurrection of the flesh, or the body, respectively, made it impossible to understand a person as soul only.

Nevertheless, ever since the early Church, the body is not at the center of Christian theology, even though this would be expected from a theology at whose center stands the incarnation of the Son of God.

In the 20th century, five impulses have contributed to the rediscovery of the body. First, the Liturgical Movement emphasized the importance of the ritual and, thereby, bodily actions for the faith. Faith is not only a cognitive attitude, but an act of the whole person.[201] Dietrich Bonhoeffer experienced the massive acts of injustice by German National Socialism. In this context, Bonhoeffer discovered that God has established the human right for physical integrity and bodily joys in the incarnation of his Son. Not only the soul, but also the body is given dignity by God. Within theology, the decisive impulse came from the Old Testament research. In his *Anthropology of the Old Testament*,[202] Hans Walter Wolff destroyed dualistic views of the human being and brought up the biblical perception of the human being as an alternative to modern anthropology. Still today, within academic theology, Old Testament scholars are advocates of bodiliness (e.g. Bernd Janowski, Othmar Keel, Norbert Lohfink, Patrick Miller, Sylvia Schroer). However, these impulses became effective only through feminist theology. The contempt for the body came alongside with a contempt for women in theology because the relation of spirit and body was understood through an analogy of the relation of man and woman. That is why feminist theology had to give impulses to a new perception of the body, especially to the life-giving qualities of the body (who is able to give birth) (e.g. Sallie McFague, Elisabeth Moltmann-Wendel, Phyllis Trible, Regina Ammicht Quinn). Finally, it was realized that in order to deal with the reductionist naturalism in a productive way, the starting point had to be the

---

201 Cf. Casel, Odo, *Die Liturgie als Mysterienfeier*, Freiburg et al.: Herder, 1922; Stählin, Wilhelm, *Vom Sinn des Leibes*, Stuttgart: Steinkopf, 1930, Guardini, Romano, *Die Sinne und die religiöse Erkenntnis: Drei Versuche*, Würzburg: Werkbund, [2]1958.

202 Wolff, *Anthropology of the Old Testament.*

body, the *Leibkörper* of the human being. Precisely those biblical and theological traditions, which put the body at the center, enable interdisciplinary dialogue (also with respect to bioethics) between theology and other disciplines.[203]

With reference to Christian congregations and churches, the following must be stated: Churches and congregations are nourished by the communication of people that are physically present, with a term from system theory: congregations live by and through interaction.[204] Only by and through the interaction of people that are physically present can trust be established. This trust is what the Christian service aims for: namely faith. Theologically speaking: God's spirit works through the bodily actions of the believers. This fact is also expressed biblically: According to Acts 9:2–5, Paul, even though he had a direct vision of Christ, at first, was not sent on mission by Christ, but was sent to the congregation of Damascus. According to Paul, faith comes from hearing (cf. Rom 10:17). The reformation has similarly connected faith with the public sermon and, thus, connected it with the assembled congregation.

Because religion wants to shape the whole person, it operates close to the body. Thus, it is not surprising that Pentecostalism, which acts in a bodily way (healings, speaking in tongues, ecstatic forms), is the fastest growing Christian movement. Similarly, in the traditional churches, a revival of healing services and the anointing of the sick can be observed.[205]

Protestantism has always counted on the interaction of people who are bodily present, but it has unilaterally focused on hearing and on the medium of the Word over other forms of interaction. Through ecumenical exchange in the 20th century, however, learning has led to a re-evaluation of the Lord's Supper, finally to a higher appreciation of all the senses. The Protestant service book explicitly says: "Liturgical action and behavior involves the whole person; it also expresses itself bodily and sensually."[206] The preached salvation shall be perceived and experienced with all senses.

This transformation has consequences with regard to pastoral care and religious pedagogy. Pastoral counseling often concentrated on the cognitive aspect,

203 Cf. Etzelmüller, Gregor / Weissenrieder, Annette (eds.), *Verkörperung als Paradigma theologischer Anthropologie*, TBT 172, Berlin / Boston: de Gruyter, 2016.

204 Cf. Dinkel, Christoph, *Was nützt der Gottesdienst? Eine funktionale Theorie des evangelischen Gottesdienstes*, PThK 2, Gütersloh: Gütersloher Verlagshaus, 2000, 114–167: Der Gottesdienst als Interaktionssystem.

205 Cf. Ernsting, Heike, *Salbungsgottesdienste in der Volkskirche: Krankheit und Heilung als Thema der Liturgie*, Leipzig: EVA, 2012.

206 *Evangelisches Gottesdienstbuch: Agende für die Evangelische Kirche der Union und für die Vereinigte Evangelisch-Lutherische Kirche Deutschlands*, Berlin et al.: Luther 1999, 16.

which was intensified by the reception of the strongly cognitive psychoanalysis. Today, however, working with the body (body care) is integrated into pastoral care.[207] Thus, the individual counseling is complemented by liturgical aspects. Also, in religious pedagogy a turn towards the bodily (and thus liturgical) learning[208] can be observed.

7 An Outline of the Practical Application of the Concept in the Present and Its Relevance for Future Developments

Christian anthropology begins with the incarnation and, therefore, puts the fundamental embodiment of the human being at the center. Such an anthropology is interdisciplinarily compatible with the sciences and medicine, but also with pragmatism and phenomenology, especially with the *Embodied Cognitive Science* and the *Philosophy of Embodiment*. Furthermore, it is able to develop theological insight in dialogue with current (scientific and philosophical) knowledge. Thus, it contributes to a realistic, interdisciplinary anthropology. It takes seriously the power and the wisdom of the body as well as the body's vulnerability, intercorporeality and finitude.

A theological anthropology of the body perceives both the power and the wisdom of the body. Thus, a theological anthropology corrects the distrust towards the body that has been deeply inscribed into Christianity. Furthermore, it helps to understand how our body contributes to the fact that our life not only succeeds, but also that aspects other than that of a mere existence come to the foreground.

> The normal and healthy subject can in large measure forget about her body in the normal routine of the day. The body takes care of itself, and in doing so, it enables the subject to attend, with relative ease, to other practical aspects of life. To the extent that the body effaces itself, it grants the subject a freedom to think of other things.[209]

The body relieves us from consciously controlling all steps of our life and, thus, gives freedom to the human being to invest his consciousness in more complex situations and relations beyond the daily routines. Our body, thus, opens up the

---

207 Cf. Naurath, Elisabeth, *Seelsorge als Leibsorge: Perspektiven einer leiborientierten Krankenhausseelsorge*, Praktische Theologie heute 47, Stuttgart et al.: Kohlhammer, 2000.

208 Cf. Silke Leonhard, *Leiblich lernen und lehren: Ein religionsdidaktischer Diskurs*, PThH 79, Stuttgart: Kohlhammer, 2006.

209 Gallagher, Shaun, *How the body shapes the mind*, Oxford: Oxford University Press, ²2013, 55.

world to us, it feels the feelings of others and operates in an appropriate way even before we become consciously aware of it.

In understanding the power of the body, we can agree with the sociologist and social philosopher, Hans Joas. He argues that a human person – in order to solve a problem – should open oneself up "for the ideas and new approaches that arise from the pre-reflexive intentionality of the human body."[210] Similarly, the psychiatrist and philosopher, Thomas Fuchs, advises that one "engage oneself in the spontaneous becoming of the body, instead of wanting to make or produce everything by oneself."[211]

Because a theological anthropology of the body highlights the body's dignity as well as its vulnerability, intercorporeality, and finitude, a theological anthropology offers ethical orientation. First, it reminds us, taking up insights from Dietrich Bonhoeffer, that God has established the dignity of the human flesh through the incarnation of his Logos.[212] The body is, therefore, nothing that must be overcome or transcended; instead, God conceives of the body as an end in and of itself.[213] This is why the human dignity includes the right for physical integrity: What is done to my body, is done to me.

The perception of the incarnation prevents a demonization of the flesh and its vitality. The incarnated is God's "Yes to what is created, to becoming, to growth, [. . .] the Yes to the flourishing of life's strength."[214] This is why the idea of the human dignity includes the right for bodily pleasures. "But if the body is an end in itself, then there is a right to bodily joys, without subordinating them to a further, higher purpose. Part of the very essence of joy is that it is spoiled by thoughts about purpose."[215] In this context, Bonhoeffer appreciates the Song of Solomon. He welcomes that the Song of Solomon "is in the Bible, contradicting all those who think being Christian is about tempering one's passions."[216] Instead, there is a justification of the natural, an appreciation of bodily joys and passions, and a "right to happiness [Glück]."[217]

---

210 Joas, Hans, *Die Kreativität des Handelns*, Frankfurt: Suhrkamp, 1992, 248–249.

211 Fuchs, Thomas, "Zwischen Leib und Körper," in: Martin Hähnel / Marcus Knaup (eds.), *Leib und Leben: Perspektiven für eine neue Kultur der Körperlichkeit*, Darmstadt: WBG, 2013, 92.

212 Cf. Etzelmüller, Gregor, "Bonhoeffers Theologie des Leibes als Wegweiser zu einer neuen ökologischen Haltung," *LuThK* 44 (2020), 179–191.

213 Cf. Bonhoeffer, Dietrich, *Ethics*, Ilse Tödt et al. (eds.), DBWE 6, Minneapolis: Fortress Press, 2005, 251.

214 Bonhoeffer, *Ethics*, 251.

215 Bonhoeffer, *Ethics*, 186.

216 Bonhoeffer, Dietrich, *Letters and papers from prison*, Christian Gremmels et al. (eds.), DBWE 8, Minneapolis: Fortress Press, 2010, 394.

217 Bonhoeffer, *Ethics*, 186.

Everybody who affirms the human right to bodily joys will also affirm sexuality as a life-affirming expression of the body. Thus, the lasting distortion towards this area of life in traditional Christianity is counteracted. Sexuality is then understood as a good gift of creation by God, in which humans may rejoice and which has to be shaped responsibly.[218] The right of the ascetic tradition of Christianity is preserved in so far as the threat that sexuality can be staged as a power discourse is made conscious. In light of the omnipresence of sexual violence, in light of the language of male adolescents who describe sexuality as conquest and war, in light of the tendency, intensified by the mass media, to abstain from bodily joys (such as eating and drinking) all the way to anorexia and to mutilate oneself through cosmetic surgery, and finally in light of the economization of sexuality by the market value "sexiness,"[219] it is necessary to realistically name the many dangers to the good gift of creation which sexuality is. Against these distortions of sexuality, the biblical "not [to] stir up or awaken love" from the Song of Solomon (2:7b; 3:5b; 8:4) must be clearly articulated.

By highlighting the vulnerability of human beings, a theology of the body contradicts an abstract conception of autonomy. The latter fails to see that the human being is not the sovereign of his life but that by living in and through his body, he is always co-shaped and influenced by others. Bodily-finite life permanently relies on the respect and care of others. The medical expression of the "morbid gain" (Krankheitsgewinn) draws attention to the fact that even those phases of life where we experience our options and possibilities as limited can be seen as an enrichment of our life. Because it is precisely then that we have the exhilarating experience that others restrain themselves in favor of me and invest time and work – and thereby love – in my life. It is striking that many people describe those experiences from early childhood in retrospect as one of the happiest experiences that they do not want to miss. But as adults, they hope to avoid situations in which they have to rely on the help of others. However, against the ideal of a non-injured life lived in pure autonomy, it must be taken into consideration that such a life would be a poor life lacking the experience that others withdraw themselves in favor of one's own life.

By highlighting the intercorporeality of the human being, clarity can be achieved with regard to current bioethical debates about abortion and surrogacy. This clarity is particularly necessary because, in the late modernity, the churches have difficulties in offering convincing orientations in this field. Because the first

---

218 Cf. Dabrock, Peter et al., *Unverschämt – schön: Sexualethik: evangelisch und lebensnah*, Gütersloh: Gütersloher Verlagshaus, 2015.

219 Cf. Illouz, Eva, *Why Love hurts: A sociological Explanation*, Cambridge: Polity Press, 2012.

and elementary expression of the human intercorporeality is the community of mother and embryo, the following becomes clear: Neither the abstract defense of the right to life of the embryo against the mother, nor the statement "My body belongs to me" do justice to the intercorporeal phenomenon of pregnancy. Pregnancy conflicts are to be solved only with and not against the mother. Taking into account that every human being exists because of a kept promise, it is decisive even for the later development of the child that in possible conflict situations, a solution is found that the woman can make her own. Thus, the legal regulation of the Federal Republic of Germany, which connects the consultation obligation with the acknowledgment of the free decision of the mother, is convincing from a theological perspective. We should not fight for the right to life of the embryo against the mother, but, in dialogue with the mother, we should search for a solution which enables a life-enhancing relationship between the mother and her child. If such a solution is not found, we have to confess our (!) guilt and have to accept the free decision of the mother.

Since the phenomenon of surrogacy reduces the intercorporeal phenomenon of pregnancy to a biological-mechanistic process, it should be critically questioned. The supporters of surrogacy overlook that already the prenatal, intercorporeal development is part of one's own life story.

By highlighting the finitude of the human being, a theology of the body introduces a life-affirming differentiation to the perception of the ill body. A theology of the body distinguishes between the phenomemon of finitude, which must be accepted, and the phenomenon of illness, which must be defeated as far as possible.

The insight that even experiences of declining vitality belong to being human is closed off by modernity. Instead, modernity pathologizes all processes of a decline in vitality beginning with the quite banal phenomena of jet lag and hair loss, but includes all forms of exhaustion and ageing. In contrast to this, the question should be posed whether it could serve humans and our humaneness to not pathologize every decline in vitality but to understand them as phenomena which are part of a human life insofar as human life is a finite life.

Therefore, the physician, Richard Smith, has suggested to separate between illness and non-illness. "Non-illness" he defines as "a human process or problem that some have defined as a medical condition but where people may have better outcomes if the problem or process was not defined in that way."[220] As examples

220 Smith, Richard, "In search of 'non-disease'," *BMJ 324* (2002), 885; cf. Körtner, Ulrich H.J., "Mit Krankheit leben: Der Krankheitsbegriff in der medizinethischen Diskussion," *ThLZ* 130 (2005), 1285.

for such "non-illnesses" he mentions lachrymal sacks, hair loss, menopause and ageing in general. There are processes of a decline in vitality which a person should accept as a sign of his or her finitude. The distinction between those illnesses that must be fought and those restrictions in life that must be accepted out of free insight, the distinction between illness and non-illness, cannot but be drawn only in the context of the individual biography of the concrete illness.

Human life is characterized by processes of a gain and a loss of vitality. This implies that also a decline in cognitive abilities is a part of life. This corresponds with the statistics that humans, the older they get, the more probable it is that they suffer from dementia.[221] Thus, it should be considered whether dementia is not at least a basic fact in human existence. Dementia reveals something deeply human: namely, that being a human includes the loss of bodily and cognitive abilities. Therefore, we should not only ask how to overcome dementia, but also which life possibilities we should create for demented people in order for them to live their dementia in dignity. "Especially the old person, who has few possibilities of his or her own, must be given possibilities by others, so that he can still be happy in his old age."[222]

With regard to dementia, the perception of the embodiment of the human being teaches us that not only the development, but also the decrease of bodily, cognitive, and psychic abilities is part of life. Not only the positive, but also the dark sides of life constitute personhood. So, a person is the unity of the positive and the dark sides of his or her existence. In this respect, the power of the body is demonstrated in two ways: On the one hand, the lived body conveys the continuity of the self.[223] The body constitutes identity through the bodily memory. On the other hand, the body – and, thus, the person that *is* the body – can in fact intensively and actively take part in life even when that same person is not consciously aware of that fact. So, with regard to an ethics of caring, it would be important to perceive bodily ways of expression and behavior of people with dementia "as an expression of self-determination."[224] Thus, a person with dementia is not reduced to a passive status, but should be appreciated in his and her relative freedom.

221 Cf. Kruse, Andreas, "Das Verhältnis Sterbender zu ihrer eigenen Endlichkeit," in: Nationaler Ethikrat (ed.), *Wie wir sterben/Selbstbestimmung am Lebensende. Tagungen des Nationalen Ethikrates in Augsburg und Münster. Tagungsdokumentationen*, Berlin, 2006, 53.

222 Jüngel, Eberhard, *Tod*, Themen der Theologie 8, Stuttgart / Berlin: Kreuz, 1971, 170.

223 Cf. Fuchs, Thomas, *Verteidigung des Menschen: Grundfragen einer verkörperten Anthropologie*, stw 2311, Berlin: Suhrkamp 2020, 282.

224 Kubik, Andreas, "Selbstbestimmung im Hinblick auf eine Diakonik der Demenz," in: Michael Coors / Martin Kumlehn (eds.), *Lebensqualität im Alter: Gerontologische und ethische Perspektiven auf Alter und Demenz*, Stuttgart: Kohlhammer, 2013, 194.

Consequently, in caring for people with dementia, their wishes and desires should not be considered "as disruptions of normal activities or at best as quirks that have to be reckoned with" but as "forms of legitimate self-determination."[225] Since a person with dementia is strongly embedded with his or her body in a concrete situation and is unable to transcend this situation cognitively, he or she necessarily relies on bodily exchange with others in order to communicate. This reliance on bodily interaction has to be acknowledged in the process of caring. That is why individual care is the only form of caring that is appropriate for people with dementia.

Partly, though not exclusively, out of fear of becoming demented, people during late modernity develop the desire to put an end to their lives with the help of others. In opposition to this desire, today's churches often reply that the human being, thus, arrogates a power for himself that is alone God's, namely the power to end life and, thus, to be the master over life and death. However, if you take seriously the paradigm of embodiment, awareness is raised that the modern medical apparatuses often do not allow the patient to die. Thus, the body's will to die is more and more suspended by modern medicine. In such a situation, the conscious will to die can represent the body that has been deprived of the possibility to die. From such a perspective, it may be possible to think about more active forms of assisted suicide also from a theological perspective.

With regard to organ donation and organ transplantation, a theological anthropology of embodiment can understand the death of the brain as a decisive turning point in the dying process of a human being. This is because "the brain does the work of integration, without which the entire organism could not exist as a unity of body and soul."[226] So, the death of the brain indicates the irreversible dying process of the human being as a whole. However, a theological anthropology of embodiment holds on to the notion that violence that is done to my body is also done to me[227] – and this conviction extends beyond death. As it conforms to human dignity to be buried with dignity, so the human dignity similarly denies an exploitation of the body without the person's consent.

To sum it up, from a theological perspective, there is no objection to the possibility of organ donation and organ transplantation – especially with regard to the biblical commandment to love your neighbor. But the removal of organs always

---

225 Kubik, "Selbstbestimmung im Hinblick auf eine Diakonik der Demenz," 197.

226 Ethikrat, Deutscher (ed.), *Hirntod und Entscheidung zur Organspende: Stellungnahme*, Berlin, 2015, 73.

227 Cf. Hegel, Georg Wilhelm Friedrich, *Grundlinien der Philosophie des Rechts oder Naturrecht und Staatswissenschaft im Grundrisse. Mit Hegels eigenhändigen Notizen und den mündlichen Zusätzen*, Werke 7, Frankfurt: Suhrkamp, 1970, 112.

requires the conscious approval of the organ donor. It is not enough that the donor has not contradicted a possible removal of organs. Instead, it has to be emphasized – under reference to the right to bodily integrity that comes along with human dignity – that a human being from whom organs are to be removed must explicitly and consciously have agreed to that practice prior to it.

Accepting finitude does not only mean accepting the decline of physical, mental, and cognitive abilities. Accepting finitude also includes accepting that life takes place in growth and decline and life wants to be lived as such. As bodily life, human life participates in the rhythm of nature that is biblically explicitly described as a blessing (cf. Gen 8:22). However, those rhythms are constantly questioned in late modernity:

> Worrying about today's experience of time is not the acceleration as such, but the missing conclusion of it, that is, the lack of tact and rhythm. Time is falling because nowhere does it come to a conclusion. Also, the (more widespread) insomnia stems from the inability to close. You have to be able to finish the day to fall asleep. Today, your eyes are closed, if at all, by fatigue and exhaustion. The eyes just shut up, which is not an end.[228]

Similar to the daily rhythm, the rhythm of the sabbath – one of the big discoveries and social-cultural innovations of the Hebrew tradition – comes under pressure, too. In the rhythm of the sabbath, the wisdom is expressed that, besides time for creativity, life needs time for leisure and recreation.

By reminding us of the finitude of life, a theology of the body simultaneously reminds us of the dignity of age and the phases of not-working. Humans are no machines that must function, but bodies that may live.

8 The Christian Hope for the Embodied and Embedded Human Being

I close with a brief reflection on eschatology. Nowhere else has theology – over the course of several centuries – preserved the focus on the body, which was given through the doctrine of incarnation, as strongly as in the expectation of the resurrection of the bodies. However, in the context of the transformation of modern Christianity, the eschatology was reduced to individual perspectives beyond death.

If eschatological perspectives want to be realistic with regard to anthropology, theology has to take into consideration that being human can only be ade-

228 Han, Byung-Chul, "Bitte Augen schließen," *Philosophie Magazin*, no. 2 (2013), 60.

quately conceived of as living an embodied life that is embedded in social and natural contexts.

1. All life is embodied. We are the body that we have. The spirit is not prior to the body. What is more, the spirit develops in the interaction of a living organism with his environment. What is easily recognized in early childhood development remains a basic feature of (human) life in general: Perception and movement, thinking and feeling are intertwined with each other.[229] The human spirit develops in the living interaction of body and world.
2. All life is embodied – in an organism that develops in social interaction with others. The human body is always already in an inter-body exchange. Human life grows in the womb and in exchange with the mother. Even the elementary shape and growth of the human being in his or her first year of life takes place in an intercorporeal exchange with others. Even seemingly pure somatic processes "such as standing up, shaping of the spine and pelvis"[230] develop in the interaction with the social environment. Through the imitation of others who walk upright, we learn the upright walk ourselves. The Biologist, Adolf Portmann, said as early as the 1940s: "We see the biological peculiarity of human existence precisely in the indissoluble, final, and unique integration of inherited faculties and social effects in the individual."[231]
3. Human life is always already embodied – in a body that stands in a permanent exchange with its environment. This fact can be illustrated by means of breathing and digestion. In addition to that, human culture is also formed in dialogue with the material world. In dealing with the material world, we discover which possibilities are offered to us. The cave paintings of our ancestors show that they did not simply paint pictures which were pre-existent in their heads on a surface, such as a rock. Rather, "motives often mirror the natural morphology of the rock surface and, thus, imitate their implicit referential context."[232] Thus, the cave paintings are somewhat the product of a

---

229 Cf. Thompson, Evan, *Mind in Life: Biology, Phenomenology, and the Sciences of Mind*, Cambridge, MA: Harvard University Press, 2007, 43; see also Sheets-Johnstone, Maxine, "Thinking in Movement: Further Analyses and Validations," in: John Stewart / Olivier Gapenne / Ezequiel A. Di Paolo (eds.), *Enaction: Toward a New Paradigm for Cognitive Science*, Cambridge, MA: MIT Press, 2010, 165–181.

230 Portmann, *Biologische Fragmente*, 125.

231 Portmann, *Biologische Fragmente*, 127.

232 Hussain, Shumon T., *Homo empathicus: Versuch einer Evolutionären Anthropologie der Empathie. Implikationen für die anthropologische Bestimmung des modernen Menschen und das Verschwinden letzter Neandertaler*, Bonn: Rudolf Habelt, 2013, 110; see also Hussain, Shumon T. / Breyer, Thiemo, "Menschwerdung, Verkörperung und Empathie: Perspektiven im Schnittfeld von Anthropologie und Paläolitharchäologie," in: Gregor Etzelmüller et al. (eds.), *Verkörperung: Eine neue interdisziplinäre Anthropologie*, Berlin / Boston: de Gruyter, 2017, 211–249.

cooperation of rock and human being. The same is true for the oldest figurine in the world.

> 250–280.000 years ago, a human individual on the Golan Heights at Berekhat Ram grabbed a piece of volcanic slag that – at least to our modern mind, accustomed to the image of a figure – is roughly reminiscent of a human woman with head, arms, breasts, abdomen, and back. [. . .] The individual took a stone tool, tracing the natural hollows along the 'neckline' and the 'arms', thus, highlighting the similarity.[233]

What does this mean for eschatology? Modernity with its distinction of soul and body could very well arrange itself with the idea of the immortality of the soul. A transient world was contrasted with an immortal spirit. But this description of the human life was increasingly questioned and shaken. The paradigm of embodiment emphasizes, at first, that spirit and body are intertwined, secondly, that human life, from the very beginning onwards, is lived in intercorporeality and, thirdly, that human life is closely embedded in its environment. Thus, the paradigm of embodiment pays attention to a network of entanglement, which is not at all unknown to Christian eschatology. Instead, we have to think the entanglement of eternal life, the resurrection of the body, the coming kingdom of God, and the new creation of all things. In classic Christian eschatology, the faith in eternal life is connected with the doctrine of the resurrection of the flesh, with the expectation of the coming kingdom of God and the new creation of all things. That means: Eternal life is understood as embodied (resurrection of the body), as intercorporeal (kingdom of God), and as profoundly embedded in its world (new creation of all things).

Obviously, the philosophy of embodiment cannot give any information about the eternal life. But it can establish a new standard: If our discourse on eternal life is to be convincing – in light of the insight that all life is embodied –, then we must not undercut the complexity of classic eschatology and we must dare to think the entanglement of eternal life, the resurrection of the flesh, the coming kingdom of God, and the new creation of all things. To convey this entanglement is presently not easy – but easy solutions do no justice to the current knowledge about the human being.

233 Haidle, Miriam Noël et al., "Die Entstehung einer Figurine? Material Engagement und verkörperte Kognition als Ausgangspunkt einer Entwicklungsgeschichte symbolischen Verhaltens," in: Gregor Etzelmüller et al. (eds.), *Verkörperung: Eine neue interdisziplinäre Anthropologie*, Berlin / Boston: de Gruyter, 2017, 251–279.

Bibliography

"The Acts of Paul", in: *The Apocryphal New Testament*, trans. James Montague Rhodes, Oxford: Clarendon Press, 1924, 270–299.

Angenendt, Arnold, "Corpus incorruptum: Eine Leitidee der mittelalterlichen Reliquienverehrung," *Saeculum* 42 (1991), 320–348.

Arendt, Hannah, *The Human Condition: Second Edition*, with a new foreword by D. Allen, introduction by M. Canovan, Chicago: The University of Chicago Press, [16]2018.

Augustine, "Confessiones," *NPNF* I/1 (1886), 27–207.

Augustine, "De bono coniugali," *NPNF* I/3 (1887), 395–413.

Augustine, *De bono coniugali and De sancta virginitate*, ed./trans. P.G. Walsh, Oxford Early Christian Texts, Oxford: Clarendon Press, 2001.

Augustine, "De civitate Dei," *NPNF* I/2 (1887), 1–511.

Augustine, "De nuptiis et concupiscentia," *NPNF* I/5 (1887), 270.

Augustine, "Enarratio in Psalmum 140," *MPL* 37 (1865), 1815–1833.

Augustine, "Morals of the Catholic Church," *NPNF* I/7 (1888), 37–63.

Augustine, "Soliloquia," *NPNF* I/7 (1888), 531–560.

Barth, Karl, *The Church Dogmatics*, vol. III/2, Edinburgh: T&T Clark 1960.

Barth, Karl, *The Church Dogmatics*, vol. III/4, Edinburgh: T&T Clark, 1961.

Barth, Karl, *Dogmatics in outline*, trans. G.T. Thomson, New York: Harper, 1959.

Bayer, Oswald, *Leibliches Wort: Reformation und Neuzeit im Konflikt*, Tübingen: Mohr Siebeck, 1992.

Beinert, Wolfgang, *Die Leib-Seele-Problematik in der Theologie*, Cologne: Karl-Rahner-Akademie, 2002.

Berger, Klaus, *Historische Psychologie des Neuen Testaments*, SBS 146/147, Stuttgart: Katholisches Bibelwerk, 1991.

Beutel, Albrecht, *In dem Anfang war das Wort: Studien zu Luthers Sprachverständnis*, HUTh 27, Tübingen: Mohr Siebeck, 1991.

Bieler, Andrea / Schottroff, Luise, *The Eucharist: Bodies, Bread & Resurrection*, Minneapolis: Fortress Press, 2007.

Böhme, Gernot, *Ethik leiblicher Existenz*, Frankfurt: Suhrkamp, 2008.

Bonhoeffer, Dietrich, *Creation and Fall: A Theological Exposition of Genesis 1–3*, DBWE 3, Minneapolis: Fortress Press, 1997.

Bonhoeffer, Dietrich, *Ethics*, Ilse Tödt et al. (eds.), DBWE 6, Minneapolis: Fortress Press, 2005.

Bonhoeffer, Dietrich, *Letters and Papers from Prison*, Christian Gremmels et al. (eds.), DBWE 8, Minneapolis: Fortress Press, 2010.

Bonhoeffer, Dietrich, "Vorlesung 'Christologie' (Nachschrift) Sommersemester 1933," in: id., *Berlin 1932–1933*, Carsten Nicolaisen / Ernst-Albert Scharffenorth (eds.), DBW 12, Gütersloh: Gütersloher Verlagshaus, 1997, 279–348.

Boyarin, Daniel, *A Radical Jew: Paul and the Politics of Identity*, Berkeley: University of California Press, 1994.

Brandt, Sigrid, "Sünde: Ein Definitionsversuch," in: ead. et al. (eds.), *Sünde: Ein unverständlich gewordenes Thema*, Neukirchen: Neukirchener Theologie, 1997, 14–34.

Brown, Peter, *The Body and Society: Men, Women and Sexual Renunciation in Early Christianity*, New York: Columbia University Press, 1988.

Buss, David M., *Evolutionary Psychology: The New Science of the Mind*, New York / London: Routledge, [6]2019.

Butler, Judith, *Bodies That Matter: On the Discursive Limits of "Sex"* [1993], Routledge Classics, London / New York: Routledge 2011.

Calvin, John, *The Institutes of the Christian Religion*, trans. Henry Beveridge, Edinburgh: Calvin Translation Society, 1846.

Casel, Odo, *Die Liturgie als Mysterienfeier*, Freiburg et al.: Herder, 1922.

Cicero, Marcus Tullius, *Hortensius – Lucullus – Academici libri: Lateinisch-deutsch*, Laila Straume-Zimmermann et al. (eds.), Düsseldorf / Zürich: Artemis & Winkler, ²1997.

Dabrock, Peter et al., *Unverschämt – schön: Sexualethik: evangelisch und lebensnah*, Gütersloh: Gütersloher Verlagshaus, 2015.

Denzinger, Heinrich, *Enchiridion symbolorum definitionum et declarationum de rebus fidei et morum: Quod emendavit, in linguam germanica transtulit et adiuvante Helmuto Hoping editit Petrus Hünermann*, Editio XLIII, Freiburg et al.: Herder, 2010.

Dinkel, Christoph, *Was nützt der Gottesdienst? Eine funktionale Theorie des evangelischen Gottesdienstes*, PThK 2, Gütersloh: Gütersloher Verlagshaus, 2000.

Di Vito, Robert A., "Old Testament Anthropology and the Construction of Personal Identity," *CBQ* 61 (1992), 217–238.

Dinzelbacher, Peter, *Körper und Frömmigkeit in der mittelalterlichen Mentalitätsgeschichte*, Paderborn: Schöningh, 2007.

Drecoll, Volker Henning, "Die 'Bekehrung' in Mailand," in: id. (ed.), *Augustin Handbuch*, Tübingen: Mohr Siebeck, 2014, 153–164.

Ernsting, Heike, *Salbungsgottesdienste in der Volkskirche: Krankheit und Heilung als Thema der Liturgie*, Leipzig: EVA, 2012.

Ethikrat, Deutscher (ed.), *Hirntod und Entscheidung zur Organspende: Stellungnahme*, Berlin, 2015.

Etzelmüller, Gregor, "Bonhoeffers Theologie des Leibes als Wegweiser zu einer neuen ökologischen Haltung," *LuThK* 44 (2020), 179–191.

Etzelmüller, Gregor, *Gottes verkörpertes Ebenbild: Eine theologische Anthropologie*, Tübingen: Mohr Siebeck, 2021.

Etzelmüller, Gregor, "Medical Anthropology and Theology on Human Destiny, " in: Michael Welker et al. (eds.), *The Impact of Health Care on Character Formation, Ethical Education, and the Communication of Values in Late Modern Pluralistic Societies*, Leipzig: Evangelische Verlagsanstalt, 2023, 175–195.

Etzelmüller, Gregor / Weissenrieder, Annette (eds.), *Verkörperung als Paradigma theologischer Anthropologie*, TBT 172, Berlin / Boston: de Gruyter, 2016.

Eusebius of Caesarea, *The Proof of the Gospel: Volume 1*, transl. W. J. Ferrar, London: SPCK, 1920.

Evangelisches Gottesdienstbuch: Agende für die Evangelische Kirche der Union und für die Vereinigte Evangelisch-Lutherische Kirche Deutschlands, Berlin et al.: Luther 1999.

Fineman, Martha Alberton / Allard, Silas W., "Vulnerability, the Responsive State, and the Role of Religion," in: Heike Springhart / Günter Thomas (eds.), *Exploring Vulnerability*, Göttingen: Vandenhoeck & Ruprecht, 2017, 185–203.

Foucault, Michel, *The Care of the Self*, The History of Sexuality 3, trans. Robert Hurley, New York: Vintage Books, 1988.

Frettlöh, Magdalene L., *Gott Gewicht geben: Bausteine einer geschlechtergerechten Gotteslehre*, Neukirchen: Neukirchener, ²2009.

Fuchs, Josef, *Die Sexualethik des heiligen Thomas von Aquin*, Cologne: Bachem, 1949.

Fuchs, Thomas, *Das Gehirn – ein Beziehungsorgan: Eine phänomenologisch-ökologische Konzeption*, Stuttgart: Kohlhammer, ⁴2013.

Fuchs, Thomas, "Non-verbale Kommunikation: Phänomenologische, entwicklungspsychologische und therapeutische Aspekte," in: Hermann Lang (ed.), *Was ist Psychotherapie und wodurch wirkt sie?*, Würzburg: Königshausen & Neumann, 2004, 85–99.

Fuchs, Thomas, *Verteidigung des Menschen: Grundfragen einer verkörperten Anthropologie*, stw 2311, Berlin: Suhrkamp 2020.

Fuchs, Thomas, "Zwischen Leib und Körper," in: Martin Hähnel / Marcus Knaup (eds.), *Leib und Leben: Perspektiven für eine neue Kultur der Körperlichkeit*, Darmstadt: WBG, 2013, 82–93.

Fuhrer, Therese, "Körperlichkeit und Sexualität in Augustins autobiographischen und moraltheoretischen Schriften," in: Barbara Feichtinger / Helmut Seng (eds.), *Die Christen und der Körper: Aspekte der Körperlichkeit in der christlichen Literatur der Spätantike*, BzA 184, Munich / Leipzig: Saur, 2004, 173–188.

Gallagher, Shaun, *How the body shapes the mind*, Oxford: Oxford University Press, ²2013.

Gertrude of Helfta, *The Herald of Divine Love*, trans./ed. Magaret Winkworth, New York / Mahwah: Paulist Press, 1993.

Gräb-Schmidt, Elisabeth, "Leiblichkeit – das Ende der Werke Gottes? Materialität und Kommunikation als Dimensionen theologischer Anthropologie," in: Bernd Janowski / Christoph Schwöbel (eds.), *Dimensionen der Leiblichkeit: Theologische Zugänge*, Neukirchen-Vluyn: Neukirchener Verlag, 2015, 98–117.

Gregory of Nyssa, "On Virginity," *NPNF* II/5 (1888), 343–371.

Greschat, Katharina, "'Teilweise auferstehen wäre eine Strafe, keine Erlösung': Tertullians Verteidigung der fleischlichen Auferstehung und des göttlichen Gerichts als Beginn des ewigen Lebens," in: Günter Thomas / Markus Höfner (eds.), *Ewiges Leben: Ende oder Umbau einer Erlösungsreligion?*, DoMo 21, Tübingen: Mohr Siebeck, 2018, 57–71.

Guardini, Romano, *Die Sinne und die religiöse Erkenntnis: Drei Versuche*, Würzburg: Werkbund, ²1958.

Haidle, Miriam Noël et al., "Die Entstehung einer Figurine? Material Engagement und verkörperte Kognition als Ausgangspunkt einer Entwicklungsgeschichte symbolischen Verhaltens," in: Gregor Etzelmüller et al. (eds.), *Verkörperung: Eine neue interdisziplinäre Anthropologie*, Berlin / Boston: de Gruyter, 2017, 251–279.

Hampe, Michael, "Anthropology," in: *Religion Past and Present*, vol. 1, H. D. Betz et al. (eds.), Leiden: Brill, 2006, 258–260.

Han, Byung-Chul, "Bitte Augen schließen," *Philosophie Magazin*, no. 2 (2013), 60–61.

Harnack, Adolf, *Dogmengeschichte*, GThW IV/3, Tübingen: Mohr, 1914.

Hasler, Ueli, *Beherrschte Natur: Die Anpassung der Theologie an die bürgerliche Naturauffassung im 19. Jahrhundert (Schleiermacher, Ritschl, Herrmann)*, BBStHST 49, Bern / Frankfurt: Lang, 1982.

Hegel, Georg Wilhelm Friedrich, *Grundlinien der Philosophie des Rechts oder Naturrecht und Staatswissenschaft im Grundrisse: Mit Hegels eigenhändigen Notizen und den mündlichen Zusätzen*, Werke 7, Frankfurt: Suhrkamp, 1970.

Herms, Eilert, "Leibhafter Geist – Beseelte Organisation: Schleiermachers Psychologie als Anthropologie: Ihre Stellung in seinem theologisch-philosophischen System und ihre Gegenwartsbedeutung," in: Arnulf von Scheliha / Jörg Dierken (eds.), *Der Mensch und seine Seele. Bildung – Frömmigkeit – Ästhetik: Akten des Internationalen Kongresses der Schleiermacher-Gesellschaft in Münster*, Schleiermacher-Archiv 26, Berlin: de Gruyter, 2017, 217–243.

Horell, David G., "Σῶμα as a Basis for Ethics in Paul," in: Friedrich W. Horn et al. (eds.), *Ethische Normen des frühen Christentums: Gut – Leben – Leib – Tugend*, Kontexte und Normen neutestamentlicher Ethik IV, Tübingen: Mohr Siebeck, 2013, 351–363.

Hussain, Shumon T., *Homo empathicus: Versuch einer Evolutionären Anthropologie der Empathie: Implikationen für die anthropologische Bestimmung des modernen Menschen und das Verschwinden letzter Neandertaler*, Bonn: Rudolf Habelt, 2013.

Hussain, Shumon T. / Breyer, Thiemo, "Menschwerdung, Verkörperung und Empathie: Perspektiven im Schnittfeld von Anthropologie und Paläolitharchäologie," in: Gregor Etzelmüller et al. (eds.), *Verkörperung: Eine neue interdisziplinäre Anthropologie*, Berlin / Boston: de Gruyter, 2017, 211–249.

Illouz, Eva, *Why Love hurts: A sociological Explanation*, Cambridge: Polity Press, 2012.

Irenaeus of Lyon, *Adversus haereses: Chapter 4–5*, ANF 9/1, Edinburgh: T&T Clark, 1869.

Janowski, Bernd, "Die lebendige naepaes: Das Alte Testament und die Frage nach der 'Seele'," in: Gregor Etzelmüller / Annette Weissenrieder (eds.), *Verkörperung als Paradigma theologischer Anthropologie*, TBT 172, Berlin / Boston: de Gruyter, 2016, 50–94.

Janowski, Bernd, "Der Mensch im Alten Israel: Grundfragen Alttestamentlicher Anthropologie," *ZThK* 102 (2005), 143–175.

Jewett, Robert, "The Anthropological Implications of the Revelation of Wrath in Romans," in: Kathy Ehrensperger / J. Brian Tucker (eds.), *Reading Paul in Context: Explorations in Identity Formation: Essays in Honour of William S. Campbell*, London / New York: T&T Clark, 2010, 24–38.

Joas, Hans, *Die Kreativität des Handelns*, Frankfurt: Suhrkamp, 1992.

Johann Wolfgang von Goethe, "To Wilhelm von Humboldt," Weimar, 17th of March 1832, *Goethes Werke*, Weimarer Ausgabe, IV. Abteilung, vol. 49, Letter 193. http://www.zeno.org/nid/20004860926.

Johnson, Luke Timothy, *The Revelatory Body: Theology as Inductive Art*, Grand Rapids / Cambridge: Eerdmans, 2015.

Jonas, Hans, "Matter, Mind, and Creation: Cosmological Evidence and Cosmogonic Speculation," in: id., *Mortality and Morality: A Search for the Good after Auschwitz*, Lawrence Vogel (ed.), Evanston, IL: Northwestern University Press, 1996, 165–197.

Jonas, Hans, *The Phenomenon of Life: Toward a Philosophical Biology*, Chicago: University of Chicago Press, 1982.

Jüngel, Eberhard, *Tod*, Themen der Theologie 8, Stuttgart / Berlin: Kreuz, 1971.

Justin the Martyr, "Dialogue with Trypho, a Jew," ANF 2 (1867), 85–278.

Kant, Immanuel, *Anthropologie in pragmatischer Hinsicht*, Hamburg: Meiner, 2000.

Kant, Immanuel, *Anthropology from a Pragmatic Point of View*, trans. Mary J. Gregor, The Hague: Martinus Nijhoff, 1974.

Karras, Valerie A., "A Re-Evaluation of Marriage, Celibacy, and Irony in Gregory of Nyssa's On Virginity," *JECS* 13 (2005), 111–121.

Körtner, Ulrich H.J., "Mit Krankheit leben: Der Krankheitsbegriff in der medizinethischen Diskussion," *ThLZ* 130 (2005), 1273–1290.

Kretschmar, Georg, "Auferstehung des Fleisches: Zur Frühgeschichte einer theologischen Lehrformel," in: *Leben angesichts des Todes: Beiträge zum theologischen Problem des Todes: Helmut Thielicke zum 60. Geburtstag*, Tübingen: Mohr Siebeck, 1968, 102–137.

Krieg, Matthias, "Leiblichkeit im Alten Testament," in: Matthias Krieg / Hans Weder (eds.), *Leiblichkeit*, ThSt 128, Zürich: Theologischer Verlag, 1983, 7–29.

Kruse, Andreas, "Das Verhältnis Sterbender zu ihrer eigenen Endlichkeit," in: Nationaler Ethikrat (ed.), *Wie wir sterben/Selbstbestimmung am Lebensende: Tagungen des Nationalen Ethikrates in Augsburg und Münster: Tagungsdokumentationen*, Berlin, 2006, 43–54.

Kubik, Andreas, "Selbstbestimmung im Hinblick auf eine Diakonik der Demenz," in: Michael Coors / Martin Kumlehn (eds.), *Lebensqualität im Alter: Gerontologische und ethische Perspektiven auf Alter und Demenz*, Stuttgart: Kohlhammer, 2013, 183–199.

Leppin, Volker, "Madensack und Tempel des Heiligen Geistes: Leiblichkeit bei Martin Luther," in: Bernd Janowski / Christoph Schwöbel (eds.), *Dimensionen der Leiblichkeit: Theologische Zugänge*, Neukirchen-Vluyn: Neukirchener, 2015, 86–97.

Link, Christian, *Schöpfung: Ein theologischer Entwurf im Gegenüber von Naturwissenschaft und Ökologie*, Neukirchen: Neukirchener, 2002.

Lohfink, Norbert, "Die Gottesstatue: Kreatur und Kunst nach Genesis 1," in: id., *Im Schatten deiner Flügel: Große Bibeltexte neu erschlossen*, Freiburg et al.: Herder, ^{2}1999, 29–48.

Löhr, Winrich, "Sündenlehre," in: Volker Henning Drecoll (ed.), *Augustin Handbuch*, Tübingen: Mohr Siebeck, 2014, 498–506.

Lona, Horacio E., *Über die Auferstehung des Fleisches: Studien zur frühchristlichen Eschatologie*, BZNW 66, Berlin / New York: de Gruyter, 1993.

Löning, Karl / Zenger, Erich, *Als Anfang schuf Gott: Biblische Schöpfungstheologie*, Düsseldorf: Patmos Verlag, 1997.

Luther, Martin, "Confession Concerning Christ's Supper," in: Robert H. Fischer (ed.), *Luther's Works*, vol. 37, Word and Sacrament III, Philadelphia: Fortress Press, 1961, 161–372.

Luther, Martin, "The Freedom of a Christian," in: id., *Three Treatises*, trans. W.A. Lambert, Minneapolis: Fortress Press, ^{2}1970, 265–316.

Luther, Martin, "Der kleine Katechismus," in: Irene Dingel (ed.), *Die Bekenntnisschriften der Evangelisch-Lutherischen Kirche. Vollständige Neuedition*, Göttingen: Vandenhoeck & Ruprecht, 2014, 852–910.

Marquardt, Friedrich-Wilhelm, *Was dürfen wir hoffen, wenn wir hoffen dürften? Eine Eschatologie*, vol. 3, Gütersloh: Gütersloher Verlagshaus, 1996.

Mathewes, Charles, "Vulnerabilty and Political Theology," in: Heike Springhart / Günter Thomas (eds.), *Exploring Vulnerability*, Göttingen: Vandenhoeck & Ruprecht, 2017, 165–183.

McCormack, Bruce, *Karl Barth's Critically Realistic Dialectical Theology: Its Genesis and Development 1909–1936*, Oxford: Oxford University Press, 1995.

Meltzoff, Andrew N. / Moore, M. Keith, "Newborn Infants Imitate Adult Facial Gestures," *Child Development* 54 (1983), 702–709.

Merleau-Ponty, Maurice, *Phenomenology of Perception* (1945), New York: Routledge, 2012.

Moxter, Michael, "Anthropologie in systematisch-theologischer Perspektive," in: Jürgen van Oorschot (ed.), *Mensch*, TdT 11, Tübingen: Mohr Siebeck, 2018, 141–186.

Naurath, Elisabeth, *Seelsorge als Leibsorge: Perspektiven einer leiborientierten Krankenhausseelsorge*, Stuttgart et al.: Kohlhammer, 2000.

Nell, Victor, "Cruelity's rewards: The gratification of perpetrators and spectators," *Behavioral and Brain Sciences* 29 (August 2006), 211–257.

Neuser, Wilhelm H., "Heidelberger Katechismus von 1563," in: Andreas Mühling / Peter Opitz (eds.), *Reformierte Bekenntnisschriften. Band 2/2: 1562–1569*, Neukirchen-Vluyn: Neukirchener Verlag, 2009, 167–212.

Origen, *Contra Celsum*, trans. Henry E. Chadwick, Cambridge: Cambridge University Press, 1965.

Origen, *Schriften vom Gebet und Ermahnung zum Martyrium*, trans. Paul Koetschau, BKV I/48, Munich: Kösel, 1926.

Peters, Ted, "The Evolution of Evil," in: Gaymon Bennett et al. (eds.), *The Evolution of Evil*, RThN 8, Göttingen: Vandenhoeck & Ruprecht, 2008, 20–52.

Pinker, Steven, *The Better Angels of Our Nature: The Decline of Violence in History and its Causes*, London: Penguin Books, 2011.
Plato, *Dialogues of Plato*, vol. 2, London: W. Sandby, 1767.
Plotinus, *Ennead IV*, trans. A.H. Armstrong, Loeb Classical Library 443, Cambridge, MA: Harvard University Press, 1989.
Portmann, Adolf, *Biologische Fragmente: Zu einer Lehre vom Menschen*, Basel: Schwabe, 1944.
Rösel, Martin, "Den Herrn aus ganzem Denken lieben (Dtn 6,5 IXX): 'Entkörperung' in der griechischen Übersetzung des Alten Testaments?," in: Gregor Etzelmüller / Annette Weissenrieder (eds.), *Verkörperung als Paradigma theologischer Anthropologie*, TBT 172, Berlin / Boston: de Gruyter, 2016, 143–158.
Sand, Alexander, "sarx," in: Horst Balz / Gerhard Schneider (eds.), *EWNT* III/2, Stuttgart et al.: Kohlhammer, ^{2}1992, 549–557.
Sandherr, Susanne, *Die heimliche Geburt des Subjekts: Das Subjekt und sein Werden im Denken Emmanuel Lévinas'*, PThH 34, Stuttgart et al.: Kohlhammer, 1998.
Schleiermacher, Friedrich Daniel Ernst, *Brouillon zur Ethik* (1805/06), Hans-Joachim Birkner (ed.), Hamburg: Meiner, 1981.
Schleiermacher, Friedrich Daniel Ernst, *Christian Faith*, A New Translation and Critical Edition, vol. 2, Catherine L. Kelsey / Terrence N. Tice (eds.), Louisville (KY): Westminster John Knox Press, 2016.
Schleiermacher, Friedrich Daniel Ernst, "Monologen: Eine Neujahrsgabe," in: id., *Schriften aus der Berliner Zeit: 1800–1802*, Günter Meckenstock (ed.), KGA I/3, Berlin: de Gruyter, 1988, 3–61.
Schleiermacher, Friedrich Daniel Ernst, *On Religion: Speeches to Its Cultural Despisers*, trans. John Oman, New York: Harper & Brothers, 1958.
Schleiermacher, Friedrich Daniel Ernst, "Rezension von Immanuel Kant: Anthropologie (1799)," in: id., *Schriften aus der Berliner Zeit: 1796–1799*, Günter Meckenstock (ed.), KGA I/2, Berlin / New York: de Gruyter, 1984, 363–369.
Schleiermacher's Soliloquies. An English Translation of The Monologen. With a Critical Introduction and Appendix by Horace Leland Friess [1926], Eugene, OR: Wipf and Stock, 2002.
Schleiermacher, Friedrich Daniel Ernst, *Vorlesungen über die Psychologie*, Dorothea Meier (ed.), KGA II/13, Berlin / Boston: de Gruyter, 2018.
Schroer, Markus, "Zur Soziologie des Körpers," in: id. (ed.), *Soziologie des Körpers*, stw 1740, Frankfurt: Suhrkamp, ^{3}2005, 7–47.
Seeliger, Hans Reinhard, "Lehre und Lebensform: Über die 'Hellenisierung' und 'Enkratisierung' des antiken Christentums," *ThQ* 196 (2016), 127–138.
Sheets-Johnstone, Maxine, "Thinking in Movement: Further Analyses and Validations," in: John Stewart / Olivier Gapenne / Ezequiel A. Di Paolo (eds.), *Enaction: Toward a New Paradigm for Cognitive Science*, Cambridge, MA: MIT Press, 2010, 165–181.
Sigurdson, Ola, *Heavenly Bodies: Incarnation, the Gaze, and Embodiment in Christian Theology*, Grand Rapids: Eerdmans, 2016.
Silke Leonhard, *Leiblich lernen und lehren: Ein religionsdidaktischer Diskurs*, PThH 79, Stuttgart: Kohlhammer, 2006.
Smith, Mark S., "The Heart and Innards in Israelite Emotional Expressions: Notes from Anthropology and Psychobiology," *JBL* 117 (1998), 427–436.
Smith, Richard, "In search of 'non-disease'," *BMJ* 324 (April 2002), 883–885.
Stählin, Wilhelm, *Vom Sinn des Leibes*, Stuttgart: Steinkopf, 1930.
Tertullian, *Adversus Marcionem*, Ernest Evans (ed.), Oxford: Oxford University Press, 1972.
Tertullian, "De exhortatione castitatis," *ANF* 4 (1885), 50–58.

Thandeka, *The Embodied Self: Friedrich Schleiermacher's Solution to Kant's Problem of the Empirical Self*, Albany: State University of New York Press, 1995.
Thandeka, "Schleiermacher's Dialektik: The Discovery of the Self that Kant Lost," *HTR* 85:4 (1992), 433–452.
Theißen, Gerd, *Biblischer Glaube in evolutionärer Sicht*, Munich: Kaiser, 1984.
Theißen, Gerd, *Erleben und Verhalten der ersten Christen: Eine Psychologie des Urchristentums*, Gütersloh: Gütersloher Verlagshaus, ^{2}2007.
Thomas Aquinas, *Contra Gentiles: Book three: Providence Part II*, trans. Vernon J. Bourke, Notre Dame: University of Notre Dame Press, 1975.
Thomas Aquinas, *Summa Theologiae*, https://www.logicmuseum.com/wiki/Authors/Thomas_Aquinas/Summa_Theologiae
Thompson, Evan, *Mind in Life: Biology, Phenomenology, and the Sciences of Mind*, Cambridge/MA: Harvard University Press, 2007.
Trible, Phylis, *God and the Rhetoric of Sexuality*, Philadelphia: Fortress Press, 1978.
Volp, Ulrich, "Der Mensch: Kirchen- und theologiegeschichtliche Perspektive," in: Jürgen van Oorschot (ed.), *Mensch*, ThTh 11, Tübingen: Mohr Siebeck, 2018, 105–140.
Wagner, Andreas, "Verkörpertes Herrschen: Zum Gebrauch von 'treten'/'herrschen' in Gen 1,26–28," in: Gregor Etzelmüller / Annette Weissenrieder (eds.), *Verkörperung als Paradigma theologischer Anthropologie*, TBT 172, Berlin / Boston: de Gruyter, 2016, 127–141.
Walter, Matthias, *Gemeinde als Leib Christi: Untersuchungen zum Corpus Paulinum und zu den Apostolischen Vätern*, NTOA 49, Freiburg / Göttingen: Vandenhoeck & Ruprecht, 2001.
Welker, Michael,"Romantic Love, Covenantal Love, Kenotic Love," in: John Polkinghorne (ed.), *The Work of Love: Creation as Kenosis*, Grand Rapids / London: Eerdmans / SPCK, 2001, 127–136.
Weizsäcker, Viktor von, "Die Medizin im Streit der Fakultäten," in: id., *Grundfragen medizinischer Anthropologie: Allgemeine Medizin*, Frankfurt: Suhrkamp, 1987, 197–211.
Weizsäcker, Viktor von, "Von den seelischen Ursachen der Krankheit," in: id., *Körpergeschehen und Neurose: Psychosomatische Medizin*, Frankfurt: Suhrkamp, 1986, 399–417.
Whitehead, Alfred North, *Process and Reality: An Essay in Cosmology*, Corrected Edition, David Ray Griffin / Donald W. Sherburne (eds.), New York: Free Press, 1978.
Wolff, Hans Walter, *Anthropology of the Old Testament*, trans. Margaret Kohl, Philadelphia: Fortress, 1974.
Wolter, Michael, *Paulus: Ein Grundriss seiner Theologie*, Neukirchen: Vandenhoeck & Ruprecht, 2011.
Wrangham, Richard / Peterson, Dale, *Demonic Males: Apes and the Origins of Human Violence*, Boston / New York: Mariner Books, 1996.

Suggestions for Further Reading

Brown, Peter, *The Body and Society: Men, Women and Sexual Renunciation in Early Christianity*, New York: Columbia University Press, 1988.
Etzelmüller, Gregor, *Gottes verkörpertes Ebenbild: Eine Theologische Anthropologie*, Tübingen: Mohr Siebeck, 2021.
Etzelmüller, Gregor / Weissenrieder, Annette (eds.), *Verkörperung als Paradigma theologischer Anthropologie*, TBT 172, Berlin / Boston: de Gruyter, 2016.
Fuchs, Thomas, *Verteidigung des Menschen: Grundfragen einer verkörperten Anthropologie*, stw 2311, Berlin: Suhrkamp, 2020.

Huyssteen, J. Wentzel van, *Alone in the World? Human Uniqueness in Science and Theology* (The Gifford Lectures. The University of Edinburgh. Spring 2004), RThN 6, Göttingen 2006.

Janowski, Bernd, *Anthropologie des Alten Testaments: Grundfragen – Kontexte – Themenfelder*, Tübingen: Mohr Siebeck, 2019.

Kelsey, David H., *Eccentric Existence: A Theological Anthropology*, two volumes, Louisville, Ky: Westminster John Knox Press, 2009.

Munteanu, Daniel, *Was ist der Mensch? Grundzüge und gesellschaftliche Relevanz einer ökumenischen Anthropologie anhand der Theologien von K. Rahner, W. Pannenberg und J. Zizioulas*, Neukirchen: Neukirchener, 2010.

Sigurdson, Ola, *Heavenly Bodies: Incarnation, the Gaze, and Embodiment in Christian Theology*, Grand Rapids: Eerdmans, 2016.

Weissenrieder, Annette / Doll, Katrin (eds.), *Körper und Verkörperung: Biblische Anthropologie im Kontext antiker Medizin und Philosophie: Ein Quellenbuch für die Septuaginta und das Neue Testament*, FoSub 8, Berlin / Boston: de Gruyter, 2019.

Welker, Michael, *In God's Image: An Anthropology of the Spirit*, Grand Rapids / Cambridge: Eerdmans, 2021.

Welton, Donn, "Biblical Bodies," in: id. (ed.), *Body and Flesh: A Philosophical Reader*, Oxford: Blackwell, 1998, 229–258.

Abbas Poya

The Concept of Body in Islam

1 Introduction

All Abrahamic religions, including Islam, define human beings through their relationship with God. God created humans and placed them as His representative on Earth. As a result, the human bears responsibility before God and is accountable to Him. How well human beings acknowledge this responsibility determines how properly they follow the religion of God (which every religion naturally claims to be), determining their status in this world and the hereafter. The religion of Islam, just like that of Judaism and Christianity, consists of teachings, the observance or neglect of which, depending on the theological intensity, places human beings on a certain level on a beatific scale. With regards to the topic of this article, we can ask which component of the human being bears responsibility before God. Which will be held accountable in the end? The body? The soul? Or perhaps both, if perceived as an entity forming the human being as such. The answer to these questions can ultimately shed light on how Islam regards the body and its position in the relationship between humans and God.

Needless to say, this article can only trace broad sketches of a very complex and controversial discourse. Different theological, philosophical, mystical, and legal schools within Islam maintain distinct attitudes towards the body. At the same time, they share some key features, on which the main focus of this articles lies.

On the whole, the basic Islamic sources – the Qur'ān and the Ḥadīṯ – speak of two components, of which the human being consists, namely the body and the spirit (or soul).[1] However, this division does not address the question of whether the essence of the human is dualistic in the sense of a categorical distinction between body and soul, or rather anti-dualistic in the sense of a unity of body and soul, nor does this explain whether the soul is material or immaterial. In addition, it fails to answer the question to which extent the Islamic religion is body- or soul-oriented.

Overall, there are two predominant views that can be identified in the Islamic tradition. The one, which I describe as the material, focuses strongly on the body. The representatives of this point of view believe in the existence of the soul, but their religiosity expresses itself rather physically. Therefore, they place more value on the actual, comprehensible, and verifiable practice of religious rites. The other viewpoint, which I refer to as the immaterial, focuses more on the soul of the human

1 The words "body" and "spirit" are discussed later in the paper.

https://doi.org/10.1515/9783110748246-003

being. It acknowledges the body, but does not place it at the center of its worldview. Rather, it centers the human's spirit and the spiritual aspects of religious messages.

Importantly, the Islamic readings of those who are more focused on the material and physical aspects of human beings primarily focus on the exterior, or the "body," of religious texts – the Qur'ān and the Ḥadīṯ. In contrast, those who centralize the human soul mainly consider the meaning, or the "soul," of the text. The first view, which harmonizes more closely with the wording of the Qur'ān, has prominently shaped Islamic theology and Islamic viewpoints in general. It is also the dominant and widespread position in Islam. Concurrently, it reflects the religious practice within Muslim communities. The second, which parallels ideas of ancient philosophy, is particularly represented by Muslim philosophers, philosophical scholars, and mystics. Broadly speaking, it represents the "educated middle-class" position within Islam.

However, the distinction between the theologians and legal scholars on the one hand and the philosophers and mystics on the other must not be strictly interpreted. There are, of course, people from all groups who tend towards diverse positions.

Additionally, the concept of the body in Islam is normatively shaped by two basic assumptions shared by Muslim scholars:

- Islamic teaching considers the human body primarily as a creation of God. As a result, it has dignity and must be treated with respect and honor.
- Since the body is a creation of God, it belongs to Him. Therefore, human beings are not allowed to simply do as they please with their bodies. Rather, handling the body must be in accordance with the basic principles of Islamic teaching. This includes the protection of human physical integrity (*ḥurma*).

2 The Dichotomy of the Body and Soul – A Philosophical and Historical Digression

It is fairly impossible to speak of the body without thinking of its counterpart: the soul, the spirit, the mind. In this respect, any consideration of the body depends on examining its relation to the soul. All cultures throughout history have dealt with questions regarding the relationship between body and soul – or, as is known in philosophical terminology, with the mind-body problem – and have, accordingly, presented a wide variety of answers. In this article, a brief overview of the general philosophical discussion of this question is presented in order to better historically classify the Islamic discourses on the human body and make their content more comprehensible.

Basically, there are two tendencies when trying to explain the mind-body problem. Some only define the world materially and trace everything related to the mental realm back to the physical. Adherents of this school of thought do not deny that there are actions or abilities such as perception, feelings, or wishes that other bearers, like mind and soul, hold. However, they understand these bearers as material things. The representatives of this view are called naturalists, materialists, or physicalists.[2]

Supporters of the other view assume that the human is more than just a physical thing. He possesses mind and soul, immaterial matters, which even constitute human's reality. This assumption is not only represented in many religious cultures, but also by ancient philosophers such as Plato and Aristotle. Over time, this view has taken on various developments. The followers of this view were sometimes called vitalists. They consider the basis of all living things to be a life force, a special substance, or the soul. In this way, they distinguish between organic and inorganic matters in nature.[3] In addition, the followers of this view were called dualists or substance dualists, as their interpretation of the world is based on two different and independent basic elements, entities, or substances: here, the material body and the immaterial soul, with the soul being the important and actual element.[4]

However, at the historical beginning of philosophical discussions of body and soul, no distinction between beings with and without mental characteristics was made, but rather simply between the animate and the inanimate. Therefore, the question was: What constitutes the essence of a living being, a human being that distinguishes itself from non-living beings and survives death? One spoke of the *psyche* as opposed to the physical. *Psyche*, which is generally translated as soul, initially meant that which distinguishes the living from the dead. Aristotle found that the soul is the reason for the living being. Plato argued upon similar lines before him.[5]

It is important to note that the first thing was not to classify the world into material and immaterial, but rather to ask what it is that gives living things (plants, animals, and people) life. Evidently, many have assumed the existence of another dimension of human existence, namely that of the soul, or the *psyche*. However, not all of them considered this an immaterial thing.

---

2 Cf. Beckermann, Ansgar, *Das Leib-Seele-Problem. Eine Einführung in die Philosophie des Geistes*, Paderborn: Fink, 2008, 7.

3 Cf. Lohff, Brigitte, "Vitalismus," in: Werner E. Gerabek et al. (eds.), *Enzyklopädie Medizingeschichte*, Berlin: Walter de Gruyter, 2005, 1449–1451.

4 Cf. Robinson, Howard, "Dualism," in: Stephen P. Stich / Ted A. Warfield (eds.), *The Blackwell Guide to Philosophy of Mind*, Malden: Blackwell, 2003, 85–101.

5 Cf. Beckermann, *Leib-Seele-Problem*, 8.

Materialists or atomists such as Titus Lucretius Carus (approx. 97–55 BCE) believed that the *psyche* is a material thing. For them, the mind and soul were physical parts of the body (such as the hand or eye) and closely related; accordingly, the mind lies in a certain place in the body, namely the chest, while the soul is spread over the whole body. The mind is the determining force that thinks, feels, and decides. The soul carries out its commands by making the limbs move as the mind wants. However, the atoms that make up the mind or soul are fine, light, and very mobile. With the onset of death, the atoms of the mind and soul are distributed everywhere. This view, which is referred to as monistic or substance-monistic, perceives the mind (*animus*), which weighs and makes decisions, just like the other limbs of the body, that is, a material part of the human being.[6]

Plato, however, assumed that the soul is an immaterial thing that is separate from the body. It has a completely different nature than the body, constitutes the actual self of the human, detaches itself from the body at death, and continues to exist thereafter. From Plato's point of view, the soul is immortal and lives on after the death of the body. This life after death is also highly desirable. As long as the soul is in the body, the capabilities of the soul are limited. It is only after death that the body no longer prevents the soul from realizing ideas. In this respect, Plato follows a dualistic, or substance dualistic view, which holds that humans consist of two completely different parts which can exist independently from one another and are only connected in life.[7]

Aristotle also assumed the existence of the soul but did not understand it as a thing or being per se, but rather as the form of a living being, i.e., a human being. He argues that all beings consist of material (matter) and form, which together build substance, the living body and the living being. However, not all living things have the same abilities, nor is the nature of their souls alike. Plants have a vegetative soul, animals an animalistic soul, and humans the soul of reason. Therefore, the powers mediated by their souls are different as well. Humans and animals share the ability to eat and grow with plants. However, only animals and humans possess the abilities of movement and perception. Moreover, it is only the human being who has the power of reason. According to Aristotle, even if the soul is not a thing, it is also not the living body, or at least the part of the soul responsible for thinking – which Aristotle calls the active spirit of the soul (*nous*

6 Cf. Beckermann, *Leib-Seele-Problem*, 9–11; Stephan, Achim, "Das Leib-Seele-Problem," in: *Lexikon der Neurowissenschaft*, Heidelberg: Spektrum Akademischer Verlag, 2000. Available under the following link: https://www.spektrum.de/lexikon/neurowissenschaft/leib-seele-problem/6967 (June 17, 2023).

7 Cf. Beckermann, *Leib-Seele-Problem*, 11–13; Stephan, "Leib-Seele-Problem."

poiethikos) – can also exist independently of the body. In this respect, his position is similar to that of Plato and can be observed as a form of dualism.[8]

In the vein of Plato and Aristotle, Descartes also takes a substance-dualistic position. He asserts that the world is divided into two completely different types of substances: the soul, for which it is essential to think (*res cogitans*), and the body as a thing, for which it is essential to extend (*res extensa*). According to Descartes, thinking in its pure form does not imply a physical substrate. In this respect, his view is similar to that of both Plato and Aristotle.[9] For Descartes, however, the soul, which he considers as a *res cogitans*, loses the function of the bearer of life. Plants and animals are alive, but do not need a soul for their different behaviors. The soul is a part of human, is responsible for mental properties, and can exist independently of the body.[10]

Today, the substance-dualistic paradigm lost favor and was replaced by a substance-monistic, materialistic paradigm. With a few exceptions, hardly any philosopher speaks of an immaterial bearer of mental properties. Rather, most believe that organisms or systems that possess a mind, in principle, consist of the same components that make up those systems that are inanimate or have no mental properties. In this respect, modern debates still distinguish between living and non-living beings. Nonetheless, they no longer focus on the question of the systematic relationship between the two supposed substances, body and soul, with one regarded as the bearer of the somatic and the other of mental properties and states. Instead, the crucial inquiry is how a thoroughly material body can have immaterial properties. For example, how is the process of memorizing possible?[11]

In summary, the following can be stated: Regardless of whether monistic or dualistic, materialistic or vitalistic, it is evident that thinkers have always distinguished between two aspects of human life: the body and the soul. The emergence of different philosophical positions goes hand in hand with the answer to the question of whether the existence of humans is ontologically based on the material, the physical, the immediately graspable, or rather, if it is the soul of the human that is real. While the body-centered view was dominant at the beginning of argument development, the mind-centered view over time achieved the upper hand. Today, the physical perspective has gained distinction, whereby the concern is no longer the investigation of the relationship between body and mind, but rather the question of how a material thing (a human being) can achieve immaterial performance, like that of memory.

8 Cf. Beckermann, *Leib-Seele-Problem*, 13–14; Stephan, "Leib-Seele-Problem."
9 Cf. Stephan, "Leib-Seele-Problem."
10 Cf. Stephan, "Leib-Seele-Problem."
11 Cf. Stephan, "Leib-Seele-Problem."

Regardless of whether a material or an immaterial explanation is sought in answering the question of the relationship between body and mind, one has generally regarded the body as earthly and menial, and the soul as heavenly and sublime.

As I will explain later, many of these philosophical debates have also been recorded in Islamic contexts, albeit with different nuances and approaches. Although the basic sources Qur'ān and Ḥadīṯ present the topic in a relatively straightforward language, Islamic scholars have obviously adopted many elements of philosophical discussions, especially of ancient and Neoplatonic philosophy, in this context for their own purposes.

3 Definitions

In the Arabic language, and thus in the texts of the Qur'ān and Ḥadīṯ, there are some terms regarding the body that should be explained in more detail.

- *badan* (pl.: *abdān* / *abdun*) is used for the human body, but especially the human torso. The term occurs once in the Qur'ān, referring to the subjective body. This lone verse (10:92) addresses the persecution of the Israelites by the Pharaoh and his multitudes. When the Pharaoh drowns in the sea as a consequence of his own actions, he demonstrates remorse and shows his commitment to God. Then God says: "Today We shall only save your body that you may be a sign for those after you [. . .]." Elsewhere in the Qur'ān (22:36), the term *budn* (sing.: *bādin*) appears, derived from the same etymological root. The term generally denotes the corporeal, fat body. In the passage mentioned in the Qur'ān, the term means camel body.
- *jism* (pl.: *ajsām* / *jusūm*) is to be principally understood in the sense of body, form, substance, mass, and is, therefore, used to signify the human body or the stature of the human body. The term occurs twice in the Qur'ān. Verse 2:247 speaks of *Ṭālūt* (Saul) as his people stand against him: "[. . .] God had chosen him over you, and had increased him broadly in knowledge and body [. . .]." Another verse (63:4) describes the hypocrites (*munāfiqūn*) to the prophet Muhammad as follows: "And when you see them, their bodies [outward appearance] may please you [. . .]."
- *jasad* (pl.: *ajsād*) is for both human and non-human body. It occurs four times in the Qur'ān (7:148; 20:88; 21:8; 38:34). While *jasad* is to be understood in the sense of the animal body (that of the calf) in the first two verses, it is used in reference to the human body in the two later verses.

- *juthmān* (pl.: *juthmānāt*) also means body. The term does not appear in the Qur'ān itself, but in subsequent Islamic traditions. In a Ḥadīṯ handed down by Muslim, prophet Muhammad describes some leaders of his community who come after him, warning them. He says the leaders do not follow his tradition, but have a satanic heart in a human body (*juthmān*).[12]
- *jirm* (pl.: *ajrām, jurum*) in the sense of a body or mass is used in philosophical and scientific texts in connection with celestial bodies.[13]

Generally, it can be assumed that the word *badan* most closely reflects the human and living body. *Jasad* is used for a lifeless human body and for lifeless bodies of living beings in general. The term *jism* can be used for any body. As stated, *jirm* is mainly reserved to describe a connection with celestial bodies.

According to the motto "things are determined by their counterparts" (*al-ashyā' tu'rafu bi-aḍdādihā*), it is important to discuss here the central counter-terms of *badan* in Arabic, in order to more precisely understand the meaning of the term body.

As an opposite of *badan*, the term *rūḥ* (pl.: *arwāḥ*; Hebrew: *rúach*) is used in the sense of spirit. *Rūḥ* is what God breathed into the human body to give it life.[14] In this respect, it can also be read as a vital force. As is explained later, *rūḥ* is understood as the counterpart of the body, but many describe it as a ray of light, something subtle, or a kind of wind (*rīḥ*). Curiously, these descriptions point toward a material understanding of mind.

Another term that is also used as an opposite of the human body is *nafs* (pl. *nufūs* / *anfus*; Hebrew: *nefesh*), in the sense of soul. *Nafs* occurs in various contexts in the Qur'ān and is used in the sense of self, life, human being, and soul. *Nafs* is also the term used in Islamic philosophy with the nuance of the Platonic soul, meaning the self. However, theologians have also viewed *nafs* as having material properties by describing it as mortal, as the Qur'ān explicitly states: "Every *nafs* is bound to taste death [. . .]."[15]

Remarkably, the Qur'ān often uses the terms *rūḥ* (spirit) and *nafs* (soul) interchangeably, and at the same time equates these with the term *insān* (human being). In the verse quoted above – "Every *nafs* is bound to taste death [. . .]" – *nafs* can be understood as simply referring to a human being. This is also the case

12 Cf. Muslim Ibn al-Ḥajjāj, Abu l-Ḥusayn, *Ṣaḥīḥ*, 5 vols., Muḥammad Fu'ād 'Abd al-Bāqī (ed.), Beirut: Dār iḥyā' at-turāth al'arabī, 1955, vol. 3, 1476, Ḥadīṯ-Nr. 1847.

13 Cf. as an example Ibn Sīnā, Abū 'Alī, *ash-Shifā'*, 10 vols., Maḥmūd Qāsim (ed.), Cairo: al-Idāra al-'āmma li-ṯ-ṯaqāfa, n. d., vol. 5, 50 ff.

14 Cf. Qur'ān 15:29 and 38:72.

15 Qur'ān 3:185.

in other verses such as "Upon the day when the *rūḥ* and the angels stand in ranks [. . .],"[16] where one might again read *rūḥ* as human being or human soul.

In this article, *badan* is used to mean human body, *jism* to refer to bodies in general, *rūḥ* for the spirit or mind, and *nafs* for the soul. This roughly corresponds to the use of these terms in Oriental studies.[17]

Islamic philosophy employs similar terminology,[18] whereby *rūḥ* and *nafs* are mostly understood as synonyms. Ibn Sīnā, for example, uses the terms *nafs* or *an-nafs an-nāṭiqa* as opposite expressions to the human body,[19] but meanwhile equates them to *rūḥ*. For example, in the chapter on *ma'ād* (the hereafter) in his major philosophical work *ash-Shifā'* (The Healing), he discusses the questions of what happens to the *rūḥ* when it leaves the body and whether there is a physical resurrection (resurrection of the philosophical body).[20] He uses the term *nafs* here and means *rūḥ*. He provides rational arguments for a spiritual resurrection.

All in all, the following table of definitions can be drawn:

badan	living human body
jism	body in general, human or not human
jasad	lifeless body
jirm	heavenly body
rūḥ	spirit, soul
nafs	soul, spirit, person, the self

4 The Body in the Qur'ān and Ḥadīṯ

The Qur'ān itself does not address the body-soul question. Clearly, the text does not see any reason to ask this question, as there not even once arises any allusion to a contradiction between mind and body. While the Qur'ān addresses the physical more dominantly than the spiritual, it does not present the two aspects as opposites

16 Qur'ān 78:38.

17 Cf. e.g. van Ess, Josef, *Theologie und Gesellschaft im 2. und 3. Jahrhundert Hidschra: Eine Geschichte des religiösen Denkens im frühen Islam*, 6 vols., Berlin: Walter de Gruyter, 1991–1997, vol. 4 (1997), 517–518.

18 Ibn Sīnā, for example, uses the word *jism* when generally referring to the body as a whole, and *badan* for the human body. Cf. Ibn Sīnā, *ash-Shifā'*, vol. 1, al-Ab Qanawātī / Sa'īd Zāyid (eds.), 61 and 423.

19 Cf. Ibn Sīnā, *ash-Shifā'*, vol. 1, 423. The title of one of his works is *Risāla fī ma'rifa an-nafs an-nāṭiqa wa-aḥwālihā*, electronic publication, Windsor: Hindawi, 2017.

20 Cf. Ibn Sīnā, *ash-Shifā'*, vol. 1, 423.

to one another. The Qur'ān thematizes the human being as such – regardless of whether the text deals with the story of the human's creation, their life in this world, or the afterlife. Moreover, the text's explanations give the impression that the Qur'ān has an eye on the physical rather than the spiritual or soulistic. The name of the prehistoric man in the Qur'ān, Ādam, is etymologically related to the words or the compound words such as *adam* (skin), *adīm* (surface), and *adīm al-arḍ* (surface of the earth). The linguistic logic behind this is that dust is the surface or skin of the earth from which Adam was created.

The human body is generally prominent throughout the Qur'ān, in the story of creation, the stories of the prophets, ritual regulations, and in the descriptions of life after death, in paradise as well as in hell.

The story of creation also refers to the spirit (*rūḥ*) as something divine that was blown into the prehistoric human (15:22). However, *rūḥ* does not occupy much space in the Qur'ān. At one point it is even explicitly said that the meaning of *rūḥ* belongs to God's realm of knowledge and that it is not accessible to the human mind (17:85).

Essentially, the story of creation is a material act in which Adam was created from dust (22:5), clay (23:12), or mud (15:26), and the angels were then asked to prostrate before him (7:11) – again, a corporeal act. The following passage in the Qur'ān clearly expresses the material perspective of the Qur'ān regarding humans: "Out of it [earth] We created you, and We shall restore you into it, and bring you forth from it a second time" (20:55). As we can see, the Qur'ān offers a thoroughly earthly and material representation of the human from the beginning to the end. There is no reference to the idea of a life of the soul, as developed by philosophers, before the creation of the body in this world nor after death.

Details of the act of creation in the Qur'ān are not further elaborated. However, they are extensively discussed in the Ḥadīṯs and Qur'ānic exegeses. Nonetheless, the descriptions of human beings remain strongly material. The well-known Qur'ān exegete aṭ-Ṭabarī (839–923) reports the story of creation based on some Ḥadīṯs as follows: After God decided to create a governor on Earth, He first sent the angel Gabriel to Earth to bring clay. After he was unable to complete the task, God sent the angel Mikail with the same assignment. He also failed to complete the mission. In the end, the angel of death (*malik al-mawt*) went to Earth to fulfill the mission. He took different colored clay from different places – red, white, and black – and brought it to God. God created the human body (*jasad*) from the mixed clay and blew into it from his spirit (*rūḥ*). When the *rūḥ* reached his head, he sneezed, when the *rūḥ* reached his eyes, he looked at the fruits of paradise, and when the *rūḥ* reached his stomach, he found an appetite for food. When *rūḥ* reached his legs, he jumped up in the direction of the fruit.[21]

It is evident that these scholars have simply understood the spirit as that which gives life to humans, a sort of life force. Their descriptions of the spirit are strongly material.[22] When interpreting the aforementioned passage in the Qur'ān (15:29), aṭ-Ṭabarī, for example, succinctly wrote: "*wa-nafakhtu fīhi min rūḥī, fa-ṣāra basharan ḥayyan*" ([. . .] and I breathe into him of My spirit, so he became a living human).[23] In reference to the topic of *rūḥ*, the philosophical Qur'ānic exegete Fakhr ad-Dīn ar-Rāzī (1149–1209) also found that it is what leads the body to life.[24]

Life after death is also represented in the Qur'ān as a basically physical process. When Abraham asks God to show him how to bring the dead back to life, God materially demonstrates the process of resurrection, as He says to Abraham: "[. . .] take four birds, and twist them to you, then set a part of them on every hill, then summon them, and they will come to you running [. . .]."[25] Later, the Ḥadīṯs explain in detail how Abraham took the four different birds – a rooster, a crow, a peacock, and a dove – dismembered them, mixed the body parts together, divided them, and put them on four different hills. Then, as God had recommended, he summoned the birds. The body parts of each of the four birds met, formed the respective birds, and came running to Abraham.[26]

This story literally demonstrates how the Qur'ān understands resurrection as a material or physical act. The text seems to suppose that Abraham and the people of his time had few concerns regarding what becomes of the mind. Whether and how the body would be revived after it had materially decayed are not presented as urgent questions.

Likewise, the Qur'ān depicts the confrontation of people in the hereafter in a very material manner. These are, for example, the physical parts – such as the ears, eyes, or skin – that will bear witness to the deeds of the people in this world:

---

21 Cf. aṭ-Ṭabarī, Abū Ja'far Muḥammad b. Jarīr, *Jāmi' al-bayān fī ta'wīl al-qur'ān*, 24 vols., Aḥmad Muḥammad Shākir (ed.), Beirut: Mu'assisa ar-risāla, 2000, vol. 1, 459.

22 Cf. below, the chapter on The Body in Theology. As determined by ancient philosophers already mentioned in the first chapter, the idea of the soul or the often synonymously used spirit as "life force" is that which gives life to the human body, is old and present in almost all traditions and myths of earlier cultures. According to the ancient Greek idea, as expressed in Homer's epics, it is the soul (*psyche*) that brings the body that is lifeless without it to life. At the moment of death, it leaves him again like a breath of air. Cf. Stephan, "Leib-Seele-Problem."

23 aṭ-Ṭabarī, *Jāmi' al-bayān fī-ta'wīl al-qur'ān*, vol. 17, 101.

24 Cf. ar-Rāzī, Fakhr ad-Dīn, *Tafsīr al-kabīr*, 32 vols., Beirut: Dār iḥya' at-turāth al-'arabī, 1420 h., vol. 21, 392.

25 Qur'ān 2:260.

26 Cf. aṭ-Ṭabarī, *Jāmi' al-bayān fī-ta'wīl al-qur'ān*, vol. 5, 485–511.

"Upon the day when God's enemies are mustered to the fire, duly disposed. Till when they are come to it, their hearing, their eyes, and their skins bear witness against them concerning what they have been doing."[27]

In principle, the rewards and punishments that people experience in the hereafter also affect the human body. The beatific people await in paradise amongst things like fruits, water, wine, bird meat, silken clothes, bracelets of gold and pearls, the Huri, and youths.[28] In contrast, the unholy people will be thrusted into the "crusher," which is then described as "urgent the fire of God kindled, roaring over the hearts, covered down upon them, in columns outstretched."[29] The inmates of hell are given oozing pus to drink (14:16), awaiting hooked iron rods (22:21), and carrying fetters and chains around their necks (40:71).

The religious practices (*ʿibāda*), which according to the Qur'ān represent the purpose of human creation,[30] essentially relate to physical action. The ritual of washing before prayer, the various bodily actions and movements, and the recitation of the Qur'ān during prayer all demonstrate a material character. Furthermore, fasting, pilgrimage, and almsgiving, which are also mentioned in the Qur'ān as religious regulations, are characterized by material performance and physical exertion.[31]

First of all, this fits better with the way in which the Qur'ān deals with the subject of human being as a whole, because it addresses more intensively the human body and body parts. Many parts of the body are mentioned in different contexts in the Qur'ān: fingers (2:19); fingertips (3:119); elbows, feet, face, hands, ankles, head (5:6); eyes, nose, ear, tooth (5:45); lips, tongue (90:9); belly (53:32); blood (2:30); among others. The Qur'ān also speaks of different categories of *nafs*, such as the *nafs* that encourages evil (12:53), that blames itself (75:2), and that which finds peace (89:27). Later, these descriptions of the *nafs* significantly inspired the mystics. However, it is not clear from the Qur'ān itself what is meant exactly by *nafs*, nor whether *nafs* represents something material or immaterial. The Qur'ān also speaks of other beings, such as *malak* (angel), *iblīs/shayṭān* (devil), and *jinn/jānn* (demons), which are generally regarded as invisible, or as definitely not visible to normal people. The Qur'ānic representation of these beings is remarkably material. For instance, the angels sometimes appear in human form and are seen by people.[32] According to the Qur'ān, the devil and the

27 Qur'ān 41:19–20.
28 Cf. Qur'ān 22:23, 52:20, 56:18–21, 76:12–20.
29 Qur'ān 104:4–9.
30 Cf. Qur'ān 51:56.
31 For more on this point, see the chapter The Body in Islamic Law.
32 Cf. Qur'ān 11:77–81.

demons are made of fire[33] and they listen to the prophet Muhammad;[34] the *jinn*, in addition to people and birds, served alongside Solomon's troops.[35] In contrast to its brief appearance in the Qur'ān, later scholars provide a fairly detailed and usually material presentation of the creation story. Aṭ-Ṭabarī, for example, uses many Ḥadīṯs to describe in detail how God created the heavens and the earth in six days, the *jinn* from fire, and the angels from light.[36]

In order to complete the image of the human or the human body in the Qur'ān, it must also be taken into account that according to the Qur'ānic representation, God is the creator of all things (13:16). He is the creator of the heavens and the Earth (6:73), and He is the lord of the heavens and the Earth and of what is between them (19:65). God owns what is in heaven and what is on Earth (2:284). According to this worldview, human beings and, thus, the human bodies belong to their creator, God, and are, therefore, subject to His will. The "rightly guided" people speak to God in the Qur'ān as follows: "[. . .] Verily we belong to God, and verily to Him do we return" (2:156). In this respect, human beings are not simply to do as they please. They must follow God and His will. Moreover, the Qur'ān describes attributes that are ascribed to humans which distinguish them from all other creatures. God breathes His spirit into them (15:29), gives them dignity (17:70), and calls on the angels to prostrate before them (7:11). These attributes not only characterize the human being, but also enable them to assume responsibility for the Earth. And this is how humans were given the position of God's viceroy on Earth (2:30). The fact that the human being is, on the one hand, a creature of God, and, on the other hand, has dignity and takes on the role of God's viceroy, shapes the basis for scholars' assumptions that humans and their bodies are to be treated with dignity and respect, in both earthly life and the hereafter. This perspective has maintained a lasting impact on the normative provisions related to the human body, whether interpreted traditionally or modernly. This topic is discussed in more detail in the chapter on the body in Islamic law.

33 Cf. Qur'ān 7:12 and 15:27.

34 Cf. Qur'ān 72:1.

35 Cf. Qur'ān 27:17.

36 Cf. aṭ-Ṭabarī, Abū Ja'far Muḥammad Ibn Jarīr, *Tā'rīkh ar-rusul wa-l-mulūk*, 11 vols., Beirut: Dār at-turāth, 1387 h., vol. 1, 32 ff., 84.

5 The Body in Islamic Theology

As is well known, the most important concern of theology in general, and Islamic theology in particular, is examining the teachings of sacred texts and argumentatively supporting them through reasoning. In this sense, al-Jāhiẓ (d. 868/9) already defines the term *kalām*, more or less the Arabic synonym for (Islamic) theology, in his "Treatise on the Preference of Talk over Silence" (*Risāla fī tafḍīl an-nuṭq ʿalā ṣ-ṣamt*) as the "cause for the recognition of the truth of the religions, for the rational closing (*qiyās*) when proving the divine greatness and the truth of the prophetic message."[37] However, theology does not arise in a void. Rather, theological perspectives are shaped by sociopolitical circumstances, historical contexts, scientific interests, and accumulated philosophical knowledge. In the Islamic context, the first major political question of who should lead the Muslim community after the death of the prophet Muhammad in the year 632, and the subsequent internal Muslim conflicts associated with it, gave the first impetus to the theological question of who is responsible for conflicts and whether the human being is fundamentally accountable for his actions. The murder of the third caliph, ʿUthmān (d. 656), by Muslim insurgents and the ensuing first civil war (*fitna*) finally brought the Muslim community out of balance and triggered great theological debates, including the question of the predetermination of human actions.[38] It must be noted that later encounters with other religious and cultural traditions, as well as ancient philosophy, continued to bring a range of new impulses into theological discussions.

The political and theological disputes of the first Islamic century gave subsequent rise to two major religious movements: the Sunnis and the Twelver Shīʿites. This divide has, of course, profoundly shaped the history of Islam. Theologically, the so-called rationalist beliefs of the Muʿtazilites originally formed and then decisively influenced Twelver Shīʿite theology. The Ashʿarite theology emerged later and continues to shape the majority-Sunni doctrine until today. The Muʿtazilites believed that the human's mind is able to find the way to God, so they tried to answer theological questions using rational methods. The Ashʿarites, in contrast, considered the Qur'ān and the Ḥadīṯ to be the only sources of theological knowledge. They also acknowledged rational argumentation if it supported the literal content of the religious texts. However, in the context of Sunni theology, the Ahl al-ḥadīth must not go unmentioned. The Ahl al-ḥadīth ("traditionalists"), who are generally associated with the Hanbali school of thought, are seen as opponents of both the Muʿtazilites and the Ashʿarites. Nevertheless, they are closer to the

37 Van Ess, *Theologie und Gesellschaft*, vol. 1, 54.
38 Cf. Berger, Lutz, *Islamische Theologie*, Vienna: Facultas, 2010, 55 ff.

Ash'arites as they, too, limit the understanding of religion to the revelation text and the statements and practices of the prophet Muhammad.[39]

As explained in the previous chapter, the general tenor of the Qur'ān indicates a strongly material view of the human being and the world at large. Since the Ash'arites and the Ahl al-ḥadīth base their perspectives on the literal meaning of the Qur'ān, it is only logical that they generally present a clearly material idea of both the world and the human. In this sense, the aforementioned Ash'arite Qur'ān interpreter Fakhr ad-Dīn ar-Rāzī distinguishes between *jism* and *rūḥ* as two distinct entities but describes the *rūḥ* as *rīḥ* (wind) that is blown into the cavities of *another* body. It is clear from this passage that he speaks of *another* body, as ar-Rāzī understood the spirit to be something physical that enters a body. According to him, the verse 15:29 – which connects the human spirit with God and says that God breathed His spirit into Adam – does not indicate that the spirit itself comes from God, but rather that it only honored humans by connecting human beings with God.[40]

The Sunni majority in Islam, including the Ash'arites and the Ahl al-ḥadīth, continue to maintain this view today. Looking at the verse above (15:29), which literally states that God breathes His spirit into Adam, the influential 20th century Hanbali scholar Muḥammad Ibn 'Uthaymīn (1929–2001) notes that the human spirit can belong neither to the essence (*dhāt*) of God nor to His attributes (*ṣifāt*). It is not part of the nature of God, as God would otherwise be divisible, but the nature of God is one and indivisible. It is not one of the attributes of God, because God's attributes cannot be separated from him: "And just like the house and the camel body are, is also the spirit body, which is blown into the living body with God's permission [. . .]; but it is a body made of a different material."[41]

The Mu'tazilite views regarding the nature of the human do not initially appear to be uniform. While the influential Hishām ibn al-Ḥakam (d. 795) believed that the human being encompasses both the body and the spirit, another Mu'tazilite, 'Abd ar-Raḥmān al-Aṣamm (816–892), assumed that the human being is that which is perceived with the eyes. That is, the human is one entity that does not have a soul, a single thing, and can be denied if not felt and recognized. Another Mu'tazilite, an-Naẓẓām (d. between 835 and 845), took the opposing view stating that the essence of the human is only the spirit which enters the body and is then

---

39 A comparative analysis of these theological schools of thought with reference to the current state of research can be found here: Suleiman, Farid, *Ibn Taymiyya und die Attribute Gottes*, Berlin: Walter de Gruyter, 2019, 43–95.

40 Cf. ar-Rāzī, *Tafsīr al-kabīr*, vol. 19, 139.

41 Ibn 'Uthaymīn, Muḥammad, *Majmū' fatāwā wa-rasā'il fadhīla ash-Shyakh Muḥammad bin Ṣāliḥ al-'Uthaymīn*, vol. 3, Fahd bin Nāṣir bin Ibrāhīm as-Sulaymān (ed.), 'Anīza: Dār ath-Thurayyā, 1413 h., 105–106.

engulfed by it. An-Naẓẓām obviously saw the body as something that weakens, restricts, and alters the spirit.[42]

Despite this partly Platonic or Neoplatonic view, it is clear that the Muʿtazilites could only imagine the spirit as something material. Like all other scholars, they believe that the spirit is different from the body. It not being a physical body, however, does not imply that it is immaterial. Generally, they perceived the spirit as a "subtle body." The previously mentioned Hishām b. al-Ḥakam, for instance, spoke of light as the nature of the spirit.[43] An-Naẓẓām also saw the spirit as a substance that is not compact, but subtle (*laṭīf*).[44]

Nevertheless, to the philosophers it was clear that the theologians held a material idea of the human. The well-known medieval Muslim philosopher, Ibn Sīnā (980–1037), for example, found the perspective of most theologians to be that the human being consists only of "his body."[45] This material world view concurs with the interests of some theologians in the theory of atomism. Among others, Muʿammar b. ʿAbbād as-Sulamī (d. 830) and Abū l-Hudhayl al-ʿAllāf (d. 840) contributed to the spread of atomism in Islamic theology. They argued that the body generally holds a geometrical structure consisting of atoms. The length is created by two atoms placed side by side: four of them arranged in a square provide the width and, thus, an area, and six or eight atoms create a body.[46] With regard to humans, atomism means they have an additional atom, which can be called *nafs*. Still, the human body is unlike any other body. The *nafs*, which defines free will and individuality, is that which makes humans human. It is a supplementary element in the human body, invisible but mortal.[47]

The Shīʿite theologians, who are usually closer to the Muʿtazilites, differ in opinions regarding the question of whether *nafs* or *rūḥ* is material or immaterial. Whereas the influential theologian al-Mufīd (d. 984) considered the *nafs* to be an immaterial and detached essence (*mujarrad*), his equally well known student ash-Sharīf al-Murtaḍā (d. 1044) argued for a material idea of the spirit and described *rūḥ* as a kind of wind.[48] These different views have continued to the present day and are based on questions of how much a scholar follows the wording of the

42 Cf. al-Ashʿarī, Abū al-Ḥasan, *Maqālāt al-islāmiyyin wa-ikhtilāf al-muṣallīn*, Hellmut Ritter (ed.), Wiesbaden: Franz Steiner, 1980, 331.
43 Cf. van Ess, *Theologie und Gesellschaft*, vol. 1, 368.
44 Cf. van Ess, *Theologie und Gesellschaft*, vol. 3, 369 ff.
45 Ibn Sīnā, *Risāla fī maʿrifa an-nafs an-nāṭiqa wa-aḥwālihā*, 9.
46 Cf. van Ess, *Theologie und Gesellschaft*, vol. 3, 67.
47 Cf. van Ess, *Theologie und Gesellschaft*, vol. 3, 81–82.
48 Cf. Nijāt, Ḥamīd Riḍā Fatḥ / Jāwdān, Muḥammad, "Dīdgāh-i shaykh mufīd dar bāra-i ḥaqīqat-i insān (The opinions of Shaykh Mufīd regarding the nature of man)," *Journal of Islamic Denominations (Pažūhishnāma-i madhāhib-i islāmī)* 9 (2018), 95–110.

Qur'ān and Ḥadīṯ on this topic and how influenced they are by rational and philosophical approaches. In the meantime, a middle position has prevailed among the philosophical Shīʿite scholars. The contemporary Qur'ānic exegete and philosopher Muḥammad Ḥusayn Ṭabāṭabāyī (1892–1981) and his student Murtaḍā Muṭahharī (1919–1979) represent the Shīʿite Mullā Ṣadrā's (1572–1640) tradition of the so-called "sublime philosophy."[49] This tradition holds the view that *nafs* is physical in its emergence, but that its further existence is spiritual (*jismāniyyat-u-l-ḥudūth wa-rūḥāniyyat-u-l-baqā'*).[50]

A certain materiality can even be observed in the idea of God. I do not refer to anthropomorphism, which had followers within Islam but is avoided by all major theological schools. All theologians strictly reject *tajsīm* (embodiment), *tashbīh* (similarization), and *tajnīs* (equalization) of God with other creatures. This assumption seems to include that God is a being that cannot be compared with other beings nor grasped with the sensory organs – at least not in this world. When scholars begin to describe Him, however, they rely on material means.

Inspired by the verse "God is the light of heavens and earth" (24:35), many theologians understand God as light. Among others, the Shīʿite scholar of law and theology, Zurāra b. Aʿyan (d. approx. 767), described God as a radiant light.[51] This teaching was later refined by saying that God moves as pure light and can become one with every body.[52]

Certainly, the vast majority of Muslims affirm that God will be seen with the naked eye in the afterlife, even if they refrain from specifying the precise way of beholding Him. The eponym of Sunni theology, al-Ashʿarī (d. 938), fundamentally rejected any similarity between God and other creatures, holding that God is eternal and thus cannot be created like other beings. He refers to the following statements in the Qur'ān: "nothing is equal to Him" (42:11) and "none is equal to Him" (112:4).[53] In another passage, al-Ashʿarī also plainly rejects that God could be a body (*jism*) because a body necessarily consists of several parts, whereas God can

49 This is how Mullā Ṣadrā's philosophical direction is described, in contrast to Suhrawardī's "Enlightenment Philosophy" and "Peripatetic Philosophy," whose main representative was Ibn Sīnā. For more on Ṣadrā's philosophy cf. Rudolph, Ulrich, *Islamische Philosophie: Von den Anfängen bis zur Gegenwart*, Munich: C.H. Beck, 2013, 99–104.

50 Cf. Ḥasanzāda, Ṣāliḥ, "Ḥaqīqat-i nafs wa-rūḥ dar qur'ān wa-ḥikmat-i islāmī," *Pažūhishnāma-i maʿārif-i qur'ānī* 25 (2016), 55–82, available under the following link: http://rjqk.atu.ac.ir/article_7085_771b1aff484fd8f93077d93dcadd4ff6.pdf (June 17, 2023).

51 Cf. van Ess, *Theologie und Gesellschaft*, vol. 1, 326. Perhaps that is also the reason why Khwarazmi classified Zurāra under anthropomorphism in his *Mafātiḥ al-ʿulūm*. Cf. ibid., 326–327.

52 Cf. van Ess, *Theologie und Gesellschaft*, vol. 1, 333.

53 Cf. al-Ashʿarī, Abū al-Ḥasan, *Kitāb al-lumaʿ fī-radd ʿalā ahl al-ziyagh wa-l-bidaʿ*, Ḥamūda Gharāba (ed.), Cairo: Maṭbaʿa miṣr, 1955, 19–20.

only be one single being. Anything other than that would mean that there was more than one God, and this would destroy life. Here he also refers to the Qur'ān, which, at one point, states that "had there been in heaven or on earth any deities other than God, both [those realms] would surely have fallen into ruin" (21:22).[54]

At the same time, in another section of the same book, al-Ash'arī vehemently argues that God will be seen with the naked eye in the hereafter because the Qur'ān says "some faces will on that day be bright. Looking up to their Lord" (75:22–23).[55] In doing so, he explicitly emphasizes that seeing is not an intangible understanding of the inside, but something that can be perceived by the eyes.[56] At the same time, he affirms that seeing God (*mar'ā*) does not mean that He has a body (*jism*), substance (*jawhar*), or accident (*'araḍ*).[57]

Aḥmad Ibn Ḥanbal, the most prominent representative of the Ahl al-ḥadīth, takes a similar stance. In the treatise *ar-Radd 'alā al-jahmiyya wa-z-zanādiqa* – which is directed against the doctrine of Jahm ibn Ṣafwān (d. 746), a pioneer of the Mu'tazilite school, and various views influenced by Manichaeism – Ibn Ḥanbal holds that it is certain that people cannot see God in this world, but that they will indeed observe Him with their own eyes (*tu'āyinu*) in paradise. In this way, Ibn Ḥanbal attempts to resolve the contradiction that some heretics (*zanādiqa*), as he called them, believed to be in the Qur'ān. According to them, there is a contradiction between verses 75:22–23, which say that bright faces look at their Lord, and verse 6:103, which says that eyes do not reach Him. According to Ibn Ḥanbal, however, these statements do not contradict each other, as the first two verses refer to the hereafter while the last verse refers to this world.[58]

However, there are some in the ranks of the Ḥanbalites whose utterances resemble *tajsīm* (representation of God as body) or *tashbīh* (similarization of God with His creatures). Abū Ya'lā Ibn al-Farrā' (d. 1065), a judge serving the Abbasids, argued, for example, that you can see God's molars and uvula when He laughs. Because of this statement, not only his opponents, but also school colleagues like Ibn al-Jawzī (d. 1201), accused him of *tajsīm*.[59]

However, it is essential to acknowledge that anthropomorphism (*tajsīm* or *tashbīh*) has developed into a problematic concept in Islamic theology, and that almost every school accuses competing theologies of this practice in order to discredit them.

54 Cf. al-Ash'arī, *Kitāb al-luma'*, 23–24 and 20–21.
55 Cf. al-Ash'arī, *Kitāb al-luma'*, 61 ff.
56 Cf. al-Ash'arī, *Kitāb al-luma'*, 63–64.
57 Cf. al-Ash'arī, *Kitāb al-luma'*, 67–68.
58 Cf. Ibn Ḥanbal, Aḥmad, *ar-Radd 'alā al-jahmiyya wa-z-zanādiqa*, Ṣabrī bin Salāma Shāhīn (ed.), n. p., n. d., 76–78.
59 Cf. Suleiman, *Ibn Taymiyya*, 79–80.

Overall, it can be said that the Ash'arites and the Ahl al-ḥadīth represent a clearly material idea of the world and the human. They understand the human as a being that consists of two components: the body and the spirit. But, they argue, it represents a material unit that is clearly not to be understood as dualistic. The Mu'tazilites, in contrast, use more rationalistic or Platonic approaches and lean towards a dualistic attitude. Nevertheless, their descriptions of the soul remain largely material.

6 The Body in Islamic Philosophy

In contrast to theologians, the primary concern of Muslim philosophers is not to explain or justify Islamic teaching. Their subjects, methods, and interests in knowledge are rational and shaped by the likes of Plato, Aristotle, and Plotinus. The Islamic philosophical discussion of the essence of human beings, on the whole, follows rational premises and clearly shows the influence of ancient philosophy.

In the following section, I discuss this topic using the significant Muslim philosopher Abū 'Alī Ibn Sīnā (980–1037) as an example. Ibn Sīnā can be seen as an icon of the philosophy of *mashshāʾī* (peripatetic) in Islam, which al-Kindī (801–866) founded and al-Fārābī (870–950) deepened, expanded, and disseminated.[60] The *mashshāʾī* philosophers combined "Aristotelian philosophy as interpreted by Alexandrian commentators – especially Alexander Aphrodisias Thermistius – [. . .] with Neoplatonism, which had reached the Muslims through the translation and paraphrasing of sections of the Enneads under the name of the Theology of Aristotle, and the pseudo-Aristotelian *Liber de Causis*, which was the epitome of Proclus' *Elements of Theology*."[61] They, however, separated the area of philosophical debate from the sphere of faith, and generally accepted religious dogmas per se as beyond their rational interpretation of the world.

It should be noted that Muslim philosophers are predominantly focused on the spirit of the human being. They commonly trace everything – life, powers, possibilities, afterlife, the decision of fate, bliss, and misery – back to the soul. As is discussed later, Ibn Sīnā significantly uses the metaphor of the rider and the mount in this context to explain the relationship between the human's body and soul. According to him, the soul represents the rider and the body represents the mount. Nevertheless, Muslim philosophers acknowledge that religious texts tend

60 Cf. Nasr, Seyyed Hossein, *Three Muslim Sages. Avicenna – Suhrawardī – Ibn 'Arabī*, New York: Caravan books, 1964, 9 ff.
61 Nasr, *Three Muslim Sages*, 9.

towards a corporeal interpretation of phenomena, such as resurrection or the ascension of the prophet Muhammad. However, they generally regard this as a matter of belief that cannot be rationally understood.

Ibn Sīnā shows special fascination for the study of the soul in his works: "That the subject clearly lies near the heart of his concern for philosophy is indicated by the fact that he devoted numerous major and minor tracts to the subject and returned repeatedly to its elaboration throughout his life."[62] He assumes that it is merely the rational soul that constitutes the human. According to him, all foundations of being human – identity, origin, and ultimate determination – lie within the soul.[63]

In two of his tracts, Ibn Sīnā explicitly dealt with the subject of the soul. He discusses the topic in the *Miʿrājnāma* (The Scripture about the Ascension),[64] which he wrote in Persian, and in *Risāla fī maʿrifa an-nafs an-nāṭiqa wa-aḥwālihā* (The Treatise on Knowledge About the Rational Soul and Its States),[65] which he wrote in Arabic. In addition, there are some indications of his attitude towards the soul in his two main works: *Kitāb ash-Shifāʾ* (The Book of Healing)[66] and *al-Ishārāt wa-t-tanbihāt* (Remarks and Admonitions).[67] Although these writings are primarily concerned with the soul, they provide helpful insight into Ibn Sīnā's understanding of the human body.

One question that has remained controversial among Muslim scholars to this day, and which illustrates the great divergence between theological and philosophical attitudes, is whether Muhammad's ascension to heaven occurred physically or mentally. The ascension of Muhammad, which partly consists of his night journey on the miraculous mount *Burāq* from Mecca to Jerusalem, and partly from there (or from Mecca, depending on the variation) upon a ladder to heaven, de-

62 Heath, Peter, *Allegory and Philosophy in Avicenna (Ibn Sīnā) with a Translation of the Book of the Prophet Muhammad's Ascent to Heaven*, Philadelphia: University of Pennsylvania Press, 1992, 53.

63 Cf. Rudolph, *Islamische Philosophie*, 49.

64 Ibn Sīnā, Abū ʿAlī, *Miʿrājnāma*, Najīb Māyil Harawī (ed.), Mashhad: Bunyād-i pazhūhishhā-i islāmī-i āstān-i quds-i raḍawī, 1986. Scholars argue whether Ibn Sīnā is the author of this relatively short script. Many assume his authorship. Some arguments for this are made by the editor of the work, Najīb Māyil Harawī. Cf. Ibn Sīnā, *Miʿrājnāma*, 67–74. Other arguments can be found in: Heath, *Allegory and Philosophy*, 201–207. Heath's argument for Ibn Sīnā's authorship of the tract concludes "that although the issue of attribution may be such that it can never be settled irrefutably, there is enough external and internal evidence pointing to Ibn Sīnā actually being the tract's author that the burden of proof falls to those who would argue otherwise." Heath, *Allegory and Philosophy*, 201.

65 Ibn Sīnā, *Risāla fī-maʿrifa an-nafs an-nāṭiqa wa-aḥwālihā*.

66 Ibn Sīnā, *ash-Shifāʾ*.

67 Ibn Sīnā, Abū ʿAlī, *al-Ishārāt wa-t-tanbihāt*, 3 vols., Qum: al-Balāgha, 1996.

scribes one of the prophetic miracles according to the Islamic tradition.[68] Verses 53:1–18 and 81:19–25 of the Qur'ān report Muhammad's encounter with God and with the other prophets at the different levels of heaven. Moreover, verse 17:1 refers to Muhammad's nighttime journey from Mecca to Jerusalem. These brief Qur'ānic explanations of what happened are then supplemented in the *Sīra* literature, the Ḥadīṯ works, and the exegesis of the Qur'ān with somewhat legend-like reports. The core motive of the story that makes it miraculous is the physical character of this trip, which according to the human and rational judgment seems impossible.

Contrary to popular belief, Ibn Sīnā argues in the *Mi'rājnāma* that the ascension of the Prophet Muhammad could not have taken place physically, but only spiritually. As a philosophical basis for his argument, he first discusses the body-soul question in a special chapter. His remarks here coincide with the views expressed in his second scripture, *The Treatise on Knowledge About the Rational Soul and Its States*, and his assumptions about *al-mabda' wa-l-ma'ād* (the beginning and resurgence) in *ash-Shifā'*.[69]

In this context, it is important to note that Ibn Sīnā's cosmology is closely related to his idea of the human being.

Ibn Sīnā first divides the cosmos in two essentially disparate parts. On the one hand, there is the "Necessary Existent" (*wājib al-wujūd*): it is one, it has no cause, and its existence is a fundamental component of its essence.[70] It is assumed that the category of *wājib al-wujūd* is ultimately a synthesis of Plato's "The Good," Aristotle's "Prime Mover," and Plotinus' "The One."[71] On the other hand, there is the "Possibly Existent" (*mumkin al-wujūd*). The concept derives from the "Necessary Existent," it can be more than one, and its existence and nonexistence have a cause.[72] The Possibly Existent is divided into "the abstract immaterial substances of the celestial spheres and the material bodies of the sublunary world."[73] The first celestial existences are the Ten Intelligences (*'uqūl*, sing. *'aql*). The First Intelligence emerges directly from the Necessary Existent and then gives rise to lower Intelligences. The Tenth Intelligence is the Active Intelligence (*'aql fa''āl*) and the Giver of Forms (*wāhib aṣ-ṣuwar*). Each Intelligence arises from a soul (*nafs*) and a heavenly body (*jirm*). According to Ibn Sīnā, the heavenly souls and bodies are

68 Heribert Busse has compiled the relevant sources and their variations of this story in "Jerusalem in the story of Muhammad's night journey and ascension," *Jerusalem Studies in Arabic and Islam* 14 (1991), 1–40.
69 Cf. Ibn Sīnā, *ash-Shifā'*, vol. 1, 435–440.
70 Cf. Ibn Sīnā, *ash-Shifā'*, vol. 1, 37 and 43.
71 Cf. Heath, *Allegory and Philosophy*, 36.
72 Cf. Ibn Sīnā, *ash-Shifā'*, vol. 1, 38.
73 Heath, *Allegory and Philosophy*, 37.

equal to those of the human: "Just as the human soul is the principle that animates our bodies, Souls are the principles that move the heavily spheres."[74] On the level of the Tenth Intelligence, matter emerges, first in the Forms of the Four Elements (Earth, Water, Air, and Fire) "and then in the compound forms that constitute the earth as we know it."[75] So begins terrestrial life.

Ibn Sīnā asserts in the *Mi'rājnāma* that God created the human from two different elements: the body (*tan*) and the spirit (*rūḥ*). While the body consists of the gathering of humors (*akhlāṭ*, sing. *khilt*) and basic elements (*arkān*, sing. *rukn*), the spirit is seen as an effect of the *intellectus agens* (*'aql fa''āl*). Ibn Sīnā suggests that spirit is a life force: Whereas the body is the "mount" (*markab*), the spirit is the "rider" (*sawār*).[76]

Ibn Sīnā speaks of three forms of the spirit which are located in three parts of the body: the animal spirit (*rūḥ haywānī*) which lies in the heart (*dil*) and is responsible for "desire" (*shahwat*), "anger" (*ghaḍab*), "sensory perception" (*ḥiss*), "imagination"(*khayāl*), and "delusion" (*wahm*); the natural spirit (*rūḥ ṭabī'ī*) situated in the liver and is responsible for "absorption" (*jaḏb*), "cessation" (*imsāk*), "digestion" (*haḍm*), and "excretion" (*daf'*); and the mental spirit (*rūḥ nafsānī*) located in the "brain" (*damāgh*) and is responsible for "cognition capacity" (*quwwat-i tafakkur*), "memory power" (*taḏakkur*), "judgment" (*tamyīz*), and "memory" (*ḥifẓ*).[77] While the animal and natural forms of the spirit, like the body, are temporal and mortal, the mental spirit is immortal and lives on after human death.[78] Later, he refers to the mental form of the spirit as the "psyche" (*rawān*), which is neither material nor physical and only represents a "force" (*quwwa*). However, the spirit, meaning the animal or natural spirit, is material or physical, albeit subtle (*laṭīf*).[79]

The mental spirit – that he sometimes calls *rūḥ-i nāṭiqa* (rational spirit), and at other times *nafs-i nāṭiqa* (rational soul) or *rūḥ-i qudsī* (holy spirit)[80] – is created by the intellect (*'aql*) that protects people from overstatement and understatement and encourages them to act fairly.[81]

---

74 Heath, *Allegory and Philosophy*, 37–38.
75 Heath, *Allegory and Philosophy*, 38.
76 Cf. Ibn Sīnā, *Mi'rājnāma*, 81.
77 Cf. Ibn Sīnā, *Mi'rājnāma*, 81.
78 Cf. Ibn Sīnā, *Mi'rājnāma*, 82.
79 Cf. Ibn Sīnā, *Mi'rājnāma*, 82.
80 Cf. Ibn Sīnā, *Mi'rājnāma*, 82–84. The phrase *rūḥ-i qudsī* (Holy Spirit) is evidently based on the Qur'ān (2:87). Cf. Ibn Sīnā, *Mi'rājnāma*, 89.
81 Cf. Ibn Sīnā, *Mi'rājnāma*, 84.

According to Ibn Sīnā, the mental spirit that he later simply calls "soul" (*nafs*), and the intellect are the same being, which is referred to differently depending on its respective circumstances and effects.[82]

A dualistic view, as the one Ibn Sīnā holds, distinguishes categorically between the body and the spirit. The spirit, or "mental spirit," ensures that humans are liberated from animal drives and natural desires and that they maintain balance. In short, the spirit or soul stands for the good and the sublime, and the body for the evil and the inferior.

Additionally, Ibn Sīnā does not understand the soul as the invisible, but rather as the immaterial – a kind of force. As described above, this point of view differs significantly from the theological conception of the human or human body and the corresponding narratives found in the Qur'ān.

In his book, *The Treatise on Knowledge About the Rational Soul and Its States,*[83] Ibn Sīnā also affirms that the *nafs*, the self, is neither bodily nor physical. Rather, it is the spiritual substance that gives life to the human body, enables knowledge and insight, and outlives the body.[84] According to Ibn Sīnā, *nafs* is what makes us human, and he presents three arguments for this assertion. First, *nafs* is what remains constant throughout life, while the body and body parts constantly change, dissolve and diminish. Therefore, the human cannot be the dissolving body, but the self which remains in every situation.[85] His second argument states that humans can imagine having done something without thinking about their body parts. This also shows that the actual human ego exists separately from the body. Finally, if a person perceives or understands something through their sensory organs or if they imagine something, the person claims to have perceived, understood or imagined it. This self, in which all these insights and activities assemble, is something different from the human body and is, therefore, not to be equated with body parts. Hence, this self, *nafs*, is neither bodily nor physical. Otherwise, like the body, it would have to change and dissolve, and would not remain constant throughout life.[86]

Ibn Sīnā further explains that *nafs* is the actual substance of humans and lives on after death. The *nafs*, which is characterized in worldly life through

---

82 Cf. Ibn Sīnā, *Mi'rājnāma*, 85–86.

83 Regarding the tract cf. Mokhtar, Mustafa Kamal, "The Treatise on Knowledge. About the Rational Soul and its States by Ibn Sina: A Critical Edition and Annotated Translation," *Akademika* 44 (1994), 45–71, here 52–54.

84 Cf. Ibn Sīnā, *Risāla fī ma'rifa an-nafs an-nāṭiqa wa-aḥwālihā*, 9.

85 Cf. Ibn Sīnā, *Risāla fī ma'rifa an-nafs an-nāṭiqa wa-aḥwālihā*, 9–10.

86 Cf. Ibn Sīnā, *Risāla fī ma'rifa an-nafs an-nāṭiqa wa-aḥwālihā*, 10.

knowledge, wisdom, and good behavior, will be received in the world of lights: divine, angelic lights.[87]

Ibn Sīnā continues by stating that human souls are divided into three categories in the hereafter. If human souls are complete in theory and practice (*al-ʿilm wa-l-ʿamal*), then they are led to the uppermost world, the world of the intellect. If they are merely accomplished in one of the two areas, they go to the middle world. At this level, they reach the souls of the heavenly bodies (*aflāk*), are cleansed of the impurity of the elementary bodies (*ʿanāṣur*, sing. *ʿunsur*), and can eventually connect to the highest world. Finally, if the human souls are deficient in both areas, they go to the lowest world and sink into the oceans of natural darkness and the depths of elementary bodies.[88]

Even though Ibn Sīnā sometimes uses the term spirit (*rūḥ*) and at other times the term soul (*nafs*) for the immaterial in humans, it can be assumed that he uses both terms synonymously.[89] His answer to whether there is a physical resurrection is, however, fairly straightforward. For him, it is obvious that only the continued existence of the spirit after death can be rationally justified, whereas a physical resurrection is a matter of faith and can only be justified by specifying the Sharia.[90]

7 The Body and Philosophical Islamic Scholars

The special focus on the immaterial or the soul of the human, which we have observed in the work of Ibn Sīnā, can be ascertained in various nuances by many other scholars who, in one way or another, have encountered certain philosophical approaches. This is noted in both traditional and contemporary scholars.

A philosophical mindset was already demonstrated by the medieval theo-philosophers, the Brethren of Purity, with whose writings Ibn Sīnā was likely familiar. To some degree, this tendency can also be observed in the works of Abū Ḥāmid al-Ghazālī (d. 1111), even though he is considered a great opponent of philosophy. His intense preoccupation with philosophy, even if to refute it, impacted his way of thinking. A similar perception of the world and the human can also be witnessed

---

87 Cf. Ibn Sīnā, *Risāla fī maʿrifa an-nafs an-nāṭiqa wa-aḥwālihā*, 11.
88 Cf. Ibn Sīnā, *Risāla fī maʿrifa an-nafs an-nāṭiqa wa-aḥwālihā*, 13–14.
89 For example, in the chapter on *maʿād* (the hereafter) in his major work *ash-Shifāʾ*, he discusses the questions of what happens to the mind when it leaves the body and whether there is a physical resurrection. He uses the term *nafs* instead of *rūḥ*, although the term *rūḥ* can also be used here. Cf. Ibn Sīnā, *ash-Shifāʾ*, vol. 1, 423.
90 Cf. Ibn Sīnā, *ash-Shifāʾ*, vol. 1, 423.

in the work of the modern Indian-Pakistani philosopher and poet Muhammad Iqbal (d. 1938).

The Ikhwān aṣ-ṣafā (the Brethren of Purity) were substantively influenced by Neoplatonic approaches and clearly represent a soul-oriented perspective. They mostly had Iranian background and first appeared at the end of the 10th century. The group shaped Islamic history in a theological, political, and philosophical way. Since Ibn Sīnā's father already knew the epistles of Ikhwān aṣ-ṣafā in Bukhara,[91] it can be assumed that Ibn Sīnā also encountered their ideas.

The Ikhwān aṣ-ṣafā obviously did not care for the human body or worldly life, they rather viewed the material world as the prison for the humans, from which they can save themselves through knowledge that has its place in the heart and soul:

> Practically every chapter of their long work reminds the reader that in this world he is a prisoner who must free himself from his earthly prison through knowledge. All the sciences they consider – whether astronomy, angelology, or embryology – are discussed, not with the aim of a purely theoretical or intellectual interpretation or for their practical application, but to help untie the knots in the soul of the reader by making him, on the one hand, aware of the great harmony and beauty of the Universe and, on the other hand, of the necessity for man to go beyond material existence.[92]

In their cosmology, a universal soul exists in addition to the material universe, just as there is a human soul in addition to the human body.[93] Moreover, the soul directs everything, in both its universal and human dimensions, and "all bodies in the universe are like tools in the hand of the universal soul which performs all actions through them in the same way a carpenter uses his tools to meet various ends. Therefore, all change in the universe is directed by the soul."[94]

They argue that the human body belongs to the animal kingdom and functions like the animal body. The only difference between the human and the animal body is that it stands upright. This is to be seen as a sign of its striving for the higher and loftier world. The difference between humans and animals is not so much in their material properties, but rather in the human soul – which is part of the universal soul, nevertheless, is profoundly different from the soul of animals.[95] They describe the human body as a city in which every link has a function. The brain is the king and the limbs are its subjects. The heart forms the

---

91 Cf. Strohmaier, Gotthard, *Ibn Sīnā*, Munich: C.H. Beck, 2006, 104.

92 Nasr, Seyyed Hossein, *An Introduction to Islamic Cosmological Doctrines. Conceptions of Nature and Methods Used for Its Study by the Ikhwān al-Ṣafā', al-Bīrūnī, and Ibn Sīnā*, Cambridge: Harvard University Press, 1964, 30.

93 Cf. Nasr, *Introduction to Islamic Cosmological Doctrines*, 56.

94 Nasr, *Introduction to Islamic Cosmological Doctrines*, 57.

95 Cf. Nasr, *Introduction to Islamic Cosmological Doctrines*, 96–97.

center of the city and is the most sublime of all body parts.[96] Essentially, humans should strive for the permanent – what is beyond mere physicality – by leaving the material behind.

The extent to which the Ikhwān aṣ-ṣafā focused on the soul and were influenced by the Platonic world view is shown in their well-known work, "The Two Islands Simile," which is clearly inspired by Plato's allegory of the cave. Below, I have summarized Ian Richard Netton's representation of the parable:

"The Virtuous City" (*al-madīna al-fāḍila*) stands on top of a mountain and has the best conditions for a good life. The people of the city live in mutual love and harmony. A group of those people then set sail and are shipwrecked on another island. They inhabit the island and interbreed with monkeys, who are the indigenous beings of the island. Life on the second island is the opposite of life on the first island. Here, life is with suffering, pain, and dissatisfaction. Ever so often, great predatory birds attack the monkeys and capture them. One day, one of the shipwrecked people, now living on the new island, returned to his native city in a dream and experienced all the amenities of a happy life. After telling his compatriots about his dream, they asked, "How can one return and be saved from this place?" They decided to cooperate and build a ship that would bring them back to their native land. While they were busy building the ship, a huge bird appeared, grabbed one of the men, and eventually dropped him off in his native city. While the delighted man, now in his homeland, wishes all others would experience the same fate, the inhabitants of the monkey island anxiously mourn his loss.[97]

According to Ikhwān aṣ-ṣafā, the island of the shipwrecked symbolizes the terrestrial world (*ad-dunyā*) with the monkeys as human beings, the great birds as death, the shipwrecked people as the "Friends of God" (*Awliyā' Allāh*), and the Virtuous City as paradise (*Dār al-Ākhira*). The lesson from this allegory is thus that the constant, valuable, and worthwhile life lies in the non-material, in the beyond. The corporeal and material side of life, in contrast, is ephemeral and worthless.

Abū Ḥāmid al-Ghazālī (1058–1111), who, with his work *Tahāfut al-Falāsifa* (The Incoherence of the Philosophers) became known as a bitter opponent of philosophy, declared Ibn Sīnā – along with al-Fārābī, Socrates, Plato, and Aristotle – unbelievers.[98] His criticism of philosophy went so far that he declared a philosopher to be an unbeliever when, for example, they denied "the resurrection of bodies and

96 Cf. Nasr, *Introduction to Islamic Cosmological Doctrines*, 98–99.
97 Cf. Netton, Ian Richard, "Private Caves and Public Islands: Islam, Plato and the Ikhwān al-Ṣafā'," in: Maha El Kaisy-Friemuth / John M. Dillon (eds.), *The Afterlife of the Platonic Soul. Reflections of Platonic Psychology in the Monotheistic Religions*, Leiden: Brill, 2009, 105–120, here 116–117.
98 Cf. Strohmaier, *Ibn Sīnā*, 131–132.

assembly of bodies" on Judgment Day or if they believed "that the rewards and punishments in the next life are only spiritual in character and not bodily as well."[99] From this, it is not difficult to conclude what his thoughts of Ibn Sīnā were, who, for example, understood only spiritual resurrection as rationally comprehensible.

Nevertheless, it can be observed that al-Ghazālī maintained a strong aversion for the body and paid special attention to the soul. This attitude is certainly related to his mystical character, but also philosophical education. Like Ibn Sīnā and the Ikhwān aṣ-ṣafā, al-Ghazālī takes a dualistic standpoint and strictly distinguishes the soul from the body: "If you want to recognize yourself, know that you are created from two things. One is this outer shell, which is called the body and can be seen with the outer eye. The other is the inside, which is at times called the soul, sometimes the spirit, and now the heart, and which can only be recognized by the inner eye."[100] According to him, the body is earthly and from the menial world, whereas the spirit is divine and from the upper world. The lower world evokes the characteristics of cattle, predators, and the devil in the human, while the upper world represents the divine. Humans struggle between these two worlds within themselves and attempt to be freed from the lower qualities so as to be made blissful by the divine.[101]

Al-Ghazālī, thereupon, calls for the knowledge of the self as it is the key to the knowledge of God: "That is why you should strive for knowledge of your true nature, what you are, where you came from, where you are going, and for what purpose you have come to this caravansary for these few days, what you are created for, what your happiness is and what you will be happy in, what your misery is, and what will make you miserable."[102] Through the knowledge of self, al-Ghazālī continues, humans will recognize that their inner beings represent their true beings. The inside of the human – which al-Ghazālī also calls the heart and equates with the soul and spirit – is both immaterial and the decisive factor: "Everything else [equivalent to the body] is only his entourage, his host, and his staff."[103] On this point, al-Ghazālī's rhetoric is reminiscent of Ibn Sīnā's metaphor of the spirit as the rider and the body as the mount.[104]

Similarly, in another of his works, *Iḥyāʾ ʿulūm ad-dīn* (The Revival of the Religious Sciences), al-Ghazālī speaks of the *qalb* (heart) as that which gives humans

---

99 Griffel, Frank, *Al-Ghazālī's Philosophical Theology*, Oxford: Oxford University Press, 2009, 101–102.

100 Al-Ghazālī, Abū Ḥāmid, *Das Elixier der Glückseligkeit*, trans. Hellmut Ritter, Wiesbaden: Marixverlag, 2016, 32.

101 Cf. al-Ghazālī, *Elixier der Glückseligkeit*, 24–25.

102 al-Ghazālī, *Elixier der Glückseligkeit*, 31.

103 al-Ghazālī, *Elixier der Glückseligkeit*, 33.

104 Cf. al-Ghazālī, Abū Ḥāmid, *Iḥyāʾ ʿulūm ad-dīn*, 4 vols., Beirut: Dār al-maʿrifa, n. d., vol. 3, 3–4.

dignity, puts them above other beings, and benefits them in this world as well as in the hereafter.[105] According to al-Ghazālī, *qalb* is the part of human that seeks God, strives for Him and follows Him. It is not a physical organ, but it leads and guides the organs.[106] Al-Ghazālī emphasized that the term *qalb* does not mean the material organ of the heart, but rather the subtle, divine, and spiritual, which is the essence of human.[107] Al-Ghazālī equates the *qalb* in this sense with the following terms: with the *rūḥ* (spirit) in the sense of the subtle, the intuition, and the cognition in the human; with the *nafs* (soul) in the sense of the self in the human recognizing God; and with the *ʿaql* (reason), in the sense of the human capacity to grasp knowledge.[108]

Even if al-Ghazālī, as a legal scholar, attaches great importance to compliance with the Sharia rules like purity, prayer, alms, fasting, and pilgrimage,[109] for him, in the end, it is the mental aspect of human existence that is fundamental.

Muhammad Iqbal (1877–1938), an Indian-Pakistani poet and philosopher, also focuses primarily on *nafs*. However, he uses the term *khūdī*, which comes from Persian and is used in Urdu. He notably discusses the concept in his book of poems *Asrār-i khūdī* (The Secrets of the Self), in which he demonstrates a consistently positive understanding of the term *khūdī* and describes it as an expression of the entirety of the human.[110] Generally, nevertheless, the expression *khūdī* holds negative connotations in Persian and Urdu. It is linked with associations such as *khūd-bīn* (conceited, narcissistic), *khūd-pasand* (complacent, presumptuous) or *khūd-khāh* (selfish, egotistical). Iqbal, however, uses it positively and believes that the development of the *khūdī* is, in fact, the goal of life.[111] According to Iqbal, love is of great importance for the development of the self, the *khūdī*. On the one hand, he refers to love in general: "This can be knowledge, that one can recognize, or it can be something in the outside world that one can act upon."[112] On the other hand, he strongly associates it with religion and connects it to God and the prophet Muhammad.[113] In the chapter on "the human ego, its freedom and immortality" in his socio-philosophical work, *The Reconstruction of Religious*

105 Cf. al-Ghazālī, *Iḥyāʾ ʿulūm ad-dīn*, vol. 3, 2.
106 Cf. al-Ghazālī, *Iḥyāʾ ʿulūm ad-dīn*, vol. 3, 2.
107 Cf. al-Ghazālī, *Iḥyāʾ ʿulūm ad-dīn*, vol. 3, 3.
108 Cf. al-Ghazālī, *Iḥyāʾ ʿulūm ad-dīn*, vol. 3, 3–4.
109 Cf. al-Ghazālī, *Elixier der Glückseligkeit*, 27.
110 Cf. Murtaza, Mohammad Sameer, *Islamische Existenzialphilosophie – Muhammad Iqbal nietzscheanisch gelesen*, Norderstedt: BoD – Books on Demand, 2016, 332.
111 Cf. Popp, Stephan, *Mohammad Iqbal. Ein Philosoph zwischen den Kulturen*, Nordhausen: Bautz, 2007, 22.
112 Popp, *Iqbal*, 25.
113 Cf. Popp, *Iqbal*, 25.

Thought in Islam, Iqbal returns to the topic and emphasizes the human's "individuality and uniqueness" based on Qur'ānic statements. He finds three references in the Qur'ān that underline the human peculiarity: a) Humans are chosen by God, b) humans are the representative of God on Earth, and c) humans are the trustees of a free personality that they accepted at their own risk.[114] The ego, according to Iqbal, represents the entirety of what is commonly referred to as the mental state. It is independent of time and space and is characterized by the privacy that reveals the uniqueness of each ego. "[T]he ego can think of more than one space-order. [. . .] The ego, therefore, is not space-bound in the sense in which the body is space-bound."[115]

Iqbal, who according to his own statements worked out of the traditions of both Islamic mysticism and Western philosophy, generally seeks divinity in the human and in the world that goes beyond the material and survives time and space.

8 The Body in Mysticism

Islamic mystics, also called Sufis, strongly focus on the spiritual aspect of the human; like the philosophers, but probably for alternative motives. On the whole, their teachings show a tendency to free themselves from the narrowness of the body and look for deeper meaning or higher value in the human being, life, and the universe at large.

Similar to the philosophers, the mystics are generally not well accepted by theologians and legal scholars. Their reading of Islam, which is based on the inner sense of religious texts, is unacceptable to legal scholars, like the philosophers' rational interpretation of the world. Nonetheless, the mystics have maintained a lasting impact on Islamic intellectual history and have even managed to influence a number of theologians and legal scholars.

The Sufis had a difficult position in Islam due to their unconventional readings of Islam, which were usually not in accord with the wording of the religious texts. They frequently endured tribulations ranging from persecution to execution. The most famous mystics who paid for their viewpoints with death include Ḥusayn ibn Manṣūr al-Ḥallāj (857–922);[116] ʿAyn-al Quḍḍāt Hamadānī (1098–1131);

114 Cf. Iqbal, Muhammad, *The Reconstruction of Religious Thought in Islam*, Moscow: Dodo Press, 2009, 105.
115 Cf. Iqbal, *The Reconstruction of Religious Thought in Islam*, 108.
116 For more about him and his ideas cf. Lerch, Wolfgang Günter, *Tod in Bagdad oder Leben und Sterben des Al-Halladsch*, Düsseldorf: Artemis & Winkler, 1997.

and the so-called "Master of the Philosophy of Enlightenment," Shihāb ad-Dīn as-Suhrawardī (1154–1191).[117]

The example of Suhrawardī shows how the mystical perception of the universe, in a sense, resembles the philosophical interpretation of the world. Ulrich Rudolph's misgivings can also be traced back to this assertion when he, after explaining Suhrawardī's teaching of illumination, noted the following: "At the latest it is here where one can ask if Suhrawardī really taught philosophy. Because much of what he represented could just as well be explained from the tradition of Sufism or as an assumption of Gnostic ideas."[118]

Suhrawardī developed his teaching of illumination in the tradition of Ibn Sīnā, but in contrast to the Peripatetics, he assumed that the truth cannot be achieved solely through a discursive method of knowledge, but only through mystical experience (*dhawq*) and divine inspiration (*munāzala*).[119] One cannot overlook the influence of Platonic and Neoplatonic philosophy in his teaching.[120]

Suhrawardī understood the act of knowledge as enlightenment because he believed that all beings consist of light, meaning that everything which exists is light in essence. This first and foremost applies to God. He is the pure light, mixed with nothing – the light of the light. The other types of beings are flooded with the light of God, but differ in the intensity thereof.[121]

Suhrawardī's ontology is rooted in a hierarchy in which bodies are at the bottom: "Bodies are governed by the heavens, the heavens by the souls, the souls by the various orders of the angels, and the angels by the Light of lights who has dominion over the whole universe."[122] Humans can, then, reach the divine light and free themselves from their dark state through knowledge. However, for this to happen, they must undergo great efforts. The task of the human is thus "to recognize existential light and to approach it, and the more he releases himself from the darkness of his own self and is penetrated by light, the closer he reaches the divine."[123]

Suhrawardī's philosophically formulated teaching ultimately aims at what mysticism in general wants to teach: namely, that the body is the prison of the

117 For more about him and his philosophy cf. Razavi, Mehdi Amin, *Suhrawardi and the School of Illumination*, Richmond: Curzon Press, 1997.

118 Rudolph, *Islamische Philosophie*, 84.

119 Cf. Turki, Mohamed, *Eine Einführung in die arabisch-islamische Philosophie*, Freiburg: Karl Alber, 2015, 153–156.

120 Cf. Walbridge, John, *The Wisdom of the Mystic East. Suhrawardī and Platonic Orientalism*, New York: State University of New York Press, 2001, 13–16.

121 Cf. Rudolph, *Islamische Philosophie*, 84.

122 Nasr, *Three Muslim Sages*, 75.

123 Schimmel, Annemarie, *Sufismus. Eine Einführung in die islamische Mystik*, Munich: C.H. Beck, 2014, 37.

spirit and that, through abstinence and ascetic life, the human suppresses physical desire in order to become enlightened and arrive at the truth (*haqīqat*).

The Iraqi Sufi and one of the most important mystical authorities Abū al-Qāsim Junayd (830–910) affirms that Sufism is not hollow talk. A mystic must go hungry, reject desires, and part with the things they like. When asked how he reached this stage of knowledge and wisdom, the Persian and equally well-known mystic Bāyazīd Bistāmī (804–874) said that he reached it through an empty belly and a naked body.[124]

In his work the *Mathnawī*, the great mystic and poet Jalāl ad-Dīn Muḥammad Rūmī (1207–1273) also refers to the dichotomy of the body and spirit and the value of the spirit and worthlessness of the body:

> O, Brother, you are the Intellect / The rest is bones and fibres.[125]

Accordingly, in another place he recommends:

> Listen to my advice. The body is a strong rope / Put the used away when you need a new one.[126]

As Scott Kugle states in his study,[127] the Sufis can also show positive attitudes towards the body while seeing it as part of the beautiful physical world through which one can recognize God. From this perspective, the Sufis view the body as the place where God's name and attributes appear. Divinity emerges through the beauty of the human body. The Sufis cite a very common Ḥadīṯ, which states that God created humanity in His own image.[128] The belief that the human body is a creation of God gives it dignity, and one should thus treat it as something valuable:

> It is this affirmation of God's immanence and fascination with God's presence that causes Sufis to value the body in ways fuller and deeper than other Muslim authorities. Their emphasis on loving God as the medium through which people can love each other gave them a special focus on the body and the subtleties of human relations that embodiment entails.[129]

In the case of the mystics, in contrast to the theologians or legal scholars, the appreciation of the body does not imply placing the physical, material, and external in the center of religious practice, but instead recognizing God and His beauty

---

124 Cf. Malakī, Taqī Āzad / Ghurāb, Nāṣir ad-Dīn, "Jāygāh-i badan dar dīn," *Muṭāliʿāt-i farhangī wa-irtibāṭāt* 18 (2010), 25.

125 Rūmī, Jalāl ad-Dīn Muḥammad, *Mathnawī maʿnawī*, Tehran: Amīr kabīr, 1993, 214.

126 Rūmī, *Mathnawī*, 260.

127 Cf. Kugle, Scott, *Sufis & Saints' Bodies. Mysticisms, Corporeality, & Sacred Power in Islam*, Chapel Hill, NC: The University of North Carolina Press, 2007.

128 Cf. Muslim Ibn al-Ḥajjāj, *Ṣaḥīḥ*, vol. 4, 2183, Ḥadīṯ-Nr. 2841.

129 Kugle, *Sufis & Saints' Bodies*, 4.

through an understanding of the body and its beauty. Likewise, the mystical understanding of God differs from the idea of God among theologians and legal scholars: "It aims not just to understand God, like theological discourse, or to obey God, like legal discourse, but also to love and be loved by God."[130]

9 The Body and Asceticism

Renunciation of worldly pleasure, as we see in the case of the Sufis, is generally considered a sign of inner strength in Islam. The Arabic term for this is *zuhd* (detachment, renunciation). The word itself does not appear in the Qur'ān, but it was already established in the early Islamic period (at the turn of the 8th century) as an attitude worth striving for. Among others, the theologian Ḥasan al-Baṣrī (642–728) is described as an ideal example of asceticism.[131] *Zuhd* means renouncing not only material things, but also immaterial things that distract people from focusing on God and life in the hereafter.[132] In this respect, either verbal conceit or a demonstrated complacency toward God could violate principles and lead to the desire of material things. Thereby, the Qur'ānic demand is understood to be that humans serve God exclusively,[133] regard worldly life as a distraction, and perceive the hereafter as more valuable.[134] There are also several Ḥadīṯs that confirm this attitude. For instance, a frequently quoted tradition states that "the world is the prison for the believers and the paradise for the unbelievers."[135]

Therefore, all trends and influences in Islam consider *zuhd* to be a positive practice. However, some Sufis maintain a particularly consistent mode of renunciation. They advocate a radical theocentric piety in which there is not even a place for desire of the hereafter. The prominent Sufi and ascetic woman Rābiʿa al-ʿAdawiyya al-Qaysiyya (718–801) vividly demonstrated this by walking through the streets of Basra with a bucket of water in one hand and a torch in the other. When asked about the meaning of her actions, she replied, "I want to pour water into hell and set fire to paradise so that these two veils will disappear and no one

130 Kugle, *Sufis & Saints' Bodies*, 1.
131 Cf. van Ess, *Theologie und Gesellschaft*, vol. 2, 45.
132 Cf. Gramlich, Richard, *Weltverzicht: Grundlagen und Weisen islamischer Askese*, Wiesbaden: Harrassowitz, 1997, 11 ff.
133 Cf. Qur'ān 51:56.
134 Cf. Qur'ān 6:32.
135 Muslim Ibn al-Ḥajjāj, *Ṣaḥīḥ*, vol. 4, 2272, Ḥadīṯ-Nr. 2956.

will worship God out of fear of hell or hope for paradise, but only for the sake of His eternal beauty."[136]

In general, anyone who endeavors beyond the obligatory religious duties can be considered an ascetic. For instance, an ascetic can be someone who, in addition to the obligatory fasting, fasts other days, even months, prays more than required, or undertakes many "small pilgrimages" (*ʿumra*) in addition to the "big pilgrimage" (*ḥajj*).

However, some scholars or mystics warn that the religious rituals themselves are not the goal. Ultimately, all physical exertion is a means of seeking closeness to God. In general, they attach little importance to the external practice of religious rituals. The mystic mentioned above, Rumi, criticizes, for example, the ritual pilgrims to Mecca in a poem that has in modern times become one of the great songs of the well-known Afghan singer, Ahmad Zahir (1946–1979). He says:

> O Pilgrims, thou art where, thou art where?
> The Beloved is neigh, come hither, come hither.
> Thy beloved is thy neighbor, behind the wall
> Lost in the desert, you are seeking and you fall;
> From house to house, you sought for proof
> Yet never ascended up to the roof.[137]

10 The Body in Islamic Law

As it is known, the subject of the Islamic law is divided into two categories. On the one hand, there is *muʿāmalāt*, which includes topics that concern interpersonal relationships, such as buying and selling, or marriage and inheritance. On the other hand, there is the category *ʿibādāt*, which refers to the relationship of humans to God, like prayer and fasting. Regardless of the question, Islamic law deals primarily with the external and material dimensions of human actions. It is fundamental for all religious acts that they are carried out with the intention (*niyya*) to obey God. Since intent can hardly be grasped or measured, the focus of the Islamic law is on the material or corporeal aspects and their regulations. This is the same with religious rites, as with the *ḥadd* punishments or the questions of organ donation and cremation. To better understand the Islamic law, two other aspects must be considered. First, in Islam it is assumed that the human is the

136 Schimmel, *Sufismus*, 16.

137 Rūmī, Jalāl ad-Dīn Muḥammad, *Kulliyyāt-i shams-i tabrīzī*, Tehran: Pagāh, 1984, 256, Ghazal-Nr. 648.

creation of God and must therefore be treated with dignity and respect. Second, humans and their bodies belong to their creator, God, and are therefore subject to divine regulations. Accordingly, humans cannot simply do as they please with their bodies. Rather, they must take care of the divine guidelines when handling their own or someone else's body.

The following examples are intended to illustrate the centrality of the body and corporeal matters in Sharia legal discussions.

10.1 The Cleansing of the Body

In general, every human action in Islam holds a dimension of worship. According to the Islamic worldview, the human is part of a creation that is in the service of God as a whole: "The seven heavens and the earth, and whosoever in them is, extol Him; nothing is that does not proclaim His praise [. . .]."[138] Humans were created to serve God, which is stated in another passage of the Qur'ān.[139] From a Muslim perspective, this attitude is shared by all "People of the Book."[140] Importantly, believers in the Qur'ān are generally described as "worshippers" (*'ibād*; sg.: *'abd*).[141]

Legal scholars, however, become more specific in the *fiqh* works and refer to certain acts as worship or liturgy (*'ibādāt*). Prayer, fasting, and pilgrimage are the most important and best-known religious rites, which I consider below.

The basis for every worship practice in Islam is body cleansing, without which worship is considered unfulfilled. The traditions repeatedly state that the indispensable condition of correct prayer is ritual ablution.[142] For this reason, cleaning the body is seen as a religious duty and thus, an act of worship. In an oft-quoted Ḥadīṯ, the cleansing of the body is even referred to as half of belief.[143] Each work of *fiqh* dedicates an independent chapter to the topic *aṭ-ṭahāra* (cleansing), in which the issue is discussed in a meticulous manner. The Qur'ān describes how ritual washing must be carried out before prayer.[144] However, the Ḥadīṯs explain the process in much greater detail, describing parts of the body and how they are to be washed with pure water.[145] If pure water is not available, the body

138 Qur'ān 17:44.
139 Cf. Qur'ān 51:56.
140 Qur'ān 3:64.
141 Qur'ān 14:31.
142 Cf. Muslim Ibn al-Ḥajjāj, *Ṣaḥīḥ*, vol. 1, 204, Ḥadīṯ-Nr. 224.
143 Cf. Muslim Ibn al-Ḥajjāj, *Ṣaḥīḥ*, vol. 1, 203, Ḥadīṯ-Nr. 223.
144 Cf. Qur'ān 5:6.
145 Cf. Muslim Ibn al-Ḥajjāj, *Ṣaḥīḥ*, vol. 1, 203–241.

must be cleaned with soil. Cleansing issues specific to women, such as cleansing during menstruation, are also discussed in detail.[146]

Islam emerged in a world in which most religious traditions had already attached great importance to corporeal cleansing and had given the body various regulations: "By the time of the rise of Islam in the seventh century C.E., the rabbinic Jews of Palestine and ʿIrāq had essentially closed the Talmud, enshrining a form of Jewish practice in which the daily life of the common believer was constrained by a complex body of purity law."[147] The Jewish believer had to consider many rules regarding eating, bodily flux, sexual intercourse, and performance of ablutions before prayer or Torah study.[148] Additionally:

> Zoroastrian purity law was, if anything, more exact than what was developed in the Jewish Halakha. Zoroastrian purity practices were distinctive in that they sought to protect not only sacred activities and places but the pure elements of fire, water, and earth from pollution [. . .]. Zoroastrians also followed a number of purity structures which focused on the human body and which strongly resembled those of other religious traditions in the region.[149]

Physical cleansing rituals as a concept are not usually associated with Christian practice, although they were also internalized in Christianity. For example, early medieval Christians followed cleansing practices similar to those of their neighboring religions. Cleaning regulations are also attributed to Christians who lived close to the Prophet Muhammad. These regulations include "that menstruating women may neither enter a church nor partake in communion." They also prescribe that "[m]arried couples are to observe three nights of sexual abstinence before taking communion."[150]

In Islam, there is a basic distinction of body cleansing between the small ritual ablution (*wuḍūʾ*), which removes small impurities, and the large ritual ablution (*ghusl*), which removes large impurities. The small impurities arise through all body fluids (e.g., urine, feces, blood) as well as, among others, through sleep, fainting, touching the genital area, wind, or touching a corpse. The major impurities occur mainly through sexual intercourse, childbirth, or menstruation, and require a complete immersion in water or a complete washing of all parts of the body.[151]

---

146 Cf. Muslim Ibn al-Ḥajjāj, *Ṣaḥīḥ*, vol. 1, 242–284.

147 Katz, Marion Holmes, *Body of Text. The Emergence of the Sunnī Law of Ritual Purity*, New York: State University of New York Press, 2002, 3.

148 Cf. Katz, *Body of Text*, 3.

149 Katz, *Body of Text*, 4.

150 Katz, *Body of Text*, 5.

151 For a detailed description of cleansing rituals cf. az-Zuḥaylī, Wahba, *Mawsūʿa al-fiqh al-islāmī wa-l-qaḍāyā al-muʿāṣira*, 14 vols., Damascus: Dār al-fikr, 2012, vol. 1, 309–553.

In Islam, this careful cleansing preparation for fulfilling acts of worship is, on the one hand, quite remarkable, and on the other hand, shows that legal scholars attach great importance to the corporeal dimension of worship. The question of whether the believer carefully carries out prayer or fasting is not decided initially by the inner attitude of the believer – their awareness of sin or regret – but rather how correct the last purification was. If believers perform the ritual ablutions correctly, this means, according to the regulations of Sharia, that they will receive God's contentment.

10.2 Ritual Practices

In Islam, the three most known, important, and symbolic practices of worship in everyday life are: five daily prayers (*ṣalāt*),[152] fasting (*ṣawm*), and pilgrimage (*ḥajj*). The external and material fulfillment of these obligations is decisive in its legal structure. For instance, it is essential that the prayer is performed under the established conditions, from ritual washing and correct recitation of certain Qur'ānic surahs to the execution of particular bodily movements. Attention is drawn to inner concentration (*ḥuḍūr al-qalb*); however, under Sharia law, this is not a prerequisite for the proper execution of prayer.[153] The ritual practices are usually accompanied by a high level of corporeal exertion, even stress. These ritual practices are also lifted as soon as they exceed the corporeal limits of the person concerned because, in such a case, they would be regarded as a breach of the Muslim's bodily integrity.[154]

Ṣalāt: Prayer consists of particular corporeal postures and movements: *qiyām* (standing up), *rukūʿ* (bending down), *sujūd* (prostration), and *julūs* (sitting up). Alongside these postures, prayers and Qur'ānic verses praising God and asking for guidance are recited.[155]

The noticeable social highlight of the prayer ritual always takes place on Friday at lunchtime. The Friday prayer not only represents a spiritual act but also the believers' closeness and unity. Whereas daily prayers can be performed either indi-

152 There are in total five individual daily prayers, namely the morning, midday, afternoon, evening, and the night prayer. The Shīʿites rule that the midday and afternoon prayer, as well as the evening and night prayer, are combined and, therefore, they actually pray three times a day.

153 For details on the prayer cf. Muslim Ibn al-Ḥajjāj, *Ṣaḥīḥ*, vol. 1, 285 ff.

154 Cf. Krawietz, Birgit, *Die Ḥurma. Schariarechtlicher Schutz vor Eingriffen in die körperliche Unversehrtheit nach arabischen Fatwas des 20. Jahrhunderts*, Berlin: Duncker und Humblot, 1991, 50.

155 For a detailed description and components of the prayers cf. az-Zuḥaylī, *Mawsūʿa al-fiqh al-islāmī*, vol. 1, 670–718.

vidually or together, Friday prayer is only to be performed in a group. The other peculiarity of the Friday prayer is the sermon (*khuṭba*) given by the preacher (*khaṭīb*) or the *imām* (prayer leader). The sermon not only addresses moral and spiritual matters but also current issues. The Friday prayer and the sermon are always viewed as a public act in Islam, and, thus, carry socio-political value. Therefore, in the past, the sermon was given either by the caliphs or their representatives.[156] This is probably the reason why Friday prayer did not play a major role with the Shīʿites before the establishment of the Islamic Republic. According to Shīʿite law, Friday prayer in the absence of the twelfth Imam is not a definite duty. As an example, before the Islamic Republic, the Shīʿites in Iran did not usually hold Friday prayer. Only with the foundation of the Islamic Republic did the Friday prayer become a religious, public, solemn, and political gathering in Iran.[157]

Ṣawm: Fasting is perhaps the most physically demanding rite in Islam. Renouncing all corporeal pleasure – from drinking and eating to sex, from sunrise to sunset for 28–30 days (depending on the length of that year's Ramadan month) – is a great challenge that believers face. Bodily cleanliness and neatness are especially important during Ramadan. This month is also characterized by the "night of divine destiny" (*lailat al-qadr*), in which the Qur'ān was sent down to Earth: "The month of Ramadan, wherein the Quran was sent down to be a guidance to the people, and as a clear sign of the guidance and the salvation. So let those of you, who are present at the month, fast it [. . .]."[158] That fasting must not lead to suffering is emphasized in the same verse: "[. . .] and if any of you be sick, or if he be on a journey, then a number of other days; God desires easy for you, and desires not hardship for you [. . .]." The end of Ramadan is celebrated with the ceremony of breaking the fast (*ʿīd al-fiṭr*) on the first day of the new lunar calendar month. The ceremony starts with a prayer in the mosque and continues with a celebration for days together with other believers and family members alongside diverse culinary offerings.[159]

Ḥajj: According to Islamic law, every Muslim who is free, of legal age, healthy, and can afford it, is obliged to perform pilgrimage to Mecca once in a lifetime.[160] This is

156 For a detailed description of Friday prayers cf. az-Zuḥaylī, *Mawsūʿa al-fiqh al-islāmī*, vol. 2, 233 ff.
157 Cf. Maʿmūrī, ʿAlī, *Namāz-i ǧumʿa, tašayyuʿ-i siyāsī wa-inqilāb-i islāmī*, Online publication. https://www.bbc.com/persian/blogs/2016/04/160416_l44_nazeran_iran_islam_fridayprayer (June 17, 2023).
158 Qur'ān 2:185.
159 For a detailed discourse on the topic of fasting cf. az-Zuḥaylī, *Mawsūʿa al-fiqh al-islāmī*, vol. 2, 497–608.
160 Cf. Qur'ān 3:97.

the so-called great pilgrimage. The small pilgrimage, *ʿumra*, which is not mandatory, can be done at any time. The *ḥajj* ritual also involves intense physical exertion. Cleansing of the body and wearing clean clothing are of great importance. In addition, male pilgrims must wrap themselves in two white unseamed cloths before the pilgrimage. One white cloth is wrapped around the waist, and the second is used to cover the upper body. Sandals or flat shoes are worn. The head remains uncovered. During this time, pilgrims are not allowed to shave, comb, or cut their hair and nails. This state of consecration is called *iḥrām*. The usual Islamic clothing regulations apply to women in the state of consecration. Overall, women are also to dress simply. The *ḥajj* ceremony, performed by pilgrims from all over the Islamic world, clearly demonstrates how the Islamic religion encompasses different cultures, colors of skin, and traditions. The pilgrimage ends with the sacrificial festival (*ʿid al-aḍḥā*), in which every pilgrim slaughters a sacrificial animal. This day is the highest Islamic holiday and is also celebrated all over the world by Muslims who have stayed at home. Following this, the state of *iḥrām* – and, thus, the aforementioned prohibitions – is lifted.[161]

In summary, with regard to ritual practices of worship, it should be noted that the perspective of Islamic law is profoundly body-centered. The correctness of religious rites is measured according to external and verifiable physical criteria. It is ensured that all of the rites, down to their smallest detail, are carried out correctly. At the same time, ensuring that the human body does not suffer due to the performing of acts of worship and that it remains intact is of great relevance.

10.3 Organ Transplantation and Organ Donation

Organ transplantation (*naql al-aʿḍāʾ*) as a modern medical achievement is performed in all Islamic countries. The womb of a woman was transplanted into another woman for the first time in Saudi Arabia in 2000, even though the operation was ultimately unsuccessful.[162] Due to the widespread assumption that humans have no right to dispose of their body or body parts, as these are in the possession of the Creator God, many scholars initially rejected organ transplantation. Over time, however, a different trend emerged. Today organ transplantation and donation are fundamentally affirmed.[163] The practice is also constitutionally approved in many Islamic coun-

161 For a detailed discourse on the *ḥajj* rituals cf. az-Zuḥaylī, *Mawsūʿa al-fiqh al-islāmī*, vol. 3, 75–376.
162 Cf. Marḥabā, Ismāʿīl, *al-Bunūk aṭ-ṭibiyya al-bashariyya wa-aḥkāmuhā al-fiqhiyya*, Riyadh: Dār Ibn al-Jawzī, 2008, 71.
163 Cf. az-Zuḥaylī, *Mawsūʿa al-fiqh al-islāmī*, vol. 13, 18–19.

tries. Nevertheless, there are always restrictions caused by religious or political reasons. Al-Qaraḍāwī, who considers organ transplantation or donation to be legitimate, prioritizes, for instance, organ donation to a Muslim before a non-Muslim.[164] The Iranian Parliament, to give another example, passed a law in 2000 that allowed organ transplantation in general.[165] In 2015, however, the country's highest organ transplant council decided that the organ recipient must only be an Iranian citizen.[166]

Apart from such attempts at restrictions, there is usually a tendency among Muslim legal scholars to meet the requirements of medical progress by generally affirming organ transplantation or donation. In legal theory, they can use the *ijtihād* toolkit and to rethink responses regarding organ transplantation or donation. *Ijtihād* summarizes Muslim legal scholars' practice of acknowledging spatiotemporal circumstances when establishing the law.[167]

The following Ḥadīṯ is often cited in connection with this subject: *kasr ʿaẓm al-mayyit ka-kasrihi ḥayyan* (breaking the bone of a dead person is like breaking their bone when they were alive).[168] This tradition speaks for the integrity of the living and dead human body and can, therefore, be interpreted as being in opposition to organ transplantation. Nevertheless, this interpretation is being abandoned in favor of preserving the human body. For this, some legal scholars rely on the principle of *ḍarūra* (emergency), which states that "necessities render illicit things as lawful" (*aḍ-ḍarūrāt tubīḥ al-maḥẓūrāt*). Others argue that the principle of *maṣlaḥa* (common good), which states that legal provisions are subject to general normative goals (*maqāṣid ash-sharīʿa*), serve the well-being of Muslims and people in general. The primary goal of Sharia law is also to protect life. Since organ donation or transplantation is aimed at protecting human life, it is, thereby, understood as permissible.[169]

By referring to the attitude of the Islamic legal tradition, scholars agree to the stipulations of the European Convention and the World Health Organization that

---

164 Cf. El-Wereny, Mahmud, "Das Konzept der maṣlaḥa mursala: Theoretische Rahmenbedingungen und praktische Anwendung zwischen Tradition und Moderne," *Electronic Journal of Islamic and Middle Eastern Law (EJIMEL)* 4 (2016), 75–95, here 92.

165 Cf. https://www.ekhtebar.ir/قانون-پیوند-اعضای-بیماران-فوت-شده-یا-بی/ (June 17, 2023).

166 Cf. http://www.salamatnews.com/news/117795/ (June 17, 2023).

167 On the scope of the term *ijtihād* cf. Poya, Abbas, *Anerkennung des Iǧtihād – Legitimation der Toleranz. Möglichkeiten innerer und äußerer Toleranz im Islam am Beispiel der Iǧtihād-Diskussion*, Berlin: Klaus Schwarz Verlag, 2003.

168 Abū Dawūd, Sulaymān b. al-Ashʿath, *Sunan*, 5 vols., Beirut: Dār al-ḥadīth, 1969–1974, vol. 3, 543–544, Ḥadīṯ number 3207.

169 Cf. Krawietz, *Ḥurma*, 178 ff.

organ donation must only be voluntary (*tabarru'*). As justification, they refer to the Islamic legal principle *sadd aḏ-ḏarā'i'*, which states that every possibility of an evil deed must be prevented. Therefore, the sale or exchange of human organs is prohibited, so organ trading remains banned.[170] However, this assumption is based on the belief that humans lack any command of their organs, and therefore cannot sell and trade them:

> Trading and selling one of the [human] organs is prohibited under Sharia law. Because the human does not have command over his organs or his body. The human body is the possession of the sublime and creative God. Consequently, every part of the body is of the owner, the sublime God. The human is not authorized to dispense with a part of the body in return for contingent consideration. The body part is only an entrusted good to humans.[171]

10.4 Suicide

According to the language of the Qur'ān and Islamic law, the topic of suicide once again makes clear that the term *nafs*, which also means soul, primarily refers to the human body and the human being as such. When the Qur'ān and Islamic law condemn suicide (*qatl an-nafs*), it can only refer to the killing of the human body, because, according to popular Islamic belief, the soul lives on after death.

The term *intiḥār* (suicide) as such does not appear in the Qur'ān. However, the Qur'ān generally condemns the unlawful killing of a person (*nafs*) in certain places: "and kill not one another."[172] In another place the Qur'ān vaguely conveys: "[. . .] and cast not yourselves with your own hands into destruction [. . .]."[173] Nonetheless, scholars agree that these verses also refer to suicide. Al-Qaraḍāwī, for example, affirms that everything in the Qur'ān regarding killing as a crime can also be applied to suicide. He further argues that, whoever kills themself, no matter by which means, kills a person whose wrongful killing is forbidden by God.[174]

However, the Ḥadīṯs discuss the phenomenon of suicide in detail, the different types of suicide, and the punishments that will accompany them in the hereafter:

> Whoever kills himself with a knife will carry his knife in his hand and lead it to hellish flames and stay within them forever. And whoever takes poison and kills himself with it will carry his poison in his hand and drink it in hellfire and remain there forever; and who-

170 Cf. az-Zuḥaylī, *Mawsū'a al-fiqh al-islāmī*, vol. 13, 17–18.
171 az-Zuḥaylī, *Mawsū'a al-fiqh al-islāmī*, vol. 13, 18.
172 Qur'ān 4:29. For more examples cf. Qur'ān 4:92; 6:151; 17:33.
173 Qur'ān 2:195.
174 Cf. al-Qaraḍāwī, Yūsuf, *al-Ḥalāl wa-l-ḥarām fī-l-islām*, Cairo: Maktaba al-wahba, 2012, 377.

ever falls from a mountain and kills himself doing it will plunge into hellfire and remain in it forever.[175]

Following such Ḥadīṯs, Muslim legal scholars categorically reject suicide and describe it as the "most rejected thing" or the "worst sin." They describe the one who commits suicide as a "wicked sinner" or "inferior coward."[176] They fundamentally consider the ban on suicide as primacy of all people and religions.[177]

The vehement rejection of suicide is also based on the consideration that through the act of suicide people cross boundaries and assume a right to which they are not entitled. Humans are not the creators of their lives, and, therefore, do not own them.[178]

10.5 Suicide Bombing

Connected to the topic of suicide, it makes sense to briefly address the controversial question of suicide bombing. No matter which position a legal scholar takes in this context, the focus of their legal decision is always on corporeal matters. They do not discuss the mental or soulistic aspects of a suicide bombing at all.

Given the increasing number of suicide bombings committed by fanatical Muslims, supposedly justified by their vocal Islamic ideologists, suicide bombing is perceived by much of the public as a practice that is inherent to Islam and the Muslim tradition. Contrary to this widespread notion, suicide bombing, in which one kills oneself in order to cause human casualties and material damage to enemies, is a new topic in Muslim legal discourse. As such, it has not been discussed in older sources.

Linguistically speaking, the word *intiḥār* (suicide) in modern Arabic is also used in reference to suicide bombings. If one aims to express the deed as something positive and religiously worthwhile, they would use the term *istishhād*, which derives from the word *shahāda* (martyrdom).

However, today's scholars, who are characterized by a wide range of sociopolitical contexts, do not hold a uniform opinion on the subject of suicide bombings. With that said, there are no mainstream scholars who would fully affirm this practice. The Saudi and respected scholar Ibn ʿUthaymīn (1929–2001) categorically rejected suicide attacks, regardless of at whom it might be aimed. He also describes

175 Muslim Ibn al-Ḥajjāj, *Ṣaḥīḥ*, vol. 1, 103–104, Ḥadīṯ-Nr. 175.
176 Krawietz, *Ḥurma*, 94.
177 Cf. Krawietz, *Ḥurma*, 92.
178 Cf. Krawietz, *Ḥurma*, 91–92; al-Qaraḍāwī, *al-Ḥalāl wa-l-ḥarām fī-l-islām*, 377.

a suicide attack that is committed against the non-believer as *intiḥār*, subsumes it under the term suicide, and declares it forbidden with reference to the previously mentioned verse (4:29).[179] Al-Qaraḍāwī, in contrast, permits Palestinian suicide bombings in Israel and calls it *istishhād*. He also points out, however, that this fatwa is an exception. This practice is only permitted for the Palestinians because of their unique situation. It is not allowed in any other area, and, if possible, the Palestinians should also seek other means of self-defense.[180] The Shīʿite scholars mainly dealt with the topic after the establishment of the Islamic Republic, and, in principle, consider suicide bombing to be inadmissible. Some consider it legitimate only as a form of defense in a war of protecting religion.[181]

In sum, it is difficult to justify suicide bombing in the context of traditional argumentation under the law. The verse "*wa-lā-taqtulū anfusakum*" (and kill not one another), quoted above, plays a key role. Whereas opponents understand suicide bombing under the general statement of the verse prohibiting the killing of another person, proponents attempt to present it as a unique exception.

10.6 Clothing Restrictions

While some today have a concrete picture of how Muslims, and especially Muslim women, must dress, the clothing regulations and practices in Islam's beginnings were in fact anything but clear. The few passages in the Qur'ān that address this subject do not provide precise clothing regulations for women; rather, they are to be understood in the sense of general requests for moral and decent clothing.

The following verse fully deals with this question:

> And say to the believing women, that they cast down their eyes and guard their private parts, and reveal not their adornment save such as is outward; and let them cast their veils over their bosoms, and not reveal their adornment save to their husbands, or their fathers, or their husbands' fathers, or their sons, or their husbands' sons, or their brothers, or their brothers' sons, or their sisters' sons, or their women, or what their right hands own, or such men as attend them, not having sexual desire, or children who have not yet attained knowl-

179 Cf. ibn ʿUthaymīn, Muḥammad, *Majmūʿ fatāwā wa-rasāʾil fadhīla ash-Shaykh Muḥammad bin Ṣāliḥ al-ʿUthaymīn*, vol. 25, Fahd bin Nāṣir bin Ibrāhīm as-Sulaymān (ed.), ʿAnīza: Dār ath-Thurayyā, 2008, 361–364.

180 Cf. al-Qaraḍāwī, Yūsuf, *Fiqh al-jihād. Dirāsa muqārana li-aḥkāmihi wa-falsafatihi fī-dhawʾ al-qurʾān wa-s-sunna*, Cairo: Dār al-kutub al-miṣriyya, 2009, 1198–1199.

181 Cf. ad-Dūkhī, Falāḥ ʿAbd al-Ḥasan, *Haqq al-ḥayāt wa-ḥukm al-ʿamaliyyāt al-intiḥāriyya*, Qum: Muʾassisa walī-ʿaṣr li-d-dirāsāt al-islāmiyya, 2015, 65–69.

> edge of women's private parts; nor let them stamp their feet, so that their hidden ornament may be known. And turn all together to God, O you believers, haply so you will prosper.[182]

The verse asks women to cover their nakedness and charms and includes a comparatively detailed description of the woman's relatives whom she cannot marry, but it does not declare any rules on how women must dress. In another place, older women are even allowed to take off their clothes: "And such women advanced in years, who no longer feel any sexual desire, incur no sin if they discard their garments, provided they do not aim at a showy display of charms, but it is better for them to abstain [from this], and God is all-hearing, all-knowing."[183] In a third place, the women or daughters of the Prophet Muhammad and those of the believers are specifically addressed: "O Prophet, say to thy wives and daughters and the believing women, that they draw their veils close to them; so it is likelier they will be known and not hurt, God is all-forgiving, all-compassionate."[184] This passage does not contain precise information on clothing regulations either, but rather indicates that they were used to distinguish and therefore protect Muslim women at the time of the Prophet.

Over time, however, clothing ideas have assumed fixed accounts in the Islamic law, with implementation differing across various areas and traditions.

Principally, clothing regulations in Islamic law are determined by two criteria. On the one hand, the form of clothing must not imitate that of the opposite sex (*ʿadam tashabbuh al-marʾa bi-r-rajul wa-r-rajul bi-l-marʾa*), because, according to a known Ḥadīṯ, Muhammad curses the imitation of men by women and vice versa. On the other hand, the form of clothing must cover women's nakedness (*satr al-ʿawra*). It is not allowed for women to disobey this, or reveal more.[185] On the basis of these assumptions, scholars then try to determine which form and style of clothing is permitted for one gender or the other. Traditional legal scholars count, apart from the hand, foot, and face, all other parts of a woman's body as nakedness (*ʿawra*) and consider covering these parts as religious duty. For men, nakedness is usually limited to the genitals. He is also not allowed to wear silk clothing or gold jewellery. However, how these two basic assumptions are interpreted is ultimately at the discretion of the individual legal scholar. For example, the question of whether a woman can wear pants is answered differently. While one sees it as an

---

182 Qurʾān 24:31.
183 Qurʾān 24:60.
184 Qurʾān 33:59.
185 Cf. Krawietz, *Ḥurma*, 256.

imitation of men and, thus, declares it forbidden, another regards pants and coats as folk clothing and, thus, permissible for both men and women.[186]

Today, there are many voices amongst both Sunnis and Shī'ites who question the traditional dress code for women. They consider the Qur'ānic statements to be vague and in no way sufficient with regards to the traditional form of women's clothing. The Ḥadīṯs used in this context are considered as either weak or solitary (*āḥād*) and, therefore, not suitable for justifying the cause. For example, the former lawyer and member of the Egyptian State Council Muḥammad Sa'īd al-'Ashmāwī (1932–2013) questioned the widespread assumption that women must wear *ḥijāb* (veils). According to him, neither the Qur'ānic verses nor the Ḥadīṯ passages cited in this context can be used to support this alleged religious provision.[187] The Iranian critical scholar Aḥmad Qābil (d. 2012) first showed, through a historical analysis, how controversially the question of *ḥijāb* or headwear has been discussed in Shī'ite law. He then concluded that the "legal principle of rational indifference" (*iṣlāla al-ibāḥa al-'aqliyya*) always applies to a controversial and not definitely clarified legal question. In accordance with this principle, it can be inferred that the dress code for women means that they may wear headscarves, but that they are not obligated to do so. Accordingly, the Qur'ānic passages are not to be understood as an obligation to cover the head, rather only as a recommendation.[188]

The Syrian Muslim intellectual Muḥammad Shaḥrūr (1938–2019) considers the term *ḥijāb* to be incorrect and prefers to speak of *libās* (clothing).[189] He summarizes clothing regulations in Islam as follows. Men must cover their genitals and the covering of the other areas of the body is subject to respective customs and sensitivities. Women generally need to cover the genitals, breasts, and armpits. How they appear in public, however, depends on respective customs, sensitivities, and spatiotemporal circumstances. Head coverings have nothing to do with Islamic belief, neither for men nor for women. It is instead subject to social customs. In some cases, however, the maximum covering of the body except for the face and hands could be required for women. The covering of the face is to be considered as exceeding Islamic limits.[190]

186 Cf. Krawietz, *Ḥurma*, 257.
187 Cf. al-'Ashmāwī, Muḥammad Sa'īd, *Ḥaqīqa al-ḥijāb wa-ḥujjiyya al-ḥadīth*, Cairo: Mu'assisa rūz al-yūsuf, 1995.
188 Cf. Qābil, Aḥmad, *Dar mawrid-i ḥijāb*, available under the following link: https://3danet.ir/ghabel-hejab/ (June 17, 2023).
189 Cf. Shaḥrūr, Muḥammad, *Naḥw uṣūl jadīda li-l-fiqh al-islāmī. Fiqh al-mar'a. al-Waṣiyya, al-irth, al-qiwāma, at-ta'addudiyya, al-libās*, Damascus: al-Ahālī, 2000, 332 ff.
190 Cf. Shaḥrūr, *Naḥw uṣūl jadīda*, 378–379.

Beyond the question of how precise the clothing regulations are for men and women in Islam, some Muslim scholars consider clothing as a goodness that God has assigned to people which protects human dignity and sets them apart from other creatures.[191] In dressing, humans follow God's rule and maintain their dignity.[192] The Qur'ānic verse is also understood in this sense, it says: "Children of Adam, we have sent down on you a garment to cover your shameful parts [. . .]."[193] The Qur'ān already mentions the corporeal covering of Adam and Eve as one of their positive properties in paradise. They were bare when seduced by Satan and had to leave paradise:

> And We made a covenant with Adam before, but he forgot, and We found in him no constancy. [. . .] And We said "Adam, surely, this [Satan] is an enemy to you and your wife; so let him not expel you both from the Garden, so that you are unprosperous. It is assuredly given to you, neither to hunger therein, nor to go naked." [. . .] Then Satan whispered to him saying "Adam, shall I point you of eternity, and a kingdom that decays not?" So, the two of them ate of it, and their shameful parts revealed to them, and they took to stitching upon themselves leaves of the Garden. And Adam disobeyed his Lord, and so he erred.[194]

10.7 Cremation

Muslim scholars generally assume that the cremation of corpses is prohibited. This consensus is based on the assumption that Islamic rules treat humans, not only the living but also the dead, with *ḥurma* (integrity) or *karāma* (dignity). To justify this assumption, scholars refer to verse 17:70, which states: "And we have honoured the children of Adam [. . .]." In addition, some Ḥadīṯs explicitly prohibit damaging the human body in general, whether it is living or not. They cite, among others, the Ḥadīṯ quoted above ("breaking the bone of a dead person is like breaking his bone when he lived"[195]).

In this respect, there is a continuing consensus among Muslim legal scholars that the cremation of corpses is prohibited. They assert that the respectful treatment of corpses is a religious requirement and is part of the dignified treatment of the body that is buried in the grave upon death.[196] The Qur'ān also illustrates how to deal with a corpse in the story of Cain and Abel. After Cain killed his

---

191 Cf. al-Ghāmidī, Nāṣir b. Muḥammad b. Mushrī, *Libās ar-rajul, aḥkāmuhu wa-ḍawābiṭuhu fī-l-fiqh al-islāmī*, Mecca: Dār ṭayyiba al-khaḍra', 1434 h, 68.

192 Cf. al-Ghāmidī, *Libās ar-rajul*, 71.

193 Qur'ān 7:26.

194 Qur'ān 20:115, 117, 118, 120, 121.

195 Abū Dawūd, *Sunan*, 543–544, Ḥadīṯ Number 3207.

196 Cf. Krawietz, *Ḥurma*, 119–121.

brother, he stood embarrassed in front of the body, and evidently did not know what to do with it: "Then God sent forth a raven, scratching into the earth, to show him, how he might conceal the vile body of his brother [. . .]."[197]

With regards to this, Islamic sources speak out against cremation. Hence, many scholars consider cremation to be an "outdated" and "barbaric" custom and a hideous and painful practice that degrades the human body.[198]

Some scholars are so consistent in their rejection that they hardly allow exceptions. Neither the danger of an epidemic nor the state-prescribed practice in hospitals to burn the bodies of miscarriages and stillbirths make them change their minds.[199] A violent dispute arose among Cairo scholars in 2017 over the question of whether Ebola-infected bodies may be cremated. While the Egyptian Fatwa Office (*dār al-iftā'*), in agreement with medical opinion, allowed the cremation of Ebola-infected bodies, many other legal scholars have spoken out and rejected the fatwa.[200] To date, cremation in the event of an epidemic threat has not found a majority acceptance among scholars.

10.8 The Punishment and Pleasure of the Grave

It seems that many of the earlier theologians, especially the Muʿtazilites, questioned the punishment of the grave.[201] Since then, both Sunnis and Shīʿites have reached a consensus that there is a punishment or a reward in the grave. This means that the life on the other side does not begin immediately after death. Muslim scholars speak of an intermediate station (*barzakh*) that lies between this world and the beyond. Lexically, *barzakh* means that which divides two things, such as a dividing wall. The technical term denotes the space between this world and the hereafter.[202] In this intermediate station, good humans experience joy and bad humans are punished. Hence, scholars like Ibn Qayyim al-Jawziyya (1292–1350) also refer to the punishment and pleasure of the grave (*ʿaḏāb al-qabr wa-naʿīmuhu*) as punishment and joy in *barzakh* (*ʿaḏāb al-barzakh wa-naʿīmuhu*).[203]

197 Qur'ān 5:31.
198 Cf. Krawietz, *Ḥurma*, 121–122.
199 Cf. Krawietz, *Ḥurma*, 122–125.
200 Cf. about this difference of opinion https://www.albawabhnews.com/2385475 (June 20, 2023).
201 Cf. Al-Ashʿarī, Abū al-Ḥasan, *al-Ibāna ʿan uṣūl ad-diyāna*, Ḥusayn Maḥmūd (ed.), Cairo: Dār al-anṣār, 1397 h., 14–15.
202 Cf. Bin Ḥaydar, Muḥammad, *Aḥādīth ḥayāt al-barzakh fī-l-kutub at-tisʿa*, Beirut: Dār ibn ḥazm, 2004, 30–31.
203 Cf. Bin Ḥaydar, *Aḥādīth ḥayāt al-barzakh fī-l-kutub at-tisʿa*, 32.

Since death is usually explained by the soul leaving the body, the scholars first had to explain how corpses could consciously experience the punishment or pleasure of the grave when lying without soul or life. Therefore, they either assumed that the soul does not leave the body immediately, or that it returns to it again.[204] When a person is in the grave, depending on the description, two, four, or six angels (or figures) come to them. The best-known grave angels are *Munkar* (the denied) and *Nakīr* (the denier). They question the dead about their beliefs. At the center of the asking procedure is the question of belief in a God and the Prophet Muhammad. According to their own beliefs, the Shīʿites also include the question of the names of their imams. If the answers contradict Islamic belief, the grave becomes narrower and more oppressive. If the answers are in the spirit of Islamic belief, the grave becomes wider and more comfortable.[205] In spite of that, there are Ḥadīṯs that report about the punishment in the grave for the believers who neglect small Islamic regulations. For example, a Ḥadīṯ tells how the Prophet Muhammad, accompanied by some of his followers, heard the punishment of two Muslims in a grave. When asked about the reason for their punishment, he said that one came into contact with his urine and the other slandered.[206]

The detailed descriptions of the punishment or joy of the grave are different and ultimately resemble those of hell or paradise. While non-believers experience fire and heat, believers live under shade in the Garden.[207] Some refer to other passages in the Qurʾān and speak of the beating of the faces and backs of non-believers.[208] It is generally difficult to prove punishment of the grave using solely the Qurʾān. Therefore, some other scholars apply the aforementioned verses to the afterlife and Great Judgment.[209]

The statements of the Ḥadīṯ regarding the intermediate station are not uniform and, in some places, can be irritating. The well-known Ḥadīṯ collector Muslim transmitted the following Ḥadīṯ of the prophet Muhammad in the chapter "The Book on Paradise and the Nature of its Comforts and Dwellers" in his Ḥadīṯ collection *Ṣaḥīḥ*:

> When a dead person has been placed in his grave and the mourners leave and he hears the roar of their sandals, then two angels come to him, who let him sit up and ask him: "What have you always said about the man [Muhammad]?" The believer then replies: "I testify

---

204 Cf. van Ess, *Theologie und Gesellschaft*, vol. 4, 528.
205 Cf. van Ess, *Theologie und Gesellschaft*, vol. 4, 528–530.
206 Cf. al-Bukhārī, Muḥammad b. Ismāʿīl, *Ṣaḥīḥ*, 9 vols., Muḥammad Zuhayr b. Nāṣir an-Nāṣir (ed.), Beirut: Dār aṭ-ṭawq an-najāt, 1422 h., vol. 1, 53, Ḥadīṯ-Nr. 216.
207 Cf. Bin Ḥaydar, *Aḥādīth ḥayāt al-barzakh fī-l-kutub at-tisʿa*, 32 ff.
208 Cf. Qurʾān 8:50; 47:27.
209 Cf. van Ess, *Theologie und Gesellschaft*, vol. 4, 528–529.

> that he is the servant and the messenger of God." Then it will said to him: "Look, there is your place made of fire, but God has replaced it with a place in paradise for you" and he will be able to see both places.[210]

Here one might ask: How can fire and paradise already be mentioned in the *barzakh* phase?

Even if the punishment or pleasure of the grave is a common idea in Islam and many scholars declare it a religious dogma in which every Muslim must believe, accepting the principle has obviously not been easy for everyone. For example, the Khārijites rejected the idea of grave punishment and joy. Some rationalists (Muʿtazilites) also struggled with the idea. Philosophers like Ibn Sīnā interpreted the text that points to a grave punishment as metaphorical and cran "expression of inner torment."[211]

In Islam, belief in the punishment of the grave has led to the practice of *talqīn* shortly before one's death. This means that the dying person (*muḥtaḍar*) is presented with the Islamic creeds and should repeat them if they are able to. This is practiced so that the dying person might not forget the foundations of the faith or make a mistake when they encounter the angels of the grave, thereby avoiding the grave's narrowness and horror. The Shīʿite scholar, Sayyid Ibn Ṭāwūs (1193–1266), is reported to have had the names of the twelve Shīʿite imams engraved on a gem, and to have asked for it to be put in his mouth as he died so that he might answer correctly the questions of the angels of the grave.[212]

As we have seen, Islamic ideas and practices associated with the dogma of the punishment and pleasure of the grave are related to material and corporeal experiences. Few rationalist theologians and philosophers clearly challenge this idea, or, as is the case with Ibn Sīnā, attempt to metaphorically interpret the punishment of the grave in relation to the human soul.

11 The Celebration of Corporeal Suffering in Shīʿite Islam

No other Muslim denomination adopts material expression of religious rituals as the Shīʿites do. The death of the third Shīʿite Imam Ḥusayn in 680 in Karbalā at the hands of the troops of the second Umayyad caliph Yazīd (647–683) is the most for-

210 Muslim Ibn al-Ḥajjāj, *Ṣaḥīḥ*, vol. 4, 51–52, Ḥadīṯ-Nr. 2870.
211 Van Ess, *Theologie und Gesellschaft*, vol. 4, 529.
212 Cf. van Ess, *Theologie und Gesellschaft*, vol. 4, 531.

mative moment in Shī'ite history. This is why some scholars, such as Heinz Halm, attribute the emergence of Shī'ism as a special religious practice in relation to this dramatic event and the rites which developed immediately thereafter.[213] Following the death of the caliph Mu'āwiya in Damascus in 680, his designated successor and son Yazīd assumed his position. The Shī'ites in Kūfa (present day Iraq) invited Ḥusayn, the grandson of the Prophet Muhammad, who lived in Medina, to come to Kūfa to lead the Shī'ites and overthrow Yazīd's rule.

Accompanied by his family and a handful of loyal relatives and friends, Ḥusayn set off for Kūfa. However, Ḥusayn and his companions were soon beleaguered by troops loyal to the government and pushed into the area of Karbalā, seventy kilometers north of Kūfa and twenty kilometers west of the Euphrates. Despite initially announcing allegiance, not a single one of his followers from Kūfa came to support him. Ḥusayn and his small group, around seventy men and some women and children, were under siege by a large contingent of roughly 4,000 soldiers. They were not allowed to leave and had no access to water. The siege lasted more than a week (2nd–10th *muḥarram*, 680) and was occasionally accompanied by skirmishes. The last few days are primarily characterized by the repeated but unsuccessful attempts by Ḥusayn and his companions to get to water. On the tenth day (*'āshūrā*), the government troops stormed the camp and put a bloody end to the uprising of Ḥusayn and his small following. Ḥusayn and all of his male companions, including his half-brother, nephew, and two of his sons, died. After the massacre, the dead were buried there and the captive women, accompanied by Ḥusayn's only surviving son, 'Alī Zayn al-'Ābidīn, were sent away to Kūfa and then to the residence of the caliph in Medina.[214]

This tragedy soon provoked remorse and the feeling of having sinned among many Shī'ites, especially those in Kūfa because, according to the Shī'ite perception, they abandoned the grandson of Muhammad in his unequal struggle against the unlawful caliphate of Yazīd. From this point on, numerous rituals developed amongst the Shī'ites, which evolved over time and partly under the influence of other cultures. On the one hand, these rituals, carried out by physical means should express their sorrow for the death of Ḥusayn and his companions. On the other hand, they are a way of expressing the Shī'ites' remorse for their absence and failure to support Ḥusayn. Furthermore, they are intended to showcase the Shī'ites' willingness to stand up for the cause of Ḥusayn, and their readiness to sacrifice themselves for him and his purposes.

---

213 Cf. Halm, Heinz, *Der schiitische Islam. Von der Religion zur Revolution*, Munich: C.H. Beck, 1994, 29.

214 Cf. Halm, Heinz, *Die Schiiten*, Munich: C.H. Beck, 2005, 17–18.

These rites are usually accompanied by great bodily exertion and at times even injuries. In the first period after the events of Karbalā, the rites consisted of making a pilgrimage to the tomb of Ḥusayn and mourning together. When believers did not visit the grave, they mourned Ḥusayn's death in their homes and sometimes in public. Some report women who exhibited their grief with loose hair in public. Later, and especially after the establishment of Shīʿism as the official religion in Iran in the 16th century, many other rites were added. These include: performing a passion play in which the tragic events of Karbalā are spectacularly depicted; beating the chest, with one or both hands in rhythm with a song of mourning; beating the head of those present, with one or both hands; performing chain scourges, in which the mourners, usually only men, hit their heads, chests, or backs with a bundle of chains; and beating with daggers, in which the mourners, usually only men, hit their heads or back with bare blades or with a bundle of chains to which small blades are attached.[215]

Even though most scholars reject these bloody and self-injurious performances and declare them inadmissible, ordinary Shīʿites continue to cultivate and develop them, because: "[T]he real core of every religion is the ritual that the believers perform together and not the web of thought with which the theologians cover afterwards. The community is constituted in the execution of the ritual, not in the commitment to dogma."[216]

Many researchers see parallels between the *ʿāshūrā* rites and some customs from other cultures and religions. Some look for the origin of these rites in the ancient oriental lament of the killed god of Spring Tammuz (Adonis) or the mythical Iranian hero Siyawush.[217] The area of the Land of the Two Rivers, which is regarded as the cradle of the Shīʿite denomination, was already familiar with the ritual forms: for instance, crying as an expression of penance and part of worship. The Manicheans in this area, as well as the Christians, Jews, and early Muslims, considered crying as something that cleanses the body of sins.[218] Heinz Halm notes "very similar motifs" between the Shīʿite and the Christian flagellants, "whose processions are first witnessed in central Italy in 1260."[219] Interestingly, like the Shīʿites, flagellation was not well received by the official church and was finally banned in 1417. The movement continued to live on, not only on the Iberian Peninsula in

215 Cf. Halm, *Die Schiiten*, 39–55.

216 Halm, *Der schiitische Islam*, 53.

217 Cf. Yarshater, Ehsan, "Taʿziyeh and Pre-Islamic Mourning Rites in Iran," in: Peter J. Chelkowsky (ed.), *Taʿziyeh: Ritual and Drama in Iran*, New York: New York University Press, 1979, 88 ff.

218 Cf. Halm, *Der schiitische Islam*, 54.

219 Halm, *Der schiitische Islam*, 94–95.

Spain, but also around the world, from areas in South America to New Mexico: "The Holy Week plays a similar role there as does *ʿāshūrā* for the Shīʿites."[220]

Beyond the question of whether and in what form foreign influences can be found in the Shīʿite *ʿāshūrā* rituals, they certainly represent to the outside world a special corporeal demonstration of one's personal religious conviction. Nonetheless, these performances are criticized by many other Muslims, and not only contemporary ones. When the aforementioned mystic Rumi observed a *muḥarram* procession at the gates of Aleppo, for instance, he sharply condemned it and considered it senseless to mourn a long-decayed body.[221] Among Shīʿites, these ritual practices are often critically assessed. Reform scholars and religious intellectuals in particular consider many *ʿāshūrā* rites and sermons to be inauthentic or inappropriate. They understand many stories of the Karbalā tragedy as fictional narratives to enhance dramatization. The idea that the performance of *muḥarram* ceremonies, such as crying, causes the individual or collective cleansing of the sin of the Shīʿa, is also considered fundamentally invalid by many.[222] On the whole, however, scholars maintain a "soft" form of *ʿāshūrā* rites – such as crying or light hand slapping on the chest – because of their own interest in not losing religious followers. However, they reject the "hard" rituals, such as flagellation and using daggers.

12 Conclusion

In summary, the following points can be considered as the outcomes of the present study on the concept of the body in Islam:

– In Islam, one generally assumes that the human consists of two basic components: the body (*badan, jism*) and the spirit (*rūḥ*) or soul (*nafs*). The body represents the visible, the comprehensible, and the explainable, while the mind, spirit, or soul represent the mysterious, the indescribable, and the puzzling.

– In the Qurʾān, Islamic theology and Islamic law, the material and body-oriented perception of the human dominates. The spirit is distinguished from the body as a life-giving force. The majority of the descriptions of the spirit also indicate a material idea. Nevertheless, from this perspective, the human can only exist as a unit (body and soul), perform religious rites, and will be resurrected after death.

220 Halm, *Der schiitische Islam*, 97.
221 Cf. Halm, *Der schiitische Islam*, 56.
222 Cf. Murtaḍā, Muṭahharī, *Ḥamāsa-i ḥusaynī*, 2 vols., Qum: Ṣadrā, 2000.

Thereby, the body is of central importance for several reasons: a) anthropologically, due to a material – and at the same time anti-dualistic – idea of the human being, b) ritually, regarding the performance of religious practices, and c) eschatologically, in terms of the belief in humans' corporeal resurrection. From this perspective, the focus is always on the material and tangible human. As such, humans are responsible for good as well as bad deeds and will experience the punishment or pleasure of the grave and the reward or punishment in the hereafter.

– Both Islamic philosophy (as briefly explained using the example of Ibn Sīnā) and Islamic mysticism, for the most part, cultivate a dualistic, Platonic perspective, while simultaneously maintaining a strong focus on the soul. From this perspective, the human body is not ascribed a major role, it rather only gains value through the soul. Whereas the body stands for the transient, mortal, evil, and menial, the immortal soul provides the liberation of humanity from animalistic and natural desires and strives for the good and sublime. From this point of view, only a spiritual resurrection could be understood. After all, mystics arguing for this understanding also emphasize the value of the human body as a divine creation, that God created in His own image. However, this assumption does not prevent them from focusing on the immaterial in humans and the soul of religious practice.

– During the early stages of Islamic history, material viewpoints were widespread in accordance with the wording of the Qur'ān, nevertheless, as time passed, Muslims increasingly looked for more complex explanations of human existence and advocated the immaterial and the spiritual as the center of their interpretations.

– The widespread view in Islam is that of body-oriented religiosity. This still shapes Muslims' everyday religious practices. The traditional educational institutions in both Sunni and Shīʿite thinking have always primarily dealt with legal teachings, which largely focus on the body. Philosophy and mysticism are generally condemned or treated by a few lateral thinkers on the margins of official teaching. Even Qur'ānic exegesis and Ḥadīṯ studies are usually neglected and mostly viewed as "service providers" for legal studies. The complexity of rational and mystical approaches made it more difficult for them to reach the Muslim masses. This intangible perspective still forms the view of the so-called educated middle class.[223]

223 Lutz Berger, in connection to the decline of the Muʿtazilites, found that due to the complexity of their teaching, they were always only accessible to the educational elite and could hardly find any willingness to teach at the Madrasas (cf. Berger, *Islamische Theologie*, 79). This can easily be transferred to philosophy and mysticism.

– People's understanding of the nature of the human being and the human body developed similarly in the three Abrahamic religions. As already mentioned, in Islam, things were initially imagined to be simple, material, physical – and thus more tangible – for ordinary people. Over time, however, discourse has become more complex and people have been increasingly looking for deeper, unseeable, and intangible motives in religion. Christoph Markschies impressively analyzes this process in his fundamental study of God's body in relation to Christianity. In his work, he describes how the physical image of God in early Christianity developed into a disembodied, and even depersonalized image of God in the modern times. While the corporeal conception of God today is generally regarded as naive, simple-minded, and infantile, the disembodied image of God corresponds to enlightened, modern, and contemporary religious understanding. The transition in the idea of God from physical to less or barely physical is directly related to the increasing influence of ancient philosophy on religious discourse and the rational explanation of religious assumptions.[224] This development can also be found in Judaism. Whereas a material and anti-dualistic understanding dominated in the earlier centuries of Judaism, in the Middle Ages, and under the influence of Aristotle and Plotinus, Jewish philosophers and theologians such as Maimonides (1135–1204) viewed the body as purely material, which can only be purified and sanctified by intellectual effort. In the Kabbalistic tradition, people look for the experience of a direct relationship with God. In the 18th and 19th centuries, however, critical Jewish philosophers and activists questioned this perception of the body and tried to revive the original Jewish concepts to centralize the body.[225]

– The last point that I would like to mention here, which could be the subject of a future study, is that there is a clear relationship between mindsets toward the human body and mindsets toward the "bodies" of religious texts. The more one focuses on the exteriors of religious texts, the more one concentrates on the external and corporeal dimensions of religion. Conversely, the more one looks at the soul, the spirit, or the insides of the human, the more one examines the meaning and soul of religious texts. Therefore, it seems only logical that a material viewpoint leads more to formalist and external religious practices, whereas immaterial viewpoints emphasize the inner religious meanings and rules.

---

224 Cf. Markschies, Christoph, *Gottes Körper. Jüdische, christliche und pagane Gottesvorstellungen in der Antike*, Munich: C.H. Beck, 2016, 19 ff.
225 Cf. Markschies, *Gottes Körper*, 21 ff.

Bibliography

Abū Dawūd, Sulaymān b. al-Ash'ath, *Sunan*, 5 vols., Beirut: Dār al-ḥadīth, 1969–1974.

Asad, Muhammad, *Die Botschaft des Koran. Übersetzung und Kommentar*, Düsseldorf: Patmos, 2009.

al-Ash'arī, Abū al-Ḥasan, *al-Ibāna 'an uṣūl ad-diyāna*, Ḥusayn Maḥmūd (ed.), Cairo: Dār al-anṣār, 1397 h.

al-Ash'arī, Abū al-Ḥasan, *Kitāb al-luma' fī-radd 'alā ahl al-ziyagh wa-l-bida'*, Ḥamūda Gharāba, (ed.), Cairo: Maṭba'a miṣr, 1955.

al-Ash'arī, Abū al-Ḥasan, *Maqālāt al-islāmiyyin wa-ikhtilāf al-muṣallīn*, Hellmut Ritter (ed.), Wiesbaden: Franz Steiner, 1980.

al-'Ashmāwī, Muḥammad Sa'īd, *Ḥaqīqa al-ḥijāb wa-ḥujjiyya al-ḥadīth*, Cairo: Mu'assisa rūz al-yūsuf, 1995.

Beckermann, Ansgar, *Das Leib-Seele-Problem. Eine Einführung in die Philosophie des Geistes*, Paderborn: Fink, 2008.

Berger, Lutz, *Islamische Theologie*, Vienna: Facultas, 2010.

Bin Ḥaydar, Muḥammad, *Aḥādīth ḥayāt al-barzakh fī-l-kutub at-tis'a*, Beirut: Dār Ibn Ḥazm, 2004.

al-Bukhārī, Muḥammad b. Ismā'īl, *Ṣaḥīḥ*, 9 vols., Muḥammad Zuhayr b. Nāṣir an-Nāṣir (ed.), Beirut: Dār aṭ-ṭawq an-najāt, 1422 h.

Busse, Heribert, "Jerusalem in the story of Muhammad's night journey and ascension," *Jerusalem Studies in Arabic and Islam* 14 (1991), 1–40.

ad-Dūkhī, Falāḥ 'Abd al-Ḥasan, *Haqq al-ḥayāt wa-ḥukm al-'amaliyyāt al-intiḥāriyya*, Qum: Mu'assisa walī-'aṣr li-d-dirāsāt al-islāmiyya, 2015.

El-Wereny, Mahmud, "Das Konzept der maṣlaḥa mursala: Theoretische Rahmenbedingungen und praktische Anwendung zwischen Tradition und Moderne," *Electronic Journal of Islamic and Middle Eastern Law (EJIMEL)* 4 (2016), 75–95.

al-Ghāmidī, Nāṣir b. Muḥammad b. Mushrī, *Libās ar-rajul, aḥkāmuhu wa-ḍawābiṭuhu fī-l-fiqh al-islāmī*, Mecca: Dār ṭayyiba al-khaḍra', 1434 h.

al-Ghazālī, Abū Ḥāmid, *Das Elixier der Glückseligkeit*, trans. Hellmut Ritter, Wiesbaden: Marixverlag, 2016.

al-Ghazālī, Abū Ḥāmid, *Iḥyā' 'ulūm ad-dīn*, 4 vols., Beirut: Dār al-ma'rifa, n. d.

Gramlich, Richard, *Weltverzicht. Grundlagen und Weisen islamischer Askese*, Wiesbaden: Harrassowitz, 1997.

Griffel, Frank, *Al-Ghazālī's Philosophical Theology*, Oxford: Oxford University Press, 2009.

Halm, Heinz, *Der schiitische Islam. Von der Religion zur Revolution*, Munich: C.H. Beck, 1994.

Halm, Heinz, *Die Schiiten*, Munich: C.H. Beck, 2005.

Ḥasanzāda, Ṣāliḥ, "Ḥaqīqat-i nafs wa-rūḥ dar qur'ān wa-ḥikmat-i islāmī," *Pažūhishnāma-i ma'ārif-i qur'ānī* 25 (2016), 55–82. Available under the following link: http://rjqk.atu.ac.ir/article_7085_771b1aff484fd8f93077d93dcadd4ff6.pdf (June 17, 2023).

Heath, Peter, *Allegory and Philosophy in Avicenna (Ibn Sīnā) with a Translation of the Book of the Prophet Muhammad's Ascent to Heaven*, Philadelphia: University of Pennsylvania Press, 1992.

Ibn Ḥanbal, Aḥmad, *ar-Radd 'alā al-jahmiyya wa-z-zanādiqa*, Ṣabrī bin Salāma Shāhīn (ed.), n. p., n. d.

Ibn Sīnā, Abū 'Alī, *al-Ishārāt wa-t-tanbihāt*, 3 vols., Qum: al-Balāgha, 1996.

Ibn Sīnā, Abū 'Alī, *Mi'rājnāma*, Najīb Māyil Harawī (ed.), Mashhad: Bunyād-i pazhūhishhā-i islāmī-i āstān-i quds-i raḍawī, 1986.

Ibn Sīnā, Abū 'Alī, *Risāla fī-ma'rifa an-nafs an-nāṭiqa wa-aḥwālihā*, Windsor: Hindawi, 2017.

Ibn Sīnā, Abū 'Alī, *ash-Shifā'*, 10 vols., Maḥmūd Qāsim (ed.), Cairo: al-Idāra al-'āmma li-th-thaqāfa, n. d.

Ibn 'Uthaymīn, Muḥammad, *Majmū' fatāwā wa-rasā'il fadhīla ash-Shaykh Muḥammad bin Ṣāliḥ al-'Uthaymīn*, vol. 3, Fahd bin Nāṣir bin Ibrāhīm as-Sulaymān (ed.), 'Anīza: Dār ath-Thurayyā, 1992.

Ibn 'Uthaymīn, Muḥammad, *Majmū' fatāwā wa-rasā'il fadhīla ash-Shaykh Muḥammad bin Ṣāliḥ al-'Uthaymīn*, vol. 25, Fahd bin Nāṣir bin Ibrāhīm as-Sulaymān (ed.), 'Anīza: Dār ath-Thurayyā, 2008.

Iqbal, Muhammad, *The Reconstruction of Religious Thought in Islam*, Moscow: Dodo Press, *2009*.
Katz, Marion Holmes, *Body of Text. The Emergence of the Sunnī Law of Ritual Purity*, New York: State University of New York Press, 2002.
Krawietz, Birgit, *Die Ḥurma. Schariarechtlicher Schutz vor Eingriffen in die körperliche Unversehrtheit nach arabischen Fatwas des 20. Jahrhunderts*, Berlin: Duncker und Humblot, 1991.
Kugle, Scott, *Sufis & Saints' Bodies. Mysticisms, Corporeality, & Sacred Power in Islam*, Chapel Hill, NC: The University of North Carolina Press, 2007.
Lerch, Wolfgang Günter, *Tod in Bagdad oder Leben und Sterben des Al-Halladsch*, Düsseldorf: Artemis & Winkler, 1997.
Lohff, Brigitte, "Vitalismus," in: Werner E. Gerabek et al. (eds.), *Enzyklopädie Medizingeschichte*, Berlin: Walter de Gruyter, 2005, 1449–1451.
Malakī, Taqī Āzad / Ghurāb, Nāṣir ad-Dīn, "Jāygāh-i badan dar dīn," *Muṭāliʿāt-i farhangī wa-irtibāṭāt* 18 (2010), 10–35.
Maʿmūrī, ʿAlī, *Namāz-i ǧumʿa, tašayyuʿ-i siyāsī wa-inqilāb-i islāmī*, Online publication. https://www.bbc.com/persian/blogs/2016/04/160416_l44_nazeran_iran_islam_fridayprayer (June 17, 2023).
Marḥabā, Ismāʿīl, *al-Bunūk aṭ-ṭibiyya al-bashariyya wa-aḥkāmuhā al-fiqhiyya*, Riyadh: Dār Ibn al-Jawzī, 2008.
Markschies, Christoph, *Gottes Körper. Jüdische, christliche und pagane Gottesvorstellungen in der Antike*, Munich: C.H. Beck, 2016.
Mokhtar, Mustafa Kamal, "The Treatise on Knowledge. About the Rational Soul and its States by Ibn Sina: A Critical Edition and Annotated Translation," *Akademika* 44 (1994), 45–71.
Murtaḍā, Muṭahharī, *Ḥamāsa-i ḥusaynī*, 2 vols., Qum: Ṣadrā, 2000.
Murtaza, Mohammad Sameer, *Islamische Existenzialphilosophie – Muhammad Iqbal nietzscheanisch gelesen*, Norderstedt: BoD – Books on Demand, 2016.
Muslim Ibn al-Ḥajjāj, Abu l-Ḥusayn, *Ṣaḥīḥ*, 5 vols., Muḥammad Fuʾād ʿAbd al-Bāqī (ed.), Beirut: Dār iḥyāʾ at-turāth al-ʿarabī, 1955.
Nasr, Seyyed Hossein, *An Introduction to Islamic Cosmological Doctrines. Conceptions of Nature and Methods Used for Its Study by the Ikhwān al-Ṣafāʾ, al-Bīrūnī, and Ibn Sīnā*, Cambridge: Harvard University Press, 1964.
Nasr, Seyyed Hossein, *Three Muslim Sages. Avicenna – Suhrawardī – Ibn ʿArabī*, New York: Caravan books, 1964.
Netton, Ian Richard, "Private Caves and Public Islands: Islam, Plato and the Ikhwān al-Ṣafāʾ," in: Maha El Kaisy-Friemuth / John M. Dillon (eds.), *The Afterlife of the Platonic Soul. Reflections of Platonic Psychology in the Monotheistic Religion*s, Leiden: Brill, 2009, 105–120.
Nijāt, Ḥamīd Riḍā Fatḥ / Jāwdān, Muḥammad, "Dīdgāh-i shaykh mufīd dar bāra-i ḥaqīqat-i insān (The opinions of Shaykh Mufīd regarding the nature of man)," *Journal of Islamic Denominations (Pažūhishnāma-i madhāhib-i islāmī)* 9 (2018), 95–110.
Popp, Stephan, *Mohammad Iqbal. Ein Philosoph*, Nordhausen: Bautz, 2007.
Poya, Abbas, *Anerkennung des Iǧtihād – Legitimation der Toleranz. Möglichkeiten innerer und äußerer Toleranz im Islam am Beispiel der Iǧtihād-Diskussion*, Berlin: Klaus Schwarz Verlag, 2003.
Qābil, Aḥmad, *Dar mawrid-i ḥijāb*, Available under the following link: https://3danet.ir/ghabel-hejab/ (June 17, 2023).
al-Qaraḍāwī, Yūsuf, *Fiqh al-jihād. Dirāsa muqārana li-aḥkāmihi wa-falsafatihi fī-dhawʾ al-qurʾān wa-s-sunna*, Cairo: Dār al-kutub al-miṣriyya, 2009.
al-Qaraḍāwī, Yūsuf, *al-Ḥalāl wa-l-ḥarām fī-l-islām*, Cairo: Maktaba al-wahba, 2012.
Razavi, Mehdi Amin, *Suhrawardi and the School of Illumination*, Richmond: Curzon Press, 1997.
ar-Rāzī, Fakhr ad-Dīn, *Tafsīr al-kabīr*, 32 vols., Beirut: Dār iḥyaʾ at-turāth al-ʿarabī, 1420 h.

Robinson, Howard, "Dualism," in: Stephen P. Stich / Ted A. Warfield (eds.), *The Blackwell Guide to Philosophy of Mind*, Malden: Blackwell, 2003, 85–101.
Rudolph, Ulrich, *Islamische Philosophie: Von den Anfängen bis zur Gegenwart*, Munich: C.H. Beck, 2013.
Rūmī, Jalāl ad-Dīn Muḥammad, *Kulliyyāt-i shams-i tabrīzī*, Tehran: Pagāh, 1984.
Rūmī, Jalāl ad-Dīn Muḥammad, *Mathnawī maʿnawī*, Tehran: Amīr kabīr, 1993.
Schimmel, Annemarie, *Sufismus. Eine Einführung in die islamische Mystik*, Munich: C.H. Beck, 2014.
Shaḥrūr, Muḥammad, *Naḥw uṣūl jadīda li-l-fiqh al-islāmī. Fiqh al-marʾa. al-Waṣiyya, al-irth, al-qiwāma, at-taʿaddudiyya, al-libās*, Damascus: al-Ahālī, 2000.
Stephan, Achim, "Das Leib-Seele-Problem," in: *Lexikon der Neurowissenschaft*, Heidelberg: Spektrum Akademischer Verlag, 2000. Available under the following link: https://www.spektrum.de/lexikon/neurowissenschaft/leib-seele-problem/6967 (June 17, 2023).
Strohmaier, Gotthard, *Ibn Sīnā*, Munich: C.H. Beck, 2006.
Suleiman, Farid, *Ibn Taymiyya und die Attribute Gottes*, Berlin: Walter de Gruyter, 2019.
at-Ṭabarī, Abū Jaʿfar Muḥammad b. Jarīr, *Jāmiʿ al-bayān fī-taʾwīl al-qurʾān*, 24 vols., Aḥmad Muḥammad Shākir (ed.), Beirut: Muʾassisa ar-risāla, 2000.
at-Ṭabarī, Abū Jaʿfar Muḥammad Ibn Jarīr, *Tāʾrīkh ar-rusul wa-l-mulūk*, 11 vols., Beirut: Dār at-turāth, 1387 h.
Turki, Mohamed, *Eine Einführung in die arabisch-islamische Philosophie*, Freiburg: Karl Alber, 2015.
van Ess, Josef, *Theologie und Gesellschaft im 2. und 3. Jahrhundert Hidschra: Eine Geschichte des religiösen Denkens im frühen Islam*, 6 vols., Berlin: Walter de Gruyter, 1991–1997.
Walbridge, John, *The Wisdom of the Mystic East. Suhrawardī and Platonic Orientalism*, New York: State University of New York Press, 2001.
Yarshater, Ehsan, "Taʿziyeh and Pre-Islamic Mourning Rites in Iran," in: Peter J. Chelkowsky (ed.), *Taʿziyeh: Ritual and Drama in Iran*, New York: New York University Press, 1979, 88–94.
az-Zuḥaylī, Wahba, *Mawsūʿa al-fiqh al-islāmī wa-l-qaḍāyā al-muʿāṣira*, 14 vols., Damascus: Dār al-fikr, 2012.

Suggestions for Further Reading

Greenberg, Yudit Kornberg, *The Body in Religion. Cross-Cultural Perspectives*, London: Bloomsbury Academic, 2017.
Kugle, Scott Alan: *Sufis & Saints' Bodies. Mysticisms, Corporeality, & Sacred Power in Islam*, Chapel Hill, NC: University of North Carolina Press, 2007.
Nasr, Seyyed Hossein, *An Introduction to Islamic Cosmological Doctrines. Conceptions of Nature and Methods Used for Its Study by the Ikhwān al-Ṣafāʾ, al-Bīrūnī, and Ibn Sīnā*, Cambridge: Harvard University Press, 1964.

Christoph Böttigheimer / Konstantin Kamp

Epilogue

Following a widespread prejudice, the three major monotheistic religions take a rather critical stance towards the human body. Thus, Christianity in particular, but to a lesser extent also Judaism and Islam are not infrequently accused of a certain body-hostility. Often, at least two closely connected reasons for this alleged devaluation of the body are given. On the one hand, the general attitude towards the body may be traced back to the negative view of sexuality that characterizes many religions. On the other hand, it also seems to be due to the transience of the body, which, from a religious point of view, could suggest that something non-corporeal, imperishable must be assumed in every human being.

As a matter of fact, in the theological and philosophical discourses that have shaped the history of the three monotheistic religions, there have been tendencies to contrast the human body with something commonly translated as "soul." What is more, in seemingly complete agreement with the above-mentioned prejudice, this soul is sometimes given priority over the body, not least because the body is transient and associated with lust and sexuality. Upon closer examination, however, things are much more complicated than they seem. First, it is far from clear what the terms "soul" and "body" exactly mean. Does the adoption of whatever is meant by the term "soul" necessarily devalue the body? Second, even if it does, it is not yet clear that such an interpretation can be found in Judaism, Christianity, and Islam alike. Instead, it is possible that a devaluation of the body is found only in one religion and not in the others. Third, it is questionable whether such an interpretation can be traced back to the Holy Scriptures of the major monotheistic religions – i.e., to the Hebrew Bible, the New Testament and the Qur'ān. It must therefore be examined whether it is not rather the result of external influences, such as Platonic philosophy or modern Cartesian dualism, which strictly distinguish the mind from everything physical.

As these few questions show, a precise analysis of the pair of terms "body" and "soul" is necessary to clarify the attitude of the three monotheistic religions toward the body. Such an analysis has been the aim of the contributions collected in this volume, which approach the phenomenon of the body from Jewish, Christian, and Islamic perspectives, respectively. In this epilogue, we want to summarize the main results of the analyses presented in the three articles. In doing so, we attempt to identify similarities and differences in the understanding of the concept of the body in the three religions.

https://doi.org/10.1515/9783110748246-004

The Concept of Body in Judaism

Judaism is an extraordinarily diverse religion, encompassing various religious movements. To name only the major branches, it may suffice to contrast Orthodox Judaism with its numerous currents – from *Haredi* (Ultra-Orthodox) Judaism to Modern Orthodoxy and Religious Zionism – with Reform Judaism. While Orthodox Judaism emphasizes strict adherence to Jewish law (*halakha*), Reform Judaism takes a liberal stance on the same issue, viewing traditional rabbinic law as no longer binding and focusing on ethical aspects instead. To make matters even more complex, there is a third group, Conservative Judaism, which maintains the binding nature of law while emphasizing its mutability.

The account of the Jewish position on the body given by Yakir Englander in this book focuses mainly on Orthodox Judaism, which usually is considered the most traditional branch of Judaism. Against this background, the results of the analysis of the role of the body in Orthodox Judaism given here may be seen as all the more surprising. Contrary to the widespread assumption that traditional religions are inherently hostile to the body, the main thesis of the article is that because of its emphasis on the observance of the religious law, Orthodox Judaism culturally chooses to be a thoroughly bodily religion. This is evident from the very fact that Jewish law, with its regulations on prayer, eating, dress, and further areas of daily life, is primarily concerned with matters of religious practice. Even more, this practice is in large part bodily, as can be seen from the consensus among halakhic scholars that the demands of the law cannot be fulfilled mentally alone, but require physical action. Specifically, this means, for example, that prayers and blessings must be recited aloud and that wearing special garments such as *tallit* or *tefillin* may be required to fulfill the halakhic obligations. Thus, halakhic literature places the human body at its center. It focuses almost exclusively on the actions a Jew should perform (or refrain from performing) with his or her body. Even though there are exceptions, halakhic authorities generally show much less interest in the thoughts, intentions, and feelings that accompany the respective actions.

The fact that halakha focuses on bodily actions shows that Judaism takes into account the human being as a whole. Since the actions a Jew is expected to perform according to the halakha are physical in nature, they shape his or her perception of the world. The article demonstrates this using Maurice Merleau-Ponty's phenomenological approach to the body, which points out that human beings do not have a body like other objects they possess, but actually *are* their body. Thus, the modern Cartesian attempt to view one's body from the perspective of an external observer fails to recognize the actual role of the body from the outset. According to Merleau-Ponty, it is impossible to observe the body like other objects in the world, because it is only in and through the body that we have access to the world. Hence, our experience of the world is always a result of our bodily encounter with the world and is essentially shaped by it. Since we have access to the world only through our bodies, what we experience and how we act in the world cannot be completely controlled by our minds. Instead, our mental consciousness of the world is influenced by our body's encounter with the world. At the same time, the way our body perceives the world is also shaped by the way we see the world and the roles we ascribe to our body. Moreover, as Judith Butler points out, our experience of the body is to a large extent influenced by society.

Given the centrality of the body for experience and perception, one can understand halakha's focus on bodily actions as a way to "implement" halakhic actions into a person's life, thereby shaping the human being in his or her entirety. When halakhic authorities emphasize, for example, the necessity of vocal and bodily prayer, they take into account that only in this way, prayer can shape the experience of the praying Jew and make him or her what one might call a "prayerful being," i.e., a person that actually *is* prayer (cf. Ps 109:4). Similarly, when the halakha prescribes praying with a fixed wording and at fixed times, it serves the purpose of forming a habitual, embodied prayer practice. Such embodied practice also finds expression in the fact that many Jews who pray according to the halakha from an early age know most of the prayers and Shabbat songs by heart. Since knowing by heart refers to a non-reflexive knowledge, it can also be described as a kind of "bodily" familiarity that involves the entire person.

Moreover, the bodily practices mentioned above also bring forth a distinctly "halakhic" society. Living according to the halakha creates a "new world," so to speak, i.e., a mental and social infrastructure that is distinctly different from a world that is not shaped by religious practices. One way of creating such a halakhic domain is the attempt to disrupt and divide natural physical actions, which are usually performed unintentionally through the body, into multiple actions that can be mentally controlled and that can be laden with religious meanings. For example, Yosef Chaim (1832–1909), also known as "Ben Ish Chai," gives detailed instructions on how to put on the *tallit*, a prayer shawl worn by male Jews during morning prayers. He places special emphasis on the fact that the *tallit* is not to be put on in the same manner as normal clothing. Instead, he divides the process of putting on the *tallit* into specific, well-defined steps, each of which has religious significance. Thus, the simple act of putting on of a garment is transformed into a ritual conveying religious meaning. Similarly, the "Ben Ish Chai" divides the act of washing hands in the morning – an act that is also performed by many secular people – into smaller acts. In this way, the everyday act of washing hands is interpreted as part of a purification ritual to which religious significance is attributed. In addition, the "Ben Ish Chai" requires the act of washing to be interrupted at certain points. These interruptions to the physical action serve the purpose of preventing the ritual from becoming habitual, thus ensuring that the ritual continues to convey its religious meaning to the performer. Of course, there is a certain tension here with the bodily familiarity of the rituals otherwise so strongly emphasized in halakhic literature. This tension between the desire to interrupt natural acts and imbue them with religious meaning and intention, on the one hand, and the formation of a halakhic habit, on the other, can be seen repeatedly throughout the history of Jewish thought.

As mentioned earlier, not only does our body shape our experience of the world and thus bring forth a corresponding society, but this society also influences our perception of the world. Since our bodies can never absorb all the data in the world, the way our bodies respond to the world and what data they process is in large part a result of the given standards of the respective society in which a person lives. That being the case, one can understand the great difference between the view of an ultra-Orthodox Jew and that of a secular person on women. While in a secular society it is normal for women to dress in whatever way they like, in an ultra-Orthodox society there are strict rules about what a woman must wear. A similar difference can be seen with regard to the relationship between women and men: while in secular societies women can be friends with men and date them as they please, in ultra-Orthodox societies the family is supposed to choose a wife for the husband. Furthermore, unlike in secular societies, sexuality is considered something strictly private that has no place in public. These differences make it understandable why, for a Jew who lives according to halakha, a secular woman may appear as a source of temptation and potentially harmful sexual experience. As should be clear by now, this is not because the Orthodox Jew consciously chooses to view a secular woman in this way. Rather, due to the sociocultural context in which he lives, the way his body perceives and responds to the woman is fundamentally different from the way a secular person perceives the same woman. Thus, when a male Orthodox Jew views women in the manner described above, he does not do so out of any intentional hostility toward the body, but because the society in which he lives makes his body perceive the female body in this way.

Because Jewish law places such an emphasis on bodily actions and sees them as a means of shaping a halakhic society, the body is often viewed quite positively in halakhic literature. However, this does not mean that *all* halakhic authorities necessarily have a positive attitude toward the body. Especially among more recent halakhic scholars, there is a tendency to devalue the body, which in some ways is reminiscent of modern Cartesian dualism. Rabbi Yechiel Michel Epstein (1829–1908), for example, while acknowledging the necessity of the body for performing the halakha, defines the human being as an essentially incorporeal being and views the body as something negative that is only a feature of this world. In addition, there are a number of authors in halakhic literature, such as Rabbi Moses Isserles (1530–1572) or Rabbi Chaim Friedlander (1923–1986), who state that the goal of halakha is to form people whose minds are in constant reflection and dominate the body. Especially in the case of Rabbi Friedlander, according to whom the halakha aims at the mind controlling not only bodily actions but also thoughts, this devaluation of the body and the related interpretation of the human being as some kind of "cogito" bears a certain resemblance to Western Cartesian dualism. As these examples show, while Orthodox Judaism is a thoroughly bodily religion in practice, it does not always recognize the centrality of the body in theory.

The Concept of Body in Christianity

Given the centrality of the doctrine of the incarnation in Christianity, it is hardly an exaggeration to say that Christianity is, or at least should be, *the* religion of the body. Its central teaching is that in the body of Jesus of Nazareth, God truly reveals Himself. As Gregor Etzelmüller underscores in his article, the body, then, is the medium par excellence of God's revelation. This central idea is already expressed in the Gospel of John, which, in its prologue, states that the Word was made flesh, *sarx* (cf. John 1:14). In this context, the term *sarx* does not imply a dualistic anthropology; instead, *sarx* encompasses the whole human being, including the body as well as what is commonly called "spirit" or "soul." The apostle Paul expresses a similar thought, albeit in different terminology, in his letters when stressing that Christ really existed in a bodily way and has to be conceived as a psychosomatic unity. Thus, the body is at the center of Christian doctrine from the very beginning of Christian theology.

Against this background, it may seem particularly surprising that the history of Christian theology is largely marked by a dualistic anthropology that tends to devalue the body. It cannot be emphasized enough, though, that this dualism is in tension, if not in contradiction, with the biblical view of the human being. For example, the widespread theological notion that human beings are created in the image of God by virtue of their rational faculties is in marked contrast to the biblical evidence. This can be seen from the fact that Gen 1:27 speaks of the human being as having been created in the *tselem* (image) of God, the term *tselem* referring to a three-dimensional statue and, thus, clearly denoting something physical. In other words, being created in the image of God does not refer to a spiritual likeness, but rather means that human beings represent God through their body. In line with this, humans are generally regarded as embodied creatures in the Old Testament. This is clear from an analysis of the use of the word *nefesh*, which is often translated "soul." Contrary to what the translation "soul" might suggest, *nefesh* in the Old Testament does not refer to a separate spiritual entity in the human being. Rather, the term *nefesh* denotes the organ for the vital needs of the human being. *Nefesh* is, thus, part of an anthropology that has no abstract concept of the body, let alone a single, unambiguous term for it, but assigns the basic functions of the body to specific organs. These organs, in turn, represent the whole human being.

Looking at how the relationship of human beings to God is described in the Bible, it becomes clear that here, too, their physicality is central. To give just one example, in the Psalms, keeping the commandments is attributed to both the heart and the belly (cf. Ps 37:31; 40:9), i.e., to two "organs" that seem to be more or less interchangeable. In general, in the Old Testament, God addresses the whole person, who cannot be separated from his or her body. A similar emphasis on the physicality of the human being is also found in the New Testament. For example, Paul refers to the human body as the "temple of the Holy Spirit" (1 Cor 6:19). By doing so, he indicates that the body is the privileged medium of the relationship between God and the human being. Paul's high esteem for the body is also evident in his description of the Christian congregation as a body.

Furthermore, Paul points out that the Christian congregation is not only a body, but is also constituted by bodily acts. Here, especially baptism and the Lord's Supper are to be mentioned. Baptism is understood by Paul as a process through which the baptized person dies, as it were, in relation to the previously valid social norms and instead lives in a new community with new social norms. In this new community, the differences – e.g., between women and men, slaves and freemen or Jews and pagans (cf. Gal 3:28) – that had shaped the previous social life are dissolved. Since these differences are often physical in nature, as the difference of circumcision between Jewish and pagan men shows, baptism "reconfigures," so to speak, the embodied person of the baptized, thereby enabling his or her body to become a "temple of the Holy Spirit."

Of course, when speaking of the baptized dying to existing social norms in baptism, Paul does not mean that the body is stripped of all social influences. Rather, what is meant is that in baptism the body is freed from harmful influences, which Paul describes as belonging to the realm of sin, and is instead received into a community with new social norms. The point, then, is that the body is freed from the powers that enslave it and is instead shaped by a spirit that liberates. Similarly, a transformation of social rules is at stake when the death and resurrection of Jesus are celebrated in the Lord's Supper. The celebration of Jesus' death not only exposes the Roman Empire's violence and hostility against the body, but by affirming that Jesus lives and will come again, it also expresses hope for an end to the powers that rule this world. It goes without saying that this reshaping of the existing social rules, which, according to Paul, can be experienced in the Christian community, requires its members to change their behavior accordingly, as Paul's repeated admonitions to the rich members of the community show.

Biblical anthropology, which is laid down in the Old Testament and on which Paul's teaching is based, is of great actuality today. It is surprisingly similar to today's Embodied Cognitive Science and the Philosophy of Embodiment in that it emphasizes that the human being is always already embodied. For the Bible, as for contemporary anthropology, the body is not something dualistically opposed and subordinate to the soul as the center of the human being. Obviously, the body is not an object that human beings possess. Instead, what was indicated above with reference to Merleau-Ponty is already visible in the Bible: Human beings *are* their bodies. At the same time, biblical anthropology does not interpret human beings naturalistically, as if they were only their body as described by natural sciences. Rather, subjectivity, freedom, and communicability also belong to human beings, so that it can be said that they are characterized by corporeality and inwardness. In other words, according to biblical understanding, human beings are both body and soul. This connection between corporeality and inwardness is evident, for example, in the principles of natality and vulnerability, which refer to the phenomena of intercorporeality and empathy that are constitutive of the human being.

If biblical anthropology emphasizes the corporeality of the human being in such a way, how is it to be explained that the history of Christian theology is to a large extent characterized by dualistic tendencies? There are at least three starting points for this already in Paul, which could be taken up in later theology. First, even though it is clear to Paul that human life is always corporeal and will remain so even beyond death, he sees a connection between what he calls living "according to the flesh" and sin (cf., e.g., Rom 7:5–6). By assuming such a connection, Paul probably wants to point out that human beings tend to put themselves first because of the knowledge of their finiteness, which is connected with carnality. Thus, as finite beings, humans often pursue their own interests at the expense of others. By using the term "flesh," Paul points out that this striving for self-preservation is something that is rooted in the biological nature of human beings. Hence, the distinction between "living according to the flesh" and "living in the spirit of Christ" does not devalue the physicality of the human being. Rather, by using it, Paul wants to indicate that living in the Christian community demands a fundamental reorientation of one's own life, away from biological self-preservation toward service to others. Nevertheless, the connection between flesh and sin could serve as a starting point for anti-bodily tendencies in Christian theology.

A second starting point for the later dualistic anthropology of the Christian theologians can be seen in the ascetic attitude of Jesus and Paul. Both lived celibate lives. In terms of theology, Paul in particular is critical of sexuality and sees its uncontrolled practice as a fundamental danger for Christians. Thus, according to him, marriage is only permitted to prevent fornication, while he prefers as many Christians as possible to lead a celibate life like him. Even though Paul's focus on the danger of sexuality may seem rather strange today, it should not be confused with a fundamental hostility toward the body. On closer examination, it becomes clear that Paul is critical of the uncontrolled practice of sexuality *because of* his great appreciation of the body. In his view, uncontrolled sexuality is problematic, because it may harm the body as a "temple of the Holy Spirit." Therefore, Paul's attitude toward sexuality can also be interpreted positively, in that he does not reject sexuality per se, but demands human relationships to be characterized by love (*agape*) and self-control for the sake of the other.

A final starting point for a critical attitude toward the body is the reception of a dualistic or tripartite anthropology in the Septuagint. There, various examples can be found that show how the image of the embodied human being visible in the Hebrew Bible was replaced by more abstract concepts. Even in Paul, there are occasional examples that point in this direction.

In the early Church Fathers, however, such as Justin Martyr (c. 100–165) or Irenaeus (c. 130–202), there is not yet a pronounced dualistic anthropology that reduces human beings to their soul. Rather, for them it is true that human beings consist equally of body and soul and are only complete if they also have a body. Accordingly, for the early Christian theologians, believing in the resurrection also includes hoping for a resurrection of the flesh. For this reason, they fight against docetist and gnostic interpretations of Christ that disregard the corporeality of human beings.

That being said, at the same time a complete rejection of sexuality developed, which went far beyond Paul's critical attitude. Already in the Acts of Paul and Thecla, written in the second century, only the person who lives chastely is referred to as "temple of God." The fact that chastity is now increasingly seen as an ideal is probably related to Christianity setting itself apart from Judaism, which does not know this ideal. In addition, celibacy can be perceived as attractive because it is associated with a massive gain in freedom, especially for women, who have been able to escape social expectations through celibacy. On the other hand, radical asceticism carries the danger of destroying social life. Thus, Tertullian (c. 155–220), for example, takes a rather moderate position, pointing out that Christians should start a family first, not least to preserve the Christian community, and only live ascetically in old age.

While Tertullian, despite his appreciation of asceticism, was not a dualist but defended the unity of body and soul, there were also theologians in early Christianity who held a strictly Platonic and thus dualistic position. Origen (185–254), for example, sees the body as an obstacle on the soul's path to God, from which it should free itself as much as possible. Thus, according to him, only the inner being of man can be considered to be made in the image of God.

Especially Augustine (354–430) advocates a strong dualism. For him, the human being is exclusively the soul, which uses the body only as a kind of tool. Since the body is characterized by passions, it usually appears to be dangerous to the soul because it is an obstacle to knowledge. Among the passions, sexual desire is of particular concern to Augustine because it possesses man to the point of completely preventing him from any mental activity. Thus, for Augustine, sexual desire is a particularly clear symptom of the human being's sinful condition after the fall. Consequently, in Augustine's view, before the fall the human body could not feel any lust, but was purely spiritual in nature. Correspondingly, after the resurrection, human beings will again have only a spiritual body.

Subsequently, Augustine's devaluation of the body and contempt for all things sexual are widely regarded as an integral part of the Christian faith. They find expression, for example, in the practice of strict fasting or flagellation in the Middle Ages. At the same time, however, there are at least occasional approaches to a slightly different view of the body. For example, in female mystics, such as Gertrude of Helfta (1256–1301/02), the body can become a place where communion with God can be experienced sensually. Following Augustine, academic theologians such as Thomas Aquinas (1225–1274) and Bonaventure (1221–1274) hold that human beings are made in the image of God only by virtue of their rational nature. At the same time, they had to find ways to reconcile this dualism with the confession of the resurrection of the flesh.

The solution offered by Aquinas is particularly interesting because it takes its cue from Aristotle. Aquinas interprets the relationship between soul and body in terms of form and matter, equating the soul with form and the body with matter. According to him, both soul and body, as form and matter, are necessary for the existence of a concrete human being. In this way, Aquinas takes a decisive step beyond Augustinian dualism. However, he still holds to the Platonic idea that at death the soul and body are separated, and that initially only the soul continues to exist in an intermediate state before the general resurrection of the dead takes place. On closer inspection, this intermediate state of the so-called *anima separata* is deeply problematic. Since even Aquinas himself calls this state unnatural (cf. SCG IV, c.79), the question arises how the soul, which is incomplete without a body, can still be considered blissful in this state.

While Aquinas' teaching on the separation of soul and body at death is influenced by Platonism and therefore shows certain inconsistencies, his recourse to Aristotle leads him to a much more positive assessment of sexuality than Augustine. Like Aristotle, Aquinas assumes that reality has a teleological structure. Accordingly, everything that exists is divinely ordered towards an end. Thus, human sexuality must also serve a purpose, which, according to Aquinas, is procreation. Since procreation is the natural end of the sexual act, this sexual act cannot be bad as long as it is directed towards its natural end. Thus, Aquinas is one of the first theologians to hold that the sexual act and the pleasure that naturally accompanies it are something good.

In sum, therefore, Thomas Aquinas' attitude toward the body can be described as ambivalent. A similar ambivalence can be found in the theologians of subsequent centuries. One example for this is Martin Luther (1483–1546). On the one hand, probably because of his monastic background, Luther emphasizes the ideal of renunciation and the necessity of disciplining the body. On the other hand, not least because of his experiences with his own wife and children, Luther holds family life in high esteem. In addition, the idea of the incarnation is of great importance to him theologically and leads to a new appreciation of the body. According to Luther, in Christ, the human body becomes the bearer of divine attributes. As such, the body is no longer seen in an exclusively negative light. Thus, in his interpretation of the Apostles' Creed, Luther can point out that God lovingly cares for the body. Finally, another example that shows Luther's appreciation for the body is the fact that, from his point of view, it is necessary for God's Word to be preached and thus communicated in a physical, sensual way.

A similar ambivalence and tension can be found in modern theology. Friedrich Schleiermacher (1768–1834), for instance, underlines that the spirit is the most important part of the human being because it is free from all restrictions. By contrast, he considers the body to be a part of the material world that must be controlled by the spirit. At the same time, Schleiermacher stresses the interaction of body and soul, claiming that both can influence each other. As is clear here, for him the distinction between body and soul is only an abstraction that arises in thought. In Schleiermacher's view, in the more primordial feeling of the universe, the human being experiences him- or herself as a psychosomatic unity that is embedded in nature. Given this experience, the mere distinction between soul and body is only secondary, since the human being in life is simply one. For this reason, an eschatological fulfillment of the human being is also inconceivable for Schleiermacher as long as it does not include corporeality.

Finally, a similar tension, but with greater recourse to the biblical view of the human person, is found in Karl Barth (1886–1968), who advocates a position he calls "concrete monism." This "concrete monism" attempts to avoid Greek dualism by describing the human being as a "besouled body." De facto, however, Barth again assumes the superiority of the soul over the body.

Overall, it is clear that, on the one hand, Christianity greatly enhances the status of the human body compared to pagan philosophy by focusing on the idea of the incarnation. On the other hand, for many centuries Christian theology has been characterized by a more or less pronounced hostility to the body and by dualistic tendencies.

The Concept of Body in Islam

Similar to Judaism as well as Christianity, Islam is an inherently multifaceted religion, encompassing various groups such as Sunnis and Shīʿites, and giving rise to different theological, philosophical, and legal traditions. Therefore, it is perhaps not surprising that there is no single teaching on the body in Islam. Rather, different views have been held throughout the history of Islamic thought.

Nevertheless, as Abbas Poya points out in his article, there are some principles on which all Muslims agree. One of these is the simple fact of distinguishing between the human body and the soul or spirit. This distinction is already evident in Islam's primary sources, the Qur'ān and the Ḥadīṯ. Since the body is considered to be created by God, another principle which all Muslims share is that the body should be treated with respect. According to Islamic belief, as God's creation, the body belongs first and foremost to its Creator. Therefore, people cannot simply do whatever they want with their bodies. Rather, they must treat their bodies as prescribed by God, i.e., according to the teachings of Islam.

Although the Qur'ān and the Ḥadīṯ distinguish between the body and the soul, this does not answer the question of how they relate to each other. After all, the distinction between the body and the soul does not necessarily mean that the two are considered separate entities. Since there are a variety of ways to understand the conceptual pair of body and soul, a close analysis of their relationship in the Qur'ān and the Ḥadīṯ is necessary. In this analysis, the first thing to note is that there are different terms in the Arabic language for what we call the "body." For example, the term *badan* refers to the living human body, whereas *jasad* is mainly used to describe the lifeless body. In addition, *jism* is used to refer to bodies in general and *jirm* when referring to a celestial body. Similarly, there is a plurality of terms referring to what we call "soul" in English. For example, one term that is used as a counterpart to the body is *rūḥ*, which is generally translated as "spirit." In the Qur'ān, *rūḥ* is often equated with another commonly used term, *nafs*. Although *nafs* is usually rendered as "soul" in Western translations, it can also have the meanings of life, self, and human being.

When analyzing the use of these terms in the Qur'ān, it is striking that the Qur'ān is not interested in the question of the relationship between body and soul. Rather, it usually addresses the human being as such, without assuming any contradiction between body and soul. On closer examination, it becomes clear that the Qur'ān conceives of humans primarily as material beings. For example, the Qur'ān describes humans as created from "dust" (Qur'ān 22:5), as already indicated by the name of the first human, Adam, and emphasizes their origin from the "earth" and their return to it (cf. Qur'ān 22:15). Even resurrection is presented in the Qur'ān as a physical act. Although there is no explanation of how exactly it happens, the Qur'ān obviously imagines it as a kind of revival of the body. Accordingly, paradise is depicted as a garden full of bodily pleasures, while hell is seen as a place of bodily torture. Furthermore, many of the acts a Muslim is required to perform, such as prayer or fasting, are bodily in character.

But what about *rūḥ* and *nafs*, which, as mentioned earlier, are also referred to in the Qur'ān as belonging to man? According to the Qur'ān, *rūḥ*, spirit, is something divine that was breathed into human beings at their creation (cf. Qur'ān 15:22). Moreover, the Qur'ān itself and the corresponding Ḥadīṯs make it clear that the term *rūḥ* refers to what makes humans alive, i.e., to a life force given by God. Especially in many Ḥadīṯs, the blowing in of this life force is described in a very material way. This is evident, for example, when *rūḥ* is presented as something that, when blown in, gradually reaches different parts of a person's body. From these descriptions, it can be concluded that the Qur'ān and the Ḥadīṯs envision *rūḥ* as something material. As for the term *nafs*, which is often translated as "soul," it is not entirely clear whether it refers to something material or immaterial. Certainly, in some places the Qur'ān conceives of *nafs* as a kind of invisible force that tempts or blames human beings. However, other invisible entities also appear in the Qur'ān, and at the same time they can be described in a very physical way. Therefore, the incorporeality of the *nafs* cannot be inferred from its invisibility.

While the Qur'ān and the Ḥadīṯs perceive human beings primarily as corporeal beings, there are different positions in later Islamic theology on the question of the relationship between body and soul. On the one hand, there are the Ash'arites and a traditionalist group called the *Ahl al-ḥadīth*, who adhere to a literal interpretation of the Qur'ān and the Ḥadīṯ. Their view of human beings is to some extent representative of the Sunni majority. Because of their strict adherence to Islamic sources, the Ash'arites and the *Ahl al-ḥadīth* view human beings almost exclusively in terms of their physicality. On the other hand, there are the Mu'tazilites, who take a more rationalist position. No unified doctrine can be discerned here. Although there are some Mu'tazilites who take a more critical attitude toward the body, in general they tend to interpret the spirit as something that is distinct from the body, but also material. Finally, in Shī'ite theology, which usually is closer to the Mu'tazilites than to the Ash'arites, there are different opinions on the question of the materiality or immateriality of *rūḥ* and *nafs*.

While Islamic theology, despite individual differences in emphasis, generally focuses on the physicality of human beings, Islamic philosophy is much more influenced by ancient philosophers such as Plato, Aristotle, and Plotinus. It therefore places greater emphasis on the soul or spirit. According to Ibn Sīnā (980–1037), for example, the human being consists of two different elements, body and spirit (*rūḥ*). With regard to the spirit, he further distinguishes three forms: the animal spirit, which is seated in the heart, the natural spirit, located in the liver, and the mental spirit or psyche, which is in the brain. In Ibn Sīnā's view, it is the mental spirit that makes someone human and can free him or her from animal drives and natural desires. The mental spirit is a kind of force that gives life to the body and is responsible for knowledge and thought. While the animal spirit and the natural spirit are somehow physical in nature, Ibn Sīnā considers the mental spirit to be immaterial and non-corporeal. Therefore, only the mental spirit constitutes the human being. Since humans are their mental spirit, only the mental spirit is immortal. Thus, while Ibn Sīnā can conceive of a continuation of the mental spirit after death, according to him, the Islamic belief in bodily resurrection cannot be rationally justified and must be regarded as a matter of faith.

A comparison of Ibn Sīnā's different writings shows that for him the mental spirit is the same as the soul (*nafs*) or the intellect (*'aql*). Overall, then, Ibn Sīnā can be said to advocate a dualism that distinguishes between the body and the soul as the two components that human beings are made of. For him, the soul represents all that is good in human beings, while the body is considered inferior. This is also evident from the fact that he compares the relationship between the soul and the body to the relationship between a rider and a mount.

Similar views on the relationship between body and soul are also held in other currents of Islamic thought. For example, the "Brethren of Purity" (*Ikhwān aṣ-ṣafā*), a secret society strongly influenced by Neoplatonism that probably emerged in the 10th century, regard the material world and the body as a prison from which human beings must free themselves. According to them, as the well-known "Two Islands Simile" shows, human beings are to strive for the permanent, non-corporeal through knowledge. The material, on the contrary, is considered worthless, which is why human beings are supposed to transcend it.

Similar views can also be found in the works of one of Islam's most important theologians, al-Ghazālī (c. 1058–1111). Although he is best known as an opponent of Ibn Sīnā and of philosophy in general, his anthropology bears certain similarities to that of Ibn Sīnā. Of course, al-Ghazālī rejects Ibn Sīnā's assumption of a purely spiritual resurrection. Apart from this, however, al-Ghazālī also takes a dualistic stand. According to him, human beings consist of an outer shell, the body, and an inside, which is the soul or the spirit. While the body originates in the earthly world and is visible to the created eye, the soul originates in the upper, heavenly world and can only be seen by the inner eye. In al-Ghazālī's view, human beings constantly struggle between these two worlds. In order for the upper heavenly world to win, people should strive for self-knowledge, through which they realize that the soul, which al-Ghazālī also equates with the heart, is their true being.

Muhammad Iqbal (1877–1938), an influential Indo-Pakistani poet and philosopher of the more recent past, also emphasizes the centrality of the human soul, insisting that it is not bound to space. In doing so, he is influenced by the Islamic mystical tradition, Sufism, which focuses in a special way on the spiritual dimension of the human being. Similar to al-Ghazālī, who is often also considered a representative of Sufism, Islamic mysticism generally holds that the body is the prison of the soul and must therefore be overcome through asceticism. Beyond this, however, there is occasionally also a more positive view of the body in Sufism, which values the body as God's creature and emphasizes its beauty, respecting it as a place of knowing and loving God.

While the importance of asceticism is particularly emphasized in Sufism, detachment and renunciation, expressed by the Arabic term *zuhd*, are generally considered very valuable in Islam. While the term *zuhd* is not found in the Qur'ān itself, it was established as an ideal already in the 8th century. In addition to giving up material possessions, *zuhd* means abandoning everything (including immaterial goods) that distracts a person from God. Renunciation is thus supposed to be a means of complying with the Qur'ānic demand to serve God alone. Physical exertion, however, is not to be considered an end in itself, but has value only as a means of ascending to God.

Finally, when we look at Islamic law, we see that it focuses almost exclusively on the material, physical dimension of human behavior. This is also due to the fact that, according to Islamic law, intention is important and must consist of the desire to obey God, but cannot be controlled by law. An example that illustrates the orientation of Islamic law towards the physical aspects of life are the regulations concerning the ritual washing of the body before the prayer. They are already laid down in the Qur'ān and the Ḥadīṯ and are considered by legal scholars not only as an indispensable prerequisite for prayer, but are themselves seen as an act of worship. Thus, the correct performance of ablutions is more important for the proper fulfillment of prayer than, for example, the inner attitude of the person praying. Prayer itself, which involves fixed bodily movements and postures and is performed in community at least on Fridays, and fasting are also among the practices prescribed by Islamic law. Fasting in Ramadan and pilgrimage, which are considered "pillars of Islam" as well, are also obviously physical in nature. This can be seen from the fact that Islamic law precisely regulates the procedure of the pilgrimage to Mecca and, for example, prescribes the wearing of certain clothes during the pilgrimage. As is clear from these examples, the correctness of the performance of religious practices according to Islamic law is always measured by external, physical criteria.

The focus of Islamic law on bodily acts can also be seen in many other areas, such as the treatment of organ transplantation, which is generally considered permissible because it aims to protect life, or suicide, which is considered forbidden because it assumes a right over the body that belongs only to God. Similarly, cremation is usually considered forbidden in Islam because it affects bodily integrity. One topic of particular interest is the regulation of women's clothing, which is exceedingly controversial, especially in Western societies. Against this background, it may come as a surprise that the Qur'ān contains only very rough regulations on this subject, merely indicating that women should cover their nakedness and charms. Only in the course of time, more detailed rules have emerged. Thus, traditional legal scholars agree that, apart from hands, feet and face, all other parts of a woman's body must be covered. Today, however, there are also scholars who cast doubt on these traditional interpretations.

Two topics which also relate to the body and are also of a controversial nature are the punishment of the grave and the celebration of bodily suffering in Shīʿite Islam. The former refers to the belief that life in the hereafter does not begin immediately after death. Instead, according to Islamic belief, humans first enter an intermediate state where good people experience joy and bad people are physically punished. Even though this doctrine can hardly be derived from the Qur'ān directly and has been disputed or interpreted symbolically by rationalist theologians such as the Muʿtazilites or philosophers such as Ibn Sīnā, it is still an integral part of Islamic faith for Sunnis and Shīʿites alike, once again demonstrating the predominantly bodily orientation of Islam. As for the celebration of bodily suffering in Shīʿite Islam, which includes passion plays and even flagellations, it seems foreign to many secular people today. According to Shīʿite belief, those rituals are performed out of mourning and as an act of penance for the murder of the third Imam Ḥusayn by the troops of the second Umayyad caliph, Yazīd, in Karbalā in 680. Although these rituals have long been criticized by many Muslim scholars, they are a particularly striking example of how one's religious beliefs can find physical expression in Islam.

In sum, it can be stated that like Christianity, Islam shows a certain ambivalence with regard to the body. On the one hand, the Qur'ān and the Ḥadīṯ, as well as classical Islamic theology and law, address humans as thoroughly corporeal beings. On the other hand, however, there are also the traditions of Islamic philosophy and mysticism, which conceive of human beings in strictly dualistic terms. Here, it is often emphasized that the body is a prison that human beings must seek to overcome. Thus, the body appears in a thoroughly negative light.

Similarities and Differences

If we compare the significance that the three monotheistic religions – Judaism, Christianity and Islam – ascribe to the body, both similarities and differences become apparent. Every dialogue, including interreligious dialogue, is well advised to start with what is common and unifying.

In the holy scriptures of all three major religions of revelation, a distinction is made between the corporeal on the one hand and the incorporeal on the other, which is referred to as *nefesh* or *nafs*. Moreover, both the Hebrew and Christian Bibles and the Qur'ān speak of man primarily as a corporeal being and unfold a largely positive image of the human body. The body is seen as the bearer of religious acts, and in Christianity even as the medium of divine revelation. Thus, the holy scriptures of the three great religions of revelation do not show dualistic features, with the exception of the Septuagint.

Beyond the holy scriptures, there are developments and movements in all three religions that also cast a negative light on the body. These tendencies are, however, mostly conditioned by external influences, for example by (Neo)Platonism, which among other things has had a lasting influence on the theology of Augustine as well as on Islamic philosophy and mysticism, or by Cartesian dualism. If dualistic tendencies can be found within all three monotheistic religions beyond their holy scriptures, it is noticeable that they have developed differently in the three religions and have had different influences. While in Christianity the main theological current was basically dualistic over many centuries, dualism in Islam rather took an outsider's position. It can be found above all in Islamic groups that are considered heterodox by many theologians and legal scholars, such as Islamic philosophy and Sufism. In Orthodox Judaism, too, the mainstream seems to be less dualistic than in Christianity because of its strict focus on bodily performance.

In the recent past, a critical attitude towards dualism can be observed in all religions. This is evident in all three contributions collected in this book, which draw primarily on those traditions and philosophical approaches that are not dualistic.

Closely connected to the view of the body or corporeality is the topic of sexuality, which is why it is addressed in all three religions. Comparing the religions with each other, it is noticeable that in connection with the more dualistic Christian doctrine and the accompanying more negative view of the body, sexuality is seen as more problematic in Christianity than in Judaism and Islam. It is not surprising, then, that sexual abstinence is given far more importance in Christianity than in the other two religions, where the ideal of sexual abstinence is seen as only one part of a much broader ascetic attitude in which sexuality is not given such a prominent position.

If, on the whole, all three monotheistic religions have historically shown an ambivalent relationship to the body and sometimes anti-body tendencies, it would be inaccurate to call them anti-body across the board.

List of Contributors and Editors

Yakir Englander is the Senior National Director of Leadership programs at the Israeli-American Council. He also teaches at the AJR (a rabbinical school) in NY. Originally from the Hasidic community of Israel, Englander obtained his Ph.D. from the Hebrew University in Jerusalem in Jewish philosophy and gender studies. He is a Fulbright scholar and was a visiting professor of Religion at Northwestern and Rutgers Universities, the Shalom Hartman Institute and Harvard Divinity School. Englander's books about body, gender and sexuality in the Ultra-Orthodox and Zionist-Orthodox communities have changed the discourse on sexuality and gender inside the Jewish religious societies in Israel. After leaving Orthodoxy, he was drafted to the Israeli military, spending most of his service in an elite unit tasked with the identification of human remains. As a result of his service, he joined as a director at Kids4Peace, an interfaith youth movement in Jerusalem and other cities in North America.

Gregor Etzelmüller is Professor of Systematic Theology at the Department of Protestant Theology at Osnabruck University (Germany). He studied at the Theological Seminary of Bielefeld-Bethel, the Ruprecht-Karls-University of Heidelberg and as doctoral research scholar at Princeton Theological Seminary. He received his Ph.D. (Dr. theol.) from the University of Heidelberg. After he has completed his habilitation at the University of Heidelberg he taught at the Universities of Heidelberg and Bochum. He was Principal Investigator of the Heidelberg research project on embodiment and speaker of the Osnabruck graduate school "Shaping religious differences. Pluralism in Christianity and Islam". His recent publications include: *Gottes verkörpertes Ebenbild: Eine theologische Anthropologie*, Tübingen: Mohr Siebeck, 2021 (an english translation is in preparation), *Migrationskirchen: Internationalisierung und Pluralisierung des Christentums vor Ort* (ed. together with Claudia Rammelt), Leipzig: Evangelische Verlagsanstalt, 2022, and "Embodied Image of God: Evolutionary Anthropology in Theological Perspective," in: Martin Breul / Caroline Helmus (eds.), The *Philosophical and Theological Relevance of Evolutionary Anthropology: Engagements with Michael Tomasello*, Routledge Science and Religion Series, Abingdon: Routledge 2023, 119–132.

Abbas Poya is Professor of Contemporary Islamic Discourses at the Department of Islamic Religious Studies (DIRS) at Friedrich-Alexander-University Erlangen-Nuremberg (FAU). In his research and teaching, he focuses on topics such as religious theology, law, Human Rights debate, tolerance, (de-) sacralization and religious-political movements in Islam. He received his doctorate from the University of Hamburg and completed his habilitation at the Albert-Ludwigs-University of Freiburg. He was a Fellow at the Freiburg Institute for Advanced Studies (FRIAS), as well the head of the junior research group Norm, Normativity and Norm Change at FAU and taught at the Universities of Hamburg, Freiburg im Breisgau and Zurich. His recent publications include: *Islamische Theologie neu denken. Gespräche mit ʿAbd al-Ǧabbār ar-Rifāʿī, Mohsen Kadivar, Hassan Yussefi Eshkevari und Arash Naraghi*, Berlin: De Gruyter, 2023 and *Sharia and Justice: An Ethical, Legal, Political, and Cross-Cultural Approach* (ed.). Berlin: De Gruyter, 2018.

Christoph Böttigheimer has held the Chair of Fundamental Theology at the Catholic University of Eichstätt-Ingolstadt since 2002. He studied Catholic theology at the Universities of Tübingen and Innsbruck (Austria), obtained his doctorate at the University of Munich in 1993 and habilitated there in 1996. He is the author of "Lehrbuch der Fundamentaltheologie", one of the most well-received and influential textbooks in the field of fundamental theology in the German-speaking world. His

https://doi.org/10.1515/9783110748246-005

works in the ongoing legacy of the Second Vatican Council, on supplicatory prayer and core questions of faith have been translated into several languages. His most recent publication, besides a new and revised edition of the famous "Lehrbuch", is "Die Reich-Gottes-Botschaft Jesu. Verlorene Mitte christlichen Glaubens" (Herder, 2020) on Jesus' teaching in the Kingdom of God. He is member of many academic research and working committees, especially in the field of ecumenical dialogue and cooperation.

Konstantin Kamp studied Catholic Theology and Philosophy in Tübingen, Munich and Rome. He is currently working as a research assistant at the Chair of Theology in Processes of Transformation and at the Chair of Fundamental Theology at the Catholic University of Eichstätt-Ingolstadt. His research interests include the tradition of negative theology, the relationship between theology and spirituality, Christology, and interreligious dialogue.

Index of Persons

Abel 142
Abraham 108
Adam 16, 61–63, 65, 107, 112, 142
Alexander Aphrodisias Thermistius 116
al-ʿAllāf, Abū l-Hudhayl 113
Ammicht Quinn, Regina 80
Aquinas, Thomas 66–68, 163–164
Arendt, Hannah 40–41
Ari *See* Luria, Isaac
Aristotle 67, 101–103, 116, 118, 123, 150, 163–164, 167
al-Aṣamm, ʿAbd ar-Raḥmān 112
al-Ashʿarī, Abū al-Ḥasan 114–115
al-ʿAshmāwī, Muḥammad Saʿīd 141
Augustine 60–63, 64, 68, 163–164, 170
ʿAyn-al Quḍḍāt Hamadānī 126

Barth, Karl 76–78, 164–165
Ben Ish Chai 4, 15–18, 157
Ben-Gurion, David 14
Bistāmī, Bāyazīd 128
Bonaventure 67, 163
Bonhoeffer, Dietrich 76, 80, 83
Bora, Katharina von 69
Butler, Judith 12–13, 23, 157

Cain 142
Calvin, John 70
Carus, Titus Lucretius 102
Celsus 38
Cicero, Marcus Tullius 60–61

Descartes, René 5–6, 9, 38, 103, 155–156, 159, 170
Dinzelbacher, Peter 66

Epiphanios of Salamis 59
Epstein, Yechiel Michel 2–3, 20, 158
Eusebius of Ceasarea 64

al-Fārābī 116, 123
Foucault, Michel 24
Francis of Assisi 65
Frettlöh, Magdalene 48
Friedlander, Chaim 23–24, 159
Fuchs, Thomas 83

Gabriel (angel) 107
Gertrude of Helfta 66, 163
al-Ghazālī, Abū Ḥāmid 121, 123–125, 167–168
Goethe, Johann Wolfgang von 75
Gregory of Nyssa 59

al-Ḥallāj, Ḥusayn ibn Manṣūr 126
Halm, Heinz 146–147
Harnack, Adolf von 76
Ḥasan al-Baṣrī 129
Heidegger, Martin 40
Humboldt, Wilhelm von 75
Ḥusayn (Imam) 145–147, 169

Ibn Ḥanbal, Aḥmad 115
Ibn al-Ḥakam, Hishām 112–113
Ibn al-Farrāʾ, Abū Yaʿlā 115
Ibn al-Jawzī 115
Ibn Paquda, Bahya 3, 7
Ibn Qayyim al-Jawziyya 143
Ibn Sīnā 106, 113, 116–124, 127, 145, 149, 167–169
Ibn ʿUthaymīn, Muḥammad 112, 138
Iqbal, Muhammad 122, 125–126, 168
Irenaeus of Lyon 56, 162
Isserles, Moses 22–24, 159

al-Jāhiẓ 111
Jahm ibn Ṣafwān 115
Janowski, Bernd 80
Jesus Christ 29, 33–36, 40–41, 43, 45–51, 57–58, 61, 70–71, 76, 78–81, 159–162, 164
Joas, Hans 83
Job 41
John (evangelist) 29–30, 159
Judas Iscariot 46
Junayd, Abū al-Qāsim 128
Justin Martyr 55, 162

Kant, Immanuel 4, 38, 72–73
Karelitz, Yeshaya 14
Karo, Yosef 22–23

https://doi.org/10.1515/9783110748246-006

Keel, Othmar 80
al-Kindī 116
Kugle, Scott 128

Lohfink, Norbert 80
Luke (evangelist) 41
Luria, Isaac 16–17
Luther, Martin 29, 68–70, 164

Maimonides, Moses 19, 150
Marcion 57–58
Markschies, Christoph 150
Mary 41, 46, 49
McFague, Sallie 80
Merleau-Ponty, Maurice 1, 4–5, 6, 7, 9–15, 17, 19–21, 23, 25–26, 156, 161
Messas, Joseph 25
Mikail (angel) 107
Miller, Patrick 80
Moltmann-Wendel, Elisabeth 80
al-Mufīd 113
Muhammad 105, 110–112, 117–118, 125, 132, 140, 144, 146
Mullā Ṣadrā 114
Muslim Ibn al-Ḥajjāj, Abu l-Ḥusayn 105, 144
Muṭahharī, Murtaḍā 114
Muʿāwiya (caliph) 146

an-Naẓẓām 112–113
Netton, Richard 123

Onesimus 46–47
Origen 58–59, 163

Paul (apostle) 29–30, 33–35, 37, 44–47, 49–56, 61–62, 77, 81, 159–162
Philemon 46–47
Plato 55, 101–103, 116, 118, 123, 167
Plotinus 116, 118, 150, 167
Pontius Pilate 46
Portmann, Adolf 89
Proclus 116

Qābil, Aḥmad 141
al-Qaraḍāwī, Yūsuf 136–137, 139

Rābiʿa al-ʿAdawiyya al-Qaysiyya 129
Rambam *See* Maimonides, Moses
ar-Rāzī, Fakhr ad-Dīn 108, 112
Rema *See* Isserles, Moses
Rudolph, Ulrich 127
Rūmī, Jalāl ad-Dīn Muḥammad 128, 130, 148

Sayyid Ibn Ṭāwūs 145
Schleiermacher, Friedrich 71–75, 164
Schneerson, Menachem Mendel 25–26
Schroer, Sylvia 80
Shaḥrūr, Muḥammad 141
ash-Sharīf al-Murtaḍā 113
Smith, Richard 85
Socrates 54
as-Suhrawardī, Shihāb ad-Dīn 127
as-Sulamī, Muʿammar b. ʿAbbād 113

aṭ-Ṭabarī, Abū Jaʿfar Muḥammad b. Jarīr 107–108, 110
Ṭabāṭabāyī, Muḥammad Ḥusayn 114
Teresa of Ávila 3
Tertullian 57–58, 64, 162
Trible, Phyllis 80
Tyrannius Rufinus 55

ʿUthmān (caliph) 111

Wolff, Hans Walter 31, 80

Yazīd (caliph) 145–146, 169
Yosef Chaim of Baghdad *See* Ben Ish Chai

Zahir, Ahmad 130
Zayn al-ʿĀbidīn, ʿAlī (Imam) 146
Zurāra b. Aʿyan 114

Index of Subjects

Acharonim 19
Ahl al-ḥadīth 111–112, 115–116, 166
anthropology 38, 40, 48, 54–55, 73, 76–77, 80, 82–83, 87–88, 159–162, 167
anthropomorphism 114–115
Arukh HaShulchan See Epstein, Yechiel Michel
asceticism 49, 52–53, 57–58, 61, 64–65, 79, 84, 162–163, 168, 171
Ash'arites 111–112, 116, 166–167
'āshūrā 146–148

badan 104–106, 148, 165
baptism 34–35, 45, 160
Ba'al Teshuva 20–21
body 1–24, 26–27, 29–40, 43–47, 49–52, 54–56, 58–90, 99–110, 112–120, 122–124, 126–129, 131–132, 135–137, 140–144, 147–150, 155–171

central theory 6–7, 9
Chazon Ish See Karelitz, Yeshaya
Chovat HaLevavot See ibn Paquda, Bahya
Christology 76
circumcision 1
contemplation 2, 5, 24, 26
creation 56, 100, 107, 109–110, 131

dualism 5, 9, 20, 29, 31, 34, 38–39, 50, 54, 58, 76, 78, 80, 99, 101–103, 116, 124, 149, 155, 159, 161–163, 165, 167–168, 170–171

embodiment 34, 39, 48, 54, 73, 82, 86–87, 89–90, 161
eschatology 56, 73, 88, 90
Eucharist 34, 36–37, 69, 77, 80–81, 160

flesh 29–30, 32, 49–52, 55–56, 58–59, 61, 63–64, 69, 71, 74–75, 78, 80, 83, 90, 159, 161–162

ḥajj 130, 133–135
halakha 1–2, 3, 4, 5, 7–8, 11–25, 132, 156–159
Haredi Judaism 10–11, 14–15, 23–24, 156, 158
Hebrew Bible 30–32, 41, 44, 47–48, 78–80, 159–162, 170
Holy Spirit 35, 51–53, 56, 70, 76
Ḥadīṯ 99–100, 104–108, 110–111, 114, 118, 128–129, 131, 136–138, 140–142, 144, 149, 165–166, 168–169
ḥurma 100, 142

Ikhwān aṣ-ṣafā 122–124, 167
immortality 74, 90
incarnation 29, 40, 55, 69, 78, 80, 82–83, 88, 159, 164–165
intercorporeality 40, 44–45, 48–49, 82–85, 90, 161
Islamic Law *See* Sharia
Israel 14

jasad 104–107, 165
Jerusalem 118
jirm 105–106, 118, 165
jism 104–106, 112, 114–115, 148, 165
juthmān 105

Kabbalah 3–4, 16, 150
kalām 111
Karbalā 145–148
Khārijites 145

Leibkörper 81
Lord's Supper *See* Eucharist

Manichaeism 115
materialism 76, 101–103
Mecca 117–118, 130, 134
Messiah 36
mind 5, 7, 24, 26, 38–39, 52, 63, 65, 70, 100–104, 106–108, 148, 155, 157
mind-body problem 67, 100–101
monism 76, 78, 102–103, 164
Mu'tazilites 111–113, 115–116, 143, 145, 166–167, 169
mysticism 3, 26, 66, 100, 109, 124, 126–130, 149, 163, 168, 170

nafs 105–106, 109, 113–114, 117–121, 125, 137, 148, 166–167, 170

https://doi.org/10.1515/9783110748246-007

natality 40–43, 49, 161
nature 12–15, 20
nefesh 31, 159–160, 170
New Covenant 32
New Testament 30, 33, 40, 46–50, 54, 76
nurture 12

Old Testament *See* Hebrew Bible
Orthodox Judaism 24, 156, 158–159, 170

phenomenology 1, 4–5, 9, 12–14, 21, 23, 25, 39, 82, 156
prayer 7–8, 19–21, 25–27, 58, 109, 125, 130–134, 156–157, 166, 168
psyche 101–102

Qur'ān 78–79, 99–100, 104–112, 114–115, 118, 120, 129, 131, 133–134, 137, 139, 141–142, 144, 148–149, 165–166, 168–170

Religious Zionism 14–15, 156
resurrection 54–56, 67, 74, 80, 90, 106, 108, 117, 121, 123, 148–149, 162–163, 166–167
Rishonim 19
rūḥ 105–108, 112–114, 119, 121, 125, 148, 165–167

ṣalāt 133
sarx *See* flesh
ṣawm 133–134
Secular Zionism 15
Sefer HaChinukh 8
Septuagint 30, 50, 54, 162, 170
sexuality 10–12, 24, 52–53, 56, 58–64, 67–69, 79, 84, 155, 158, 162–164, 171
Shabbat 3, 20–21, 88, 157
Sharia 121, 125, 130–131, 133, 136–137, 140, 148, 168–169
Shīʿa Islam 111, 113–114, 134, 139, 141, 143–149, 165, 167, 169
siddur 7
sin 8, 29, 35, 37, 41, 44–45, 49–52, 74–75, 160–161
Son of God *See* Jesus Christ
soul 7, 21, 26–27, 29, 31–32, 39, 54–56, 58, 60, 62–67, 70–74, 76, 78, 80, 87, 90, 99–107, 112, 116–125, 127, 137, 144–145, 148–150, 155, 159–160, 162–168
spirit 8, 39, 50, 52, 54, 56, 61, 65, 68, 72, 74–75, 89–90, 99–100, 102, 106, 108, 110, 112–113, 116, 119–121, 124–125, 128, 148, 159–160, 164–168
Sufism 126–129, 168, 170
Sunnī Islam 111–112, 141, 143, 149, 165–166, 169

tallit 1, 15–18, 156–157
Talmud 19, 25–26, 132
tefillin 1, 13, 19, 156
Torah 2, 8, 22, 132
tselem 31

Ultra-Orthodox Judaism *See* Haredi Judaism

virgin birth 40
vulnerability 40, 44–46, 79, 82–83, 161

World to Come 2–3

Zoroastrianism 132

www.ingramcontent.com/pod-product-compliance
Lightning Source LLC
Chambersburg PA
CBHW031402230426
43670CB00006B/617
* 9 7 8 3 1 1 0 7 4 8 1 7 8 *